Elizabeth's Sea Dogs
and their
War Against Spain

Elizabeth's Sea Dogs and their War Against Spain

Brian Best

AN IMPRINT OF PEN & SWORD BOOKS LTD
YORKSHIRE – PHILADELPHIA

First published in Great Britain in 2021 by
FRONTLINE BOOKS
an imprint of Pen & Sword Books Ltd
Yorkshire – Philadelphia

ISBN 978-1-52678-285-4

Typeset by Concept, Huddersfield, West Yorkshire, HD4 5JL.
Printed and bound in England by TJ Books Limited, Padstow, Cornwall.

Pen & Sword Books Ltd incorporates the Imprints of Aviation, Atlas, Family
History, Fiction, Maritime, Military, Discovery, Politics, History, Archaeology,
Select, Wharncliffe Local History, Wharncliffe True Crime, Military Classics,
Wharncliffe Transport, Leo Cooper, The Praetorian Press, Remember When,
White Owl, Seaforth Publishing and Frontline Books.

For a complete list of Pen & Sword titles please contact
PEN & SWORD BOOKS LTD
47 Church Street, Barnsley, South Yorkshire, S70 2AS, England
E-mail: enquiries@pen-and-sword.co.uk
Website: www.pen-and-sword.co.uk
or
PEN & SWORD BOOKS
1950 Lawrence Rd, Havertown, PA 19083, USA
E-mail: uspen-and-sword@casematepublishers.com
Website: www.penandswordbooks.com

Contents

Introduction 1

1. Spain's Early Raiders 5

2. The Rise of the Sea Dogs 9

3. John Hawkins 15

4. The Captives 35

5. Francis Drake 43

6. Drake's Circumnavigation (1): the Doughty Incident 55

7. Drake's Circumnavigation (2): Drake's Fortune 63

8. Drake's Circumnavigation (3): The East Indies and Home 69

9. Thomas Cavendish 77

10. The Military Elizabethans 83

11. The Execution of Mary Queen of Scots 127

12. Cadiz 135

13. The Spanish Armada 141

14. Ireland and Scotland 159

15. The Deaths of the Sea Dogs 169

16. The Capture of Cadiz 175

17. The End of an Era 179

Bibliography 187

Index 189

Introduction

The reigns of four monarchs coloured and dominated the early lives of England's first maritime seamen who turned the country into a nation that has ruled the waves for four centuries. In doing so, England accumulated a vast empire. One of the main catalysts was Henry VIII's infatuation with Anne Boleyn and his determination to divorce Catherine of Aragon. After a lengthy examination of Henry's declaration that as he had married his brother's wife Catherine, so he should be allowed a legitimate parting from her, Pope Clement decided against this ruling and, in the ensuing debate, excommunicated Henry. Although he kept the Catholic doctrines, Henry severed ties with Rome and established the Church of England, so ushering in a new form of Christianity: Protestantism. The seminal figure in the Protestant Reformation was the German priest Martin Luther. The movement gathered pace during the next three decades, leading to a lengthy period of religious upheaval.

When Henry died in 1547, he left a well-equipped Royal Navy numbering fifty-three vessels, which was something the country had never known before. Sadly, in the next two reigns the Navy was neglected and by the time Elizabeth ascended the throne in 1558, the Royal Navy was reduced to just twenty-nine fighting ships.

In 1544 it was settled that Henry's three children – Edward, Mary and Elizabeth – would succeed him in that order. On his death, he was succeeded by his 9-year-old son, as Edward VI. The young king's health had always been a concern. When he was 4 he fell gravely ill with malaria, a condition that further weakened him. The Guardian and Protector who ruled in Edward's place was the Duke of Somerset, a staunch Protestant. Henry's retention of the Catholic doctrines was overthrown and in just six years England became a Protestant country. In 1549, two years after Henry's death, *The Book of Common Prayer* was printed in English, further eroding the Latin-based Catholic religion. Henry's closure and desecration of Catholic churches and monasteries continued under Edward. The proceeds extracted from the Catholics were used to fund five schools within the Birmingham area named after the young king. In 1551

Somerset was swept from power by the ambitious Duke of Northumberland. With Northumberland acting as Protector, the country became increasingly Protestant. Soon, the sickly king's health took its final toll and in 1553 the 16-year-old Edward died of tuberculosis.

Aware that he was dying, the young king wrote his last will, in which he stated that his cousin, Lady Jane Grey, should ascend the throne after him, with the proviso that she must marry a nobleman. This was done to prevent a female becoming ruler. Edward's guardian, Northumberland, put forward his son, 17-year-old Guildford Dudley, and the pair were married in May 1553. Assembling an army, Northumberland sought to thwart any attempt by Mary to re-establish the Roman Catholic religion among the English people. Instead, the public supported Mary, with the Catholic nobles forming their own army, which easily defeated Northumberland. Lady Jane Grey's brief nine-day reign ended with her execution.

Catherine of Aragon's daughter Mary, a devout Catholic, now ascended the throne and swiftly reversed England's religion, taking the country back to Roman Catholicism. There followed a five-year reign of terror during which at least 287 Protestant heretics were burned at the stake, with many more executed or imprisoned. The new queen earned the epithet 'Bloody Mary' and her short reign drove a wedge between the two religions that further divided the English. Mary married Philip II of Spain but her hopes for a male heir were dashed by several miscarriages, and her unhappy marriage ended in 1558 when she died of uterine cancer.

In 1558 Elizabeth, the last of Henry's three children, succeeded to the throne. She was mildly Protestant and reinstated her father's Church of England rules. This greatly annoyed King Philip, who ordered the capture of every English vessel that could be found. This included Francis Drake's inherited barque, forcing Drake out of business. Elizabeth had inherited a country in religious turmoil and the expectation was that the young queen would not reign for long. The Venetian ambassador remarked that 'statecraft is no business for the ladies', and in the same year John Knox, the Scottish Protestant preacher, said, 'It is more than a monster in nature that a woman should reign and bear empire over man.' (He was probably talking about Mary Queen of Scots and not the new ruler of England, but his message was clear.) Fortunately, Elizabeth was strong-minded and carefully chose her closest ministers: Sir William Cecil, her chief adviser, and Sir Francis Walsingham, Secretary of State (and popularly known as the queen's 'spymaster'.) Although Cecil came to disagree with both slavery and privateering, he was still devoted to the queen and served her for forty years. Despite initial expectations, Elizabeth's reign came to be regarded as a period of stability in which she avoided a religious war and followed the middle way between the two religions, avoiding the extremes to which Mary had been so inflexibly attached.

Elizabeth was by turns teasing, flirtatious, romantic, haughty, procrastinating and secretly supportive of the Sea Dogs. She proved to be one of England's most influential monarchs and essentially rewrote the rules of queenship. During the Elizabethan era the country made one of its periodical advancements, inspiring national pride, cultural flowering and international expansion leading to naval supremacy. It was the maritime advancement that produced the wealth, albeit in a morally dubious manner. Elizabeth, after initial wavering, encouraged and sometimes discreetly financed the exploits of her unique band of sea captains: the Sea Dogs. She had inherited from her siblings a legacy of poverty, with the country struggling to cope with high inflation and poor harvests. England was impoverished compared with the wealth of Spain, then the world's superpower. Elizabeth, along with her ministers, had the determination to reverse this trend and one of the ways was to trade with Spain's New World possessions.

Philip II was a Habsburg and son of Charles V, ruler of both the Spanish Empire and the Holy Roman Empire. Philip had inherited a Golden Age when Spain led the world in exploration, colonisation and the amassing of wealth. Encouraged by the exploits of Magellan, Balbo, de Gama and, earlier, Christopher Columbus, Spain set about conquering the Americas. *Conquistadores* and their small armies were sent to the New World, exploring and conquering areas from Florida to Mexico to Peru. They subjugated the Native American populations, including the Aztecs, Mayas and Incas. In doing so, they found a vast wealth of gold and silver, together with precious stones and pearls. Probably no country in Europe was less fitted for the task of developing America than Spain; the Spanish were exploiters rather than colonisers, and their main aim was to send gold back to Spain instead of developing the country. With the largest number of ships in the western world under their command, the Spanish began to carry this treasure back to the home country. This enormous wealth was dissipated, swallowed up in paying duties and bribes, and Spain became reliant on loans from Genoese bankers to fund her position as the wealthiest country in the western world – and the most vulnerable.

Spanish dependence on foreign supplies from foodstuffs to military hardware had grown over the previous century and left Spain without a skilled workforce. Spain only produced a fraction of the goods it needed, and as a result, almost everything – ships, cannon and weapons, and basic commodities like grain, iron and textiles – had to be obtained or manufactured abroad and imported at vast expense. Unlike many of Queen Elizabeth's courtiers, Spanish noblemen found no honour in commerce, trade or industry.

Chapter One

Spain's Early Raiders

The treaty of Tordesillas, confirmed by Spain and Portugal on 7 June 1494, stated that all lands lying west of the Cape Verde Islands (off the west coast of Africa) belonged to these two countries. It also excluded those heretical countries including Huguenot France, the Netherlands and England, who took a while to realise that Spain and Portugal were importing vast wealth from the New World. It was not until 1521 that French Huguenot privateers became aware of the trade in treasure, with which Spain hoped to convert the rest of Europe to Catholicism. In 1522 Jean Fleury, the captain of a fleet belonging to Jean Angelo of Dieppe, captured two Spanish galleons carrying Hernan Cortes' Aztec treasure from Mexico to Spain. Fleury also captured another treasure ship sailing from Santo Domingo, and over the years such successes encouraged the Dutch 'Sea Beggars' and other corsairs to join in the attacks on the treasure ships, seizing them with comparative ease.

The reasons for the attacks were probably largely mercenary but there was also a religious element involved as the Protestant French and Dutch regarded their raids as striking a blow against Catholic Spain and Portugal. It was not until the death of Mary Tudor in 1558 that the English, once again Protestant, joined the piracy or privateering against Europe's dominant country, Spain.

The Huguenots were the real thorn in the Spanish side, sending their nimbler vessels to capture ships and ports. Between 1536 and 1568 no fewer than 152 ships were captured in the Caribbean and another thirty-seven between Spain, the Canary Islands and the Azores. The Huguenots attacked not only ships on the high seas but also coastal ports and towns on the Spanish Main. In 1544 the Colombian city of Cartagena was plundered by five ships and a thousand men under the command of Jean-Francois Roberval. Taking advantage of the fact that Cartagena's walls had yet to be erected, the Huguenots attacked and took the city, forcing a ransom to be paid. In 1553 the French laid waste the settlements on the northern coast of Hispaniola (today's Dominican Republic), all but forcing the Spanish colonists to abandon the island.

On 10 July 1555 one of the most devastating raids took place on Cuba when Jacques de Sores of La Rochelle led his men in the sacking of Santiago de Cuba. The governor and population fled inland, leaving a small number of soldiers to put up a token resistance. Finding little in the way of riches, de Sores' men desecrated churches and killed those who had remained. They then advanced into the surrounding countryside to seek out and kill the colonists, but were rebuffed by the Spanish soldiers. Withdrawing his forces, de Sores then ordered the town to be burned.

The following year de Sores returned to attack Santa Maria, an island off the mainland, with similar raids on Campeche in Mexico and Trujillo in Honduras. In the same year, together with Francois de Clerc, de Sores seized Havana. De Clerc, known as 'Jambe de Bois' (Peg Leg), had been granted the first official privateer's licence allowing him to capture Spanish vessels in the Americas. This gave him *carte blanche* to raid where he liked in the Caribbean. During one raid de Clerc discovered and seized a huge cache of treasure, bringing the flow of Spanish treasure ships to a standstill for nearly seven years.

The Huguenots' piratical range extended from Calais to Spain and even as far as the Azores. By 1574 there were sixty privateering ships sailing in this area, coming mainly from La Rochelle. This was also the base for the activities of the Dutch privateers (*zelandais*) in the service of Willem, Prince van Oranje. He greatly appreciated and supported the Huguenots' contribution in attacking the Spanish ships and depriving the Spanish troops in Spanish Burgundy of supplies and money. The Huguenots used their light vessels for two purposes: cod fishing on the Grand Banks near Canada and, with added ordnance, raiding the Spanish ships. The main organiser of the Huguenots' privateering war was Admiral Gaspard de Coligny, who became involved in the founding of colonies in the Americas and sought to eventually defeat the Spanish by attacking her vessels from the closer American ports. He had some influence over young King Charles IX and proposed a combined army of French Catholics and Huguenots to join the Dutch in their fight against the Spanish in the Netherlands.

In 1572 de Coligny was in Paris to attend the wedding of the Protestant Margaret, sister of Henry III of Navarre, and the Catholic Charles IX. This led to the St Bartholomew's Day Massacre in which a huge number of Protestants were killed: reports of the death toll varied from 3,000 to 30,000. During the fighting de Coligny was fired upon, but he survived this attempted assassination – but not for long. Taken to rest in a nearby house, he was grabbed from his bed by some French Catholics and flung from the upstairs window before being beheaded. This notorious day of blood-letting proved to be the death-blow for the Huguenot movement.

The Dutch 'Sea Beggars' (*Watergeuzen*) were members of the irregular Dutch rebel forces. From 1569 Willem van Oranje issued 'letters of marque' to the Sea Beggars, turning criminal pirates into official privateers, and making them into an effective and organised fighting force against Spain under the command of a succession of daring and reckless leaders. The Eighty Years' War (fought for Dutch liberation from Spain) was a complicated conflict. It was a war of independence, but also a religious and civil war in which economic and political factors played major roles. Both sides often committed pointless atrocities. The *Watergeuzen* and the northern Protestant insurgents regarded all Spaniards and Catholic Dutchmen as their enemies. They attacked churches, monasteries and Catholic villages and towns, killing priests, monks and representatives of the Spanish crown, as well as Catholic citizens. In return, the Spanish army – mostly mercenaries from Germany and Switzerland – took delight in sacking Protestant towns and murdering innocent victims.

During the Dutch revolt – secretly supported by England and the Huguenots – any plunder the *Watergeuzen* took from the Spanish was carried to French and English ports. For several years their bases of operations included Emden, La Rochelle and Dover. Then in 1572, under pressure from Spain, England denied the Dutch access to her ports, but this only lasted a short time. Although the Sea Beggars primarily fought for their independence, they also tied up the occupying army in the Spanish Netherlands, which added to King Philip's woes. The Burgundian province was in the most dangerous part of Europe, being at the narrow end of the English Channel and subject to continuous harassment by Protestant France, Holland and England.

In 1585 Willem, Baron de Lumey, supported by Willem van Oranje and the Dutch government, captured several more low-lying coastal towns. These were promptly besieged by the Spanish, but the Dutch countered by opening the sluices and flooding the surrounding countryside. The siege-works became submerged, as did the Spanish soldiers, and in this way the Dutch controlled the country north of the river Scheldt. By 1585 the Spanish army was laying siege to the important rebel-held port of Antwerp. The Duke of Parma encircled the town so that the Dutch could not use the rivers and waterways leading to the sea, his siege works linked by an 800-yard-long pontoon bridge built across the river Scheldt. In April, however, the Sea Beggars launched a daring attack against the bridge with explosives and fire-ships (known as 'hell-burners'). The ebb-tide carried the fire-ships towards the pontoon bridge, blowing apart the protective boom before setting the bridge ablaze. Despite losing some 800 men, the Duke of Parma's men repulsed the Dutch and Antwerp eventually fell to the Spanish in August. After this episode, the role of the *Watergeuzen* decreased. From their decline sprang the Dutch navy under the command of Willem van Oranje and his general staff, who issued letters of marque with the following instructions:

> The Sea Beggars had to conform to the Articles of War. Each commander was to maintain a minister aboard his ship. All Prizes were to be divided and distributed by a prescribed rule. Command functions should be occupied by native Dutchmen unless expressly commissioned by the Prince van Oranje. No persons were to be received on board, either sailors or soldiers, save folk of good name and fame.

By 1585 Queen Elizabeth was openly siding with the Dutch rebels and she encouraged her own Sea Dogs to aid in their fight. Francis Drake attacked the coast of Spain, inflicting considerable damage, while Walter Raleigh attacked the Spanish fishing fleets on the Grand Banks. Previously she had sent Sir John Norreys, the most acclaimed soldier of his day, to aid the Dutch resistance. During Elizabeth's reign Norreys had taken part in the Wars of Religion in France, the Eighty Years' War, the Anglo-Spanish War and the brutal suppression of Ireland in the 1570s. In 1578 he helped defeat the Spanish at the Battle of Rijmenam, during which he had three horses shot from under him.

Christopher Carleill, an English military and naval commander, went to support the Dutch resistance as early as 1572. He was present at the sieges of Middelburg, Steenwijk and the fortress at Zwarte Sluis. Following his service with the Dutch, he travelled to Russia and then, from 1584 to 1588, he served in Ireland. Another noteworthy soldier sent to help the Dutch was Francis Vere, a 25-year-old who joined the Earl of Leicester with some 3,000 men. Leicester failed to support Vere at Sluys and was relieved of his command. Having spent two years fighting, Vere returned to England for the winter, during which he was acclaimed by the public as the country's pre-eminent soldier. Not yet 30 years old, he was elevated to the rank of Sergeant-Major-General and appointed second-in-command of all the English forces in the Netherlands. After years of fighting, in 1609 the Dutch Republic was finally recognised by Spain and other European countries. Even so, the Eighty Years War rumbled on until 1648, when the Netherlands was definitively recognised as an independent country and no longer a part of the Holy Roman Empire.

Chapter Two

The Rise of the Sea Dogs

One gets the impression that Spain was solely involved in fighting the English Sea Dogs in the Caribbean. In 1556 Philip II had inherited a vast empire which he was incapable of ruling; it included the seventeen provinces of the Burgundian Netherlands, thus bringing the devoutly Catholic Spanish closer to England. This also gave the English Catholics a base from where they could hatch their plots against Elizabeth when she ascended the throne in 1558. Following in the footsteps of her father Henry VIII, she was pragmatic in her attitude to religion. Despite her support for science and the arts, the author Neil Hanson described her court in his book, *The Confident Hope of a Miracle*, as 'a snake-pit of favourites and sycophants – a glittering misery, full of malice and spite' and her government as 'venal and corrupt'.

Compared with Spain, England was second-class and impoverished. Elizabeth needed to fill the country's coffers and her eyes were drawn to the treasures that Spain was bringing from the New World. To this end, in 1560 she formed a small discreet maritime group named the 'Sea Dogs'. Their ships were well armed, comparatively nimble and perfectly capable of raiding the Spanish Main. They were captained by experienced men, mostly from the West Country, with navigational ability, determination and leadership skills. They infuriated the Spanish and Portuguese, who regarded them as being pirates, although the English preferred the term privateer. Piracy was a common calling, not highly respected but widely tolerated and easily accepted. In these early years the English Sea Dogs often allied themselves with the French Huguenots and the Flemish Dutch, both Protestant and fiercely anti-Catholic.

In 1522 the French captain Jean Fleury led the first raids against three Spanish treasure ships en route from Cuba to Seville. For the first time other European nations became aware of the vast wealth Spain was transporting from her New World colonies. The French Huguenots saw it as an open invitation to plunder the Spanish colonies, which they did for some thirty years with the blessing of their king. This ended in September 1572 with the St Bartholomew's Day Massacre (see Chapter One) when between 3,000 and 30,000 Huguenots were massacred in Paris by a large Spanish force. Many Huguenots fled from France to Protestant countries like England, the Netherlands, Sweden and Denmark. The French made a point of dismissing the Huguenots from establishing a colony in America.

After Henry VIII's break with Rome, there was a loosening of English ties with Spain. Until then, they had been closely allied in their opposition to France. When Mary Tudor died, a new age opened for England and her seamen. Elizabeth's succession to the throne in 1558 inevitably caused a religious and political split with Catholic Spain and gave birth to a new age of English exploration, trade and, above all, raiding. A government licence was passed granting English ships privateering commissions to seize the cargo of enemy ships. The only problem was that England was not at war with Spain. The Sea Dogs got around this snag by carrying 'Letters of Marque', a legal licence that allowed them to capture merchant ships and bring their cargos before a court. Essentially, a privateer was a privately owned merchant ship armed with cannon and small-arms, which was given free rein to take or plunder enemy vessels. The crews of privateers received no wages but took a share of the captured booty. Also, very discreetly, Elizabeth herself shared in the spoils, which helped to boost the exchequer. Unless operating directly under the orders of the queen, most expeditions were speculative and were financed by backers hoping for a healthy profit.

The term Sea Dogs came into use in 1560 as a way of bridging the gap between the navies of Spain and England. The Sea Dogs were a quasi-military branch of the navy authorised by Elizabeth to attack and loot Spanish ships under the flimsy justification provided by the Letters of Marque. Also covered by English law were Letters of Reprisal, related to Spanish impounding of English cargoes, which gave the English another reason to attack Spanish vessels. The Sea Dogs were referred to as privateers, but the Spanish regarded them as little better than pirates. Men like Hawkins and Drake would, if captured, be swiftly executed. To the English of the Elizabethan era, trade and plunder were one and the same. Whether it was carried out by smugglers, pirates or the nobility, looting Spanish treasure ships was regarded as a patriotic act in the struggle against Catholicism. There was a fine line between privateers and pirates: privateers attack their country's enemies, while pirates attack anybody, irrespective of nationality. But even this tentative line was often overstepped, the authorities turning a conveniently blind eye to acts of piracy.

At the heart of the Sea Dogs' activities lay neither patriotism nor Protestantism, but enrichment. Investors and speculators formed consortia to back men like John Hawkins and Francis Drake, who would hopefully return from their trans-Atlantic expeditions to the New World laden with treasure. The Spanish sent their annual 'treasure fleet' (*flota*) from Seville south to the Cape Verde Islands, where the ships would catch a fair wind to take them to the Caribbean. Once there, they would split up, with the smaller vessels sailing to ports like Nombre de Dios and Rio Hacha to collect treasure transported by mule train from Peru, the Pearl Islands and Columbia. Several raids by the privateers on these smaller ports persuaded the Spanish to build forts and shore batteries to defend them against the raiding privateers, but it was not enough. All ideas had to be laboriously submitted for approval by King Philip, who relished the huge amount of paperwork that crossed his desk at the El Escorial. But in the process many good ideas were lost in the welter of paper.

To the Spanish, these attacks by the English Sea Dogs amounted to piracy but to Queen Elizabeth and her subjects they were a sturdy bulwark against the reimposition of Roman Catholicism. Queen Elizabeth during her long reign professed to be unaware of her marauding seamen and gave innocent answers to her Spanish rival. With the support of the West Country gentry and authorities, the pirates were at least partially legitimised. Small-scale piracy, mostly in the English Channel, continued throughout the early part of Elizabeth's reign, with only a half-hearted attempt to suppress it. Major figures like the mayors of Southampton and Dartmouth regularly released captured pirates, and the latter incumbent was even fined – but he was not dismissed. The problem was that the Protestant officials who could have ended piracy often stood to gain from it, and in practice had little incentive to clamp down on it.

The typical English ship of that period was a three-masted vessel with square canvas sails on the bowsprit, fore and mainmasts, and a lateen sail on the mizzenmast towards the stern. This design engendered a manoeuvrability that was unavailable to two-masted or one-masted rigs. For such a maritime nation, it is remarkable that England imported timber, canvas, pitch, tar, hemp, cordage and other materials from Danzig and other ports on the Baltic. The retired pirate Sir Henry Mainwaring, not a supporter of English shipbuilding techniques, rated Mediterranean cables the best, followed by Flemish and Russian, with the English coming last.

Various types of ship were common during the Elizabethan era. The *galleon* was a large transport ship weighing around 500–800 tons, which carried the treasures amassed in the New World. Principally merchant ships, galleons could also be fitted with cannon and were regarded as powerful vessels. They became known as the 'battleships' of their day. The *race-built galleon* was the brain-child of John Hawkins, an experienced sailor who was elevated to the Royal Navy. These vessels had a longer hull length to beam ratio, giving them a more streamlined profile. They also reduced the towering superstructures favoured by the Spanish and were far more nimble. *Galleys* and *galleasses* were used mostly in the Mediterranean Sea, with prisoners chained to their oars. The usual length of sentence was twelve years, after which they were put in prison, where they would invariably die. These vessels were unsuited for the Atlantic Ocean or the Caribbean, but some did take part in the 1588 Armada. *Carracks* were three-masted ships with square sails, and were the standard merchant ships of the period. *Caravels* were unarmed three-masted merchant vessels, weighing between 100 and 200 tons. *Hulks* or *urcas* (a term which nowadays means an abandoned wreck) were used by the Spaniards as supply ships, having none of the ornamentation and towering superstructures of the fighting ships. The *pinnace, shallop* or *hoy* was a small auxiliary vessel used by the English. It had a 50ft keel and a beam of 17ft and weighed approximately 60 tons. The similar *patche* or *zebra* was a two-masted vessel, very light and shallow, used mainly for surveillance.

The petty piracy close to home expanded into the plundering of the Spanish Main during the 1570s and 1580s, which inevitably led to war with Spain. The large numbers of men inducted into service by press-gangs were supervised by tough and expert captains and used to board captured Spanish and Portuguese ships. They were not paid but received a portion of the plunder and cargo, which made some of them wealthy men. But it was a harsh life; the longer voyages brought starvation and sickness, while the close living conditions of the crew and the lack of hygiene bred disease. With no way of preserving fruit or vegetables in the heat off the coast of West Africa or in the Caribbean, scurvy was rife; it was a serious problem that would not be addressed for another 200 years. Some captains provided citrus fruits for their crews, which prevented scurvy, but this was not common practice. It was only when Drake and Cavendish sailed to the islands in the west Pacific, where they could provision with fruit and vegetables, that they were able to prevent any major outbreaks. The crews lived mainly on ship's biscuit, rock-hard squares of petrified oats – and inedible for those suffering from scurvy. In addition the men were fed salted beef, pork or fish, peas meal, butter (which soon turned rancid) and cheese. Food and beer soon rotted or went off in the warm climate and the crews were often forced to forage ashore for something edible.

Poor food was not the only problem the privateers faced. On the fringe of the civilised world, Central America and the islands of the West Indies gained a fearsome reputation for fatal tropical diseases. In the following centuries the British Army sent regiments to defend its colonies or put down rebellions, and in consequence they suffered an enormous amount of deaths through sickness. As a result, West Indian regiments were established as black Caribbean soldiers proved better adapted to tropical service.

As depicted in the cartouches of maps of that period, the typical loose dress of an Elizabethan seaman comprised baggy breeches with woollen stockings, with a thigh-length blouse or a short jerkin reaching the waist; in addition, some wore a tall, hairy hat or a flat wide beret. Many favoured wearing a horizontal red and white or blue and white striped shirt and most preferred to work barefoot. On longer voyages the Sea Dogs took with them soldiers who were experienced at fighting on land and were useful in subduing any suggestion of mutiny. This eventually led to the establishment of the Royal Marines as part of the ship's crew. Even a puritanical captain like Francis Drake had difficulty in controlling his crew. After weeks at sea many captains found their men insolent and even mutinous. Sir George Carew, senior officer aboard the *Mary Rose*, declared that he commanded 'the sort of knaves whom he could not rule'.

Despite these dangers, the rewards were enormous. Spain had become incredibly rich and was the known-world's strongest country, but despite her huge naval and mercantile fleets, she neglected to adequately defend her possessions. This gave first the Huguenots and then the English the opportunity to attack the Spanish treasure ships and rob them of their wealth. When Elizabeth came to the throne she chose a religious middle way, in contrast to her sister Mary's murderous rule. But during the 1570s Catholicism was making great strides, and this was the time when Elizabeth was at her most vulnerable. It was also a period when the Protestants conducted fierce searches for Catholics. For years Elizabeth avoided all-out war with Spain by procrastination, ordering time-wasting investigations and pleading ignorance of her seafaring privateers. In fact, they often cooperated with their Protestant allies in the undeclared war against Spain. In the years 1560 to 1590 Elizabeth amassed a fortune, stolen from her former Spanish brother-in-law by her beloved Sea Dogs. She also encouraged, especially after the Armada, 'the development of this supplementary navy'.

William Cecil disapproved of the 'discriminating piracy' ventures of Hawkins, Drake and many other Sea Dogs. He feared war with Spain now that they had inherited the Spanish Netherlands. He believed that slavery and piracy, which Elizabeth secretly approved of, would inevitably lead to Mary Queen of Scots replacing her on the throne of England and the country reverting to Catholicism. Victorian historians, writing for a generation of empire builders, gilded the lily somewhat with their exaggerated exploits of the Sea Dogs.

Chapter Three

John Hawkins

John Hawkins was born in 1532 in his father's fine house in Kinterbury Street, Plymouth. He was the second son of William and Joan (née Trelawney) Hawkins. His brief education enabled him to read, write and become numerate but it was more important that he learned the rudiments of navigation and shipbuilding in order to succeed his father, who was a prominent owner of a merchant fleet. One of the richest men in Plymouth, John's father was a tough businessman who displayed a vicious streak. In 1543 he escaped punishment after he was accused of nearly beating to death another townsman. Indicative of the lawless nature of that time, he was not even brought to trial.

William's ships traded with nearby European countries but were always prepared to fight off attempts by pirates from France, the Netherlands and even England to board his vessels. William Hawkins was well known to Henry VIII, as in 1528 he became the first Englishman to sail to the New World. He was also fairly ambivalent regarding religion and did not involve himself in the machinations of this vexed subject. This ambivalence did not stop him benefiting from the dissolution of the monasteries. He fitted out a 200-ton ship named *Paul of Plymouth* and set sail for Brazil. He made three trips between 1530 and 1533, taking goods such as 'elephant's teeth' (tusks) from the Guinea coast to trade with the natives in Brazil. On his second trip in 1530 William persuaded a native chief to return to England with him and left one of his seamen, Martin Cockeram, as a hostage and to show good faith. Once they returned to England, the chief was presented to King Henry at Whitehall, where he made a big impression. The court was intrigued by the holes in his cheeks where small bones had been inserted. William explained that these were indicative of the chief's great bravery in allowing this to be done.

After spending a year in England, William and the chieftain boarded a ship bound for Brazil, but unfortunately the chieftain died before reaching his native land. When William explained what had happened, the natives accepted their chief's loss and, to the relief of the English, released the agitated Martin Cockeram. When William arrived back in his home port, he was elected Mayor of Plymouth. This was not a ceremonial position but one where he was in charge of the city's militia and responsible for its defences. In 1535 he was chosen to represent the borough of Plymouth in Parliament, and he remained a Member of Parliament until his death in 1554. As a prominent sea captain he received the King's Commission in 1544 to 'annoy the King's enemies'. This gave him *carte blanche* to plunder any foreign vessel he came upon. He soon overstepped the mark and was imprisoned for a short time. When he died in 1554, his estate was left to his two sons with William, his eldest, managing the business at home and John taking charge of the company's ships.

John Hawkins grew up to become an astute businessman with a charming manner. His first sea voyage in charge of a ship was to Bordeaux to bring back barrels of French wine. From then on he frequently made trips to France, the Canary Islands, Portugal and Spain. But he had inherited his father's ready temper along with his business acumen, and at the age of 20 he became involved in an argument in a Plymouth tavern with a barber and bully called John White. Seaports were notorious places, for away from the fine buildings the majority of the people lived in slums where life was dangerous and squalid. As was usual in those times, both men were armed with daggers. White came at Hawkins but the latter managed to get the better of his opponent and deliver a fatal stab wound. An inquest was held and Nicholas Slannyng, the King's Coroner, listened to the witnesses who all said that White had started the fight. The coroner declared John Hawkins pardoned on the grounds of self-defence. Slannyng may also have been swayed by the fact that John's father was a former Mayor of Plymouth, a Member of Parliament and a very prominent businessman who was able to offer a financial inducement.

Despite his temper, John Hawkins had a winning personality and made friends easily. As a result, when he and his brother inherited their father's business, John became involved in the negotiations with the Spanish ambassador over the marriage of Queen Mary and Philip of Spain. Some of the Spanish emissaries travelled through Plymouth and John performed some sort of service to King Philip, possibly as an officer of the royal convoy performing a feat of seamanship that safeguarded the king. According to Spanish sources, John was knighted by Philip for this service. This was probably an exaggeration, but Hawkins referred to the Spanish king as 'his old master'. In turn, he was also known to the Spanish as Juan Aquines, a direct translation of his English name.

Philip married Mary in 1555, confirming the Anglo-Spanish alliance. This amicable association lasted until 1558, when Mary died and Elizabeth ascended the throne. In the same year John married Katherine Gonson, the daughter of Captain Benjamin Gonson, the Navy Treasurer. The following year their only child Richard was born. Katherine's brother, Sir David Gonson, had served as a Knight of St John in the Mediterranean. This Catholic Order of Malta had been banned by King Henry in 1540, the year that Sir David returned to England. He was arrested and imprisoned in the Tower of London and condemned to death for denying the king in spiritual matters. On the day of his execution, he was taken across the Thames to Southwark, where he was hanged, drawn and quartered. He was regarded as a martyr and in 1929 the Pope declared him a saint.

By 1561 John had a house in London and he joined a syndicate of wealthy merchants eager to make profits from trade with the Canary Islands. During visits to the islands, Hawkins learned that the Spanish colonists in the Caribbean were in need of African slaves. They had all but exterminated the native Caribs and needed slaves to work the plantations and mines. At this time the Spanish allowed the trading of slaves on condition that the slavers paid a 7.5 per cent tax. The Spanish government sold as many as 17,000 licences for colonists to import slaves from Africa to the West Indies. In the sixteenth century slavery was considered a normal branch of trade and had been practised for nearly a century by the Spanish, following the example of the Arabs, who had been involved in over a thousand years of human slavery, capturing natives from West and North Africa. Even the Church gave this cruel trade its blessing. One man, Fernando Ochoa, held a monopoly over the slave trade and oversaw the importing of over 23,000 African slaves between 1553 and 1560.

Hawkins saw chance of a profit by carrying slaves to the Caribbean in exchange for precious metals, jewellery and pearls. He persuaded Edward Bysshe, Surveyor of Victuals to the queen's Fleet, to provide sacks of dried beans for feeding the slaves. This aroused the suspicions of the Spanish ambassador, who asked Elizabeth for her assurance that the Spanish monopoly over the slave trade would not be affected. Giving a rather opaque answer, Elizabeth claimed that the expedition was bound for 'Elmina' (Ghana) to compensate for the sinking of the *Mary Fortune* the previous summer. This ship had been sunk by a Portuguese warship and the crew imprisoned. The queen had complained to the Portuguese king, but received no satisfaction.

Now the English were about to join this shameful trade and soon became Europe's leading slavers. At first the speculators in London were reluctant to risk such a venture but eventually Hawkins won a local group round to his plan. His first voyage left Plymouth on October 1562; it was a small-scale enterprise supported by a Plymouth-based group. It did have support from the Crown, and Elizabeth contributed ordnance, munitions and small on-board boats ready to counter any opposition from Spain. Hawkins left England with three ships for his first trans-Atlantic voyage; he himself commanded the 120-ton *Solomon*, along with the smaller *Swallow* and *Jonas*.

Hawkins sailed to the Canaries before making for the African coast. In December, off Sierra Leone, he captured two Portuguese slave ships, seizing 300 Africans, 35,000 ducats (currency used throughout Europe) and ivory. Instead of following his father's practice of journeying to Brazil, he sailed for the Caribbean. Hawkins sold 200 captives at Santo Domingo, in today's Dominican Republic, at a much lower price than the Spanish charged the colonists, but to his chagrin he was told he must forfeit the remaining hundred slaves as a deposit. As he had exchanged the slaves for gold, silver, pearls, sugar, ginger and hides, he accepted this ruling. The sugar and hides exceeded 260 tons, so he chartered two Spanish vessels to carry these goods back to Spain, where he would be paid for them. Under the supervision of Captain Thomas Hampton, both vessels put into Spain where their cargo was impounded. Hampton narrowly made his escape and reported to Hawkins that his goods had been seized.

Hawkins arrived back in Plymouth in late August 1563. Despite the loss of the sugar and hides, the expedition had made a good profit from the precious cargo and the syndicate, including Queen Elizabeth (who had contributed 'ordnance, munitions and small on-board boats'), was keen that Hawkins should repeat his voyage. To Hawkins' dismay, Spain now closed the door on foreigners trading with their New World colonies. The governors of the towns and regions enforced this edict but the colonists needed the slaves to work their plantations and mines. As Philip Gosse's book about Sir John Hawkins points out: 'From America came her [Spain's] vast wealth, and in America she was practically defenceless.' In other words, Spain had neglected the defences of her overseas possessions. It was too good an opportunity to miss. Ignoring the protestations of the Spanish ambassador and Elizabeth's Secretary of State, William Cecil, Lord Burghley, another expedition was planned. Despite the Spanish protests, a new business association formed that was keen for Hawkins to collect more slaves to trade with the small ports around the Caribbean. As well as the queen, the Earl of Pembroke and Lord Robert Dudley were among those who joined the new syndicate. The queen's discreet contribution was to rent Hawkins the old 700-ton ship *Jesus of Lübeck*. Among the crew Hawkins took along his young cousin, Francis Drake.

Hawkins made two more slavery expeditions between 1564 and 1568, carrying some 1,200 Africans to sell to the Spanish settlers. This established a miserable route known as 'the Triangle' (England–West Africa–the Caribbean), which was subsequently followed by many other slavers.

The second voyage was on a larger scale, employing *Jesus of Lübeck*, leading three other Hawkins-owned ships, the *Solomon*, the 50-ton *Tiger* and the 30-ton *Swallow* (a different vessel from the one on the first voyage). Hawkins' investors included his father-in-law, Benjamin Gonson, Treasurer of the Navy, and Sir William Winter, Naval Surveyor and Master of the Ordnance. The remaining investors were Sir William Garrad, Sir William Chester, Edward Castlyn, Lord Robert Dudley and Lord Edward Clinton, the Lord High Admiral. Surprisingly, Sir William Cecil was one of the backers despite his opposition to slavery. Although she was a substantial vessel, *Jesus of Lübeck* proved to be a liability, her great capacity nullified by her lack of speed and strength. An old leaky Baltic trader, she had been marked for the breaker's yard but was reprieved. Built to ply her trade in the cold northern European waters, she was ill-suited to the sun and warm waters of the Caribbean.

Elizabeth herself interviewed Hawkins, and instructed him that her fleet was in the Caribbean to prevent French pirates from attacking the Spanish. As the queen's officer, Hawkins was to sail under the Cross of St George and Elizabeth's royal standard. The fleet departed Plymouth on 18 October 1564 bound for West Africa. On the way they put into Tenerife in the Canaries, where they found the Spaniards no longer friendly after Hawkins' first voyage. Chronicler John Sparke wrote in his journal of seeing a strange animal, which turned out to be a camel. On the way to the Guinea coast he wrote of an accident that occurred at sea:

When five days from Tenerife, an incident happened which shows how capable a navigator Hawkins must have been. A brisk breeze was blowing when a pinnace which was sailing alongside the *Jesus* capsized. By the time the ship could be put about, the pinnace was a long way out of sight. Nevertheless, Hawkins had a longboat launched and manned by twenty-four of the strongest rowers in the ship, and himself directed the course they would take, having marked by the sun the exact spot where the accident occurred. To the surprise and joy of all on board, the upturned pinnace was found with two occupants perched on the keel, and both men and pinnace were saved.

Sailing on to the Guinea coast, they found the natives hostile – with good reason after the previous raid. Reaching the coast of Sierra Leone, they found very few natives; most had melted into the jungle. John Sparke described sailing up the Callowsa river in search of slaves. On 22 December he wrote:

> Hawkins had been assured by the Portuguese factors on the coast that the neighbouring town of Bymba was worth his attention being rich in stores of gold and in potential slaves which merely waited to be gathered up. For once in his life Hawkins was careless and underestimated his opponents, for he took a small force of forty men, in armour, guided by a Portuguese, to attack the town. Unfortunately, tales of gold hidden in Bymba had demoralised Hawkins' soldiers, for when the town was entered the men wandered off in parties of two or three and began to search the native huts for plunder. Hawkins himself with a dozen men had marched right through the town to look for slaves and on returning found his insubordinate men in full flight before some 200 armed natives and it was only Hawkins' coolness that saved them from utter disaster. As it was, he was fortunate to get away at all with a casualty list of seven dead and twenty-seven wounded. Among those killed was Captain Field of the *Solomon* ... a heavy price to pay for the ten slaves they managed to bring away ...

So far the numbers of slaves seized had been disappointing. It was left to the smaller *Tiger* and *Swallow* to sail further up the Callowsa and capture enough prisoners to make the Atlantic crossing worthwhile. Finally departing from the African coast on 29 January 1564, the fleet experienced eighteen days of flat calm, which depleted their supplies of food and fresh water. The overcrowded ships were similar to prison-hulks, stifling in the heat and disease-ridden. Soon the bodies of those slaves who had succumbed to the heat and disease were being heaved overboard. Hawkins' small fleet was finally saved by a favourable wind that sprang up so they were able to reach 'the island of cannibals', now Haiti and Dominican Republic. Sailing on to the main city of San Domingo, which was the seat of government for the Spanish Main, the ships were able to replenish their supplies before sailing south to Bonburata off the coast of western Venezuela. Hawkins tried to negotiate with the Spanish colonists, but they had received strict instructions from Spain not to trade with slavers. Frustrated, on 16 April Hawkins landed with a hundred well-armed men and marched on the town. The governor soon relented and Hawkins sold half of the slaves for silver.

Now Hawkins had to use all his negotiating skills to sell his wares, even though he had been banned by the Spanish authorities. The Spanish colonists were anxious to buy the slaves but were governed by the rules from Madrid. In addition, the Spanish public accountant had imposed a tax on the trading of slaves in exchange for materials that would make a profit in England. At Rio de la Hacha, after much haggling and backed by his men in armour, Hawkins repeated the same tactic until the colonists agreed to strike a deal and he was able to exchange the last of his slaves.

Hawkins then spent time surveying the coast and islands in preparation for his next voyage. It may be that at this time his expedition was the first to discover the potato, for John Sparkes wrote: 'These potatoes be the most delicate roots that may be eaten, and do far exceed our carrots and parsnips.' On 31 May the little fleet turned for home, but the Caribbean current pushed the ships to the west of Hispaniola. After six weeks they reached the north coast of Cuba, and headed for the Florida coast, looking for the French Huguenot colony of Fort Caroline, established two years before. At the entrance to the May river, now the St John's river, they found two deserted ships at anchor. Hawkins took a pinnace and sailed upriver, where he found the fort and the wretched survivors of the French colony, only days from starvation. From the French leader, Réné Laudonnière, Hawkins learned that there had been a serious mutiny and two ships had been seized, along with most of the rations. Apparently, the mutineers had embarked on a piratical spree which netted them considerable plunder. Overconfident and flushed with success, they lowered their guard – only to be captured and executed by the Spaniards.

On 20 July 1565 John Sparke's journal notes the first example of tobacco being smoked by the occupants of Fort Caroline. The most common date given for tobacco's introduction into England is 27 July 1586, when Sir Walter Raleigh brought tobacco leaves back from America. Hawkins offered to take the remaining colonists back to France but this suggestion was rejected because, as Laudonnière said, they did not know 'how the case stood between the French and the English'. Instead Hawkins offered Laudonnière his smallest ship, the *Swallow*, to enable them to sail home.

Soon after Hawkins' ships left Florida, French colonial forces arrived in strength and occupied the fort. About the same time the Spanish also sent large numbers of troops but they found the French had already established themselves. Instead, they moved a little further down the coast and built strong fortifications at St Augustine. The French decided to attack the Spanish fort before more reinforcements arrived. Luck was not with them: a heavy storm broke and drove their ships onto the rocky shoreline, destroying any chance of victory. The Spanish seized the opportunity to attack the almost defenceless French fort, inflicting many deaths. Those survivors who laid down their arms and surrendered were butchered by the Spaniards, so ending France's attempt to colonise Florida.

The same great storm blew Hawkins' fleet north to Newfoundland, where they came upon two French Huguenot fishing boats. Much to the Frenchmen's surprise and delight, Hawkins paid the full value for the fish. His ships eventually limped into Padstow on 20 September. Despite the storm, and the difficulties of the voyage, the expedition was hailed as a great financial success, with its backers making a 60 per cent profit. Out of the 150 men who had embarked, only twenty had been lost. John Hawkins was regarded by his influential backers as a skilful and prudent commander, who was able to bring back to England substantial profits. The queen granted him a coat of arms, bearing a lion *passant* and a crest topped with an African slave in chains. Although Hawkins intended to make another voyage the following year, the queen's Council, in the shape of Lord Burghley, wrote him a letter forbidding him to sail for the West Indies or to break any laws that Philip had put into effect. Bizarrely, Burghley also asked for a £500 bond that would enable Hawkins' ships to sail without him. The fleet duly sailed without Hawkins, but the ship's commanders followed a similar route; little is known of the trip, except that it brought a profit.

In late 1566 Hawkins was preparing to sail again.Elizabeth loaned the venerable *Jesus of Lübeck* but distanced herself from appointing Hawkins as an officer in royal service. Nevertheless, Hawkins did command the *Jesus* and five other ships: *Minion, Swallow, Angel, Judith* and *William and John*. Francis Drake served as third officer on the *Jesus* until he was later given command of the 50-ton *Judith*. This third voyage was Hawkins' largest and the most disastrous. The fleet left Plymouth on 2 October 1567, only to run into a violent storm a week later off Cape Finisterre. The storm raged for four days and the *Jesus* barely came through it, springing several leaks below the waterline. It took much plugging to prevent the great ship from foundering, but when the storm abated she was able to sail on to Tenerife accompanied by *Swallow* and *Judith*.

While they waited at Tenerife for the rest of the fleet to arrive, a dispute broke out between one of the sea officers, George Fitzwilliam, and a gentleman soldier, Edward Sutton, the 4th Earl of Dudley. When Dudley went ashore fully armed to fight a dual with Fitzwilliam, Hawkins ordered Fitzwilliam to remain on board. Hawkins then went to find Dudley and pleaded with him to postpone the dispute and not to fight 'in the midst of our enemies, the Spaniards'. When Dudley refused, Hawkins struck him with his fist, whereupon Dudley, losing his temper, drew his dagger, which was 2ft long, and lunged at Hawkins, who at once drew his weapon and the two set about each other: 'Before the bystanders could drag Dudley away, his hand and arm were cut, while Hawkins received an ugly stab just above his right eye. The crowd of officers and men rushed angrily at Dudley, and would have killed him had not the Captain forbidden them to hurt him.' Instead, Dudley was brought aboard the *Jesus* and the whole ship's company was assembled to hear Hawkins say,

> If the offence had only been a personal one to himself, he could have overlooked it. But considering the place where they were, and the ships the queen's, and so many men that Her Grace had given him charge of, that by his disobedience all might be put in danger, he must be punished therefore.

Hawkins then called for an harquebus to be loaded with two bullets and told Dudley to prepare himself for execution. When the weapon was loaded and primed, Hawkins told his prisoner to offer his last prayer. Dudley was distraught, weeping and imploring Hawkins to spare him. Just as it appeared he would shoot the prisoner, Hawkins put aside his gun and ordered the fetters removed from Dudley and embraced him. The matter was now closed. This was typical of Hawkins; he was stern but merciful, which was not a characteristic of most seafaring commanders of the time. Some accounts say that Edward Dudley died in 1566 during the voyage between West Africa and the Caribbean and was succeeded by his infant son, the 5th Earl of Dudley.

Hawkins found the remainder of his ships at anchor at another island in the Canaries and on 4 November the whole fleet sailed for the coast of Africa. Hawkins sent his pinnaces into the shallow waters of the rivers to try to capture some natives. An internal war in Sierra Leone led Hawkins to assist the chieftain in subduing the other African tribes. In exchange, he wanted to keep the 260 captured prisoners to take to the Caribbean. On one of these raids, a pinnace was sunk by a hippopotamus and two men drowned. Off Elmina, Hawkins also intercepted the Portuguese slave ship *Madre de Deus*, carrying a cargo of 500 slaves. According to the slavers' accounts, they probably killed three times that number of natives. In response, the Portuguese and some African allies attacked the English with a hail of poisoned arrows, one of which wounded Hawkins. Fortunately an African witchdoctor supplied an antidote, which restored Hawkins to health. Finally they had captured enough slaves to make the journey to the Caribbean worthwhile. Some captains fed their men on citrus fruits which did prevent scurvy, but this was the exception. The enterprise was not a happy one and religious discontent was rife amongst the crew of *Jesus of Lübeck*. One sailor described how: 'Everybody on board the ship would assemble around the mainmast, kneeling and bareheaded, and the quarter-master praying, and everyone would recite the Psalms of David, Our Father, and the Creed, in the English tongue.' Later, a captive seaman, under cross-examination by the Inquisition in Mexico, stated that anyone who showed any inclination to abstain from these drum-head services would be rewarded by the quarter-master with a rope's end.

Leaving the African coast, they were becalmed in one of the worst of doldrums, with hardly a breath of wind. Many of the slaves succumbed to heatstroke and poor food and their bodies were heaved overboard, so reducing the numbers Hawkins had to sell. It was not until 9 March that the ships finally sighted Dominica, having endured a mixture of calms and high winds. Going ashore, they found no fresh water aside from puddles of rainwater. Hawkins sailed south to Margarita Island and Borburata off the South American coast, where he managed to trade most of his slaves for some silver and pearls. Margarita was a poor little island whose main industry was the pearl fisheries. Having worked their slaves to death, they were in need of a fresh labour. In exchange for pearls, Hawkins traded some of his slaves, most of whom were in poor condition. He then sailed on to Borburata and opened a slave market on the beach, with his armed ships keeping the hovering pirates at a distance.

Continuing westward, Hawkins arrived at Rio Hacha. After a brief exchange of fire, the outnumbered Spaniards retreated into the surround-ing jungle. After a few days the King's Treasurer agreed to pay 5,000 pesos for eighty slaves. In addition, Hawkins put ashore about a hundred more slaves, mostly the elderly and children, in compensation for torching the town. After Hawkins withdrew, Lazaro de Vallejo Aldrete, the governor, wrote a long account of the sacking of his town, including a plea to the Spanish king to defend the ports where the treasure fleets collected their spoils:

We entreat your majesty to remedy the grievous conditions prevail-ing today in the Indies. For every two ships that come hither from Spain, twenty corsairs appear. For this reason not a town on all this coast is safe, for whenever they please to do so they take and plunder these settlements. They go so far as to boast that they are lords of the sea and of the land, and as a matter of fact daily we see them seize ships, both those of the Indies trade and also some that come home from Spain itself. They capture towns, and this so commonly that we see it every year. Unless your majesty deign to favour all this coast by remedying the situation, all the settlements must necessarily be abandoned, from which will result grave detriment to your majesty's royal patrimony and an end to inter-Indies traffic ...

Hawkins then went on to Cartagena but soon departed empty-handed. He had been joined by a Huguenot, Captain Blondel of the caravel *Gratia Dei*. Two more days were spent becalmed before Hawkins turned his fleet to the return journey back to England.

There is some uncertainty in other accounts of why Hawkins went to San Juan de Ulua. He had previously made enquiries about the cost of slaves at the nearby town of Vera Cruz and he still had fifty-seven slaves to sell, valued at £160 each (£9,120 total) and he may have sailed to the port to try to sell them. The hurricane season was nearly upon the fleet, so he was either blown westward or took the chance to sell his remaining prisoners. Passing Cape San Antonio, the western point of Cuba, the ships ran into a violent storm, possibly a hurricane, and they had no choice but to run before it. On the third day, the fleet parted company with *William and John*, which managed to escape through the Straits of Florida and reached Ireland the following February. Tragically, she sank with all hands when she undertook the short voyage to England.

By this time the crew on *Jesus* were alarmed at the unseaworthy condition of their vessel. On either side of her stern-post, the planks kept opening and closing, causing so many leaks that fish were swimming about in the water on the ship. The crew attempted to plug the gaps with cloth and kept the pumps going all day. They even resorted to cutting away the upper works, the weight of which was tearing the hull to pieces. These efforts kept the *Jesus* afloat; as the storm abated, Hawkins looked along the west coast of Florida for a place to refit his battered fleet, but found it was too shallow. The lull in the storm lasted only a few days before another sprang up and pushed the fleet further westward into the Gulf of Mexico.

This was an unfamiliar area for English seamen, as the Spaniards tried to keep it from other nations. On 11 September a sail was spotted and Hawkins' ships gave chase, soon catching a Spanish ship bound for the harbour at San Juan de Ulua, the only port on the Mexican side of the Gulf. Hawkins, having no pilot, followed the Spanish vessel for four days, arriving on 15 September. It was found that the principal Spanish fleet was due to arrive at the end of the month to collect gold, silver and other valuables for shipping back to Spain. Hawkins took the chance to bring his battered vessels into the harbour, hoping to repair them and leave before the *flota* arrived.

The port at San Juan de Ulua occupied a low-lying spit of land some 200 yards in length and 400 yards offshore. On the landward side stood a collection of huts, a chapel and a battery of cannon protecting the entrance. The climate there was unhealthy for Europeans, and only a small community worked in the port. The facilities were extremely rudimentary, with all the Spanish colonists living in Vera Cruz, some 15 miles away. As his little fleet drew close to the mouth of the harbour, Hawkins ordered that all the flags of St George should be replaced by flags showing the royal arms. The Spaniards, thinking they were the treasure fleet from Spain, allowed Hawkins' fleet to enter. The only signs of life were the Spanish masters and African slaves acting as stevedores. With their bows overhanging the small island, the ships were able to tie up on the land-side using chains anchored to the spit. Hawkins gave a graphic description of the port:

> Now it is to be understood that the port is made by a little island of stones not three foot above the water in the highest place, and but a bow shoot of length any way ... this island stands from the main land two bow shoots or more, also it is to be understood that there is not in all the coast any other place for ships to arrive in safety, because the north wind hath there such violence, that in less [unless] the ships be very safely moored with their anchors fastened upon the island there is no remedy for these north winds but death ... also the place of the haven was so little, that of necessity the ships must ride one aboard the other ...

As his vessels entered the harbour, it was noted that there were eight Spanish ships at anchor containing about £200,000 worth of gold and silver waiting to be transferred to the Treasure Fleet. Hawkins, resisting the temptation, assured his hosts that all he wanted was to repair his ships and be on his way. He also took the precaution of taking control of the cannon covering the harbour's entrance, and moved some of the cannon from the *Jesus* onto the spit to guard against any Spanish aggression.

The next day Hawkins' men saw an unwelcome sight: the Spanish Treasure Fleet was approaching the harbour two weeks ahead of schedule. Hawkins sent a messenger to parley with the new Viceroy of Mexico, Don Martin Enriquez de Almansa, and for three days messages went back and forth. Meanwhile, Hawkins' men kept the cannon at the port's entrance aimed at the Treasure Fleet. Finally, the Spanish agreed to allow the

English time to repair their ships in exchange for entering the harbour. They also agreed that no Spanish soldier would set foot on the spit until the English were ready to sail. In the cramped conditions, it took two days to enable the thirty-four vessels of the Treasure Fleet to tie up alongside the six ships of Hawkins and Blondel.

Don Martin, aware that John Hawkins was within his grasp, broke his agreement and sent a message asking for Spanish soldiers to come from Vera Cruz to San Juan de Ulua under cover of darkness. Covertly, he filled an empty hulk between the English and Spanish ships with soldiers, cutting fresh portholes in the hulk's side through which to bring extra guns to fire on the *Minion*. The soldiers from Vera Cruz hid among the Spanish ships ready to rush ashore and seize the English batteries. As if promoting good relations with the English crewmen, some Spaniards went ashore and mingled with Hawkins' gun-crews.

On Thursday morning, 23 September, the English became suspicious when Spanish crews were spotted shifting weapons between ships. Hawkins sent Robert Barret, the captain of the *Jesus*, to Don Martin to request that they cease their threatening activities. Realising that the plot had been discovered, guards seized Barret as the blast of a trumpet signalled for the attack to begin. Rushing onto the deck of the *Jesus*, Hawkins saw enemy soldiers from the hulk boarding the *Minion*. Calling on his crew to repulse the enemy attack, Hawkins led his men onto the deck of the *Minion* and, in a clash of swords and pikes, managed to drive the Spaniards back onto the hulk. Meanwhile, three Spanish ships had drawn alongside the *Jesus* and attempted to board her. Hawkins and his men returned to the queen's ship, driving back the enemy.

Hawkins knew he had lost his men on the shore but now looked desperately for a way to break out of the harbour. He ordered the mooring ropes on the *Jesus* and *Minion* to be cut, allowing them to drift out to midstream. This enabled him to fire broadsides at the Spanish ships still tethered to the chains on the spit. The two biggest ships, the *Capitena* and *Almirata*, were pummelled and the latter caught fire; when a gunpowder cask exploded, the former sank in the shallows.

Although the guns on the Spanish warships were silenced, those on the island kept firing at the English ships bottled up in the harbour. Twenty guns kept up a steady fire at short range and it became impossible to withstand it any longer. The *Angel* was sunk and the crew of the *Swallow* were forced to abandon ship. The *Minion* was so badly knocked about that she was forced to withdraw out of range. Francis Drake's *Judith* was poorly armed and unable to help. She was also stationed at the end of the line and so escaped the worst of the cannon fire.

The French commander Robert Blondel set the *Gratia Dei* on fire and joined Hawkins on the *Jesus*. The old ship was not very manoeuvrable and was soon riddled with shot; the decision was taken to abandon her as unseaworthy. Under cover of darkness, *Minion* pulled alongside her stern, shielded from the guns, and the crew began to transfer the gold and silver from the *Jesus*. She held the bulk of the treasure they had previously collected, but not all of it could be transferred. They were interrupted by the Spaniards who let loose a fire-ship – the worst sight for any seaman. In panic, and without warning, the crew cut the ropes holding the *Minion* to the *Jesus*. There was a mad scramble to climb aboard the *Minion*, and Hawkins was the last one to cross. A year later, before the Admiralty Court, Hawkins gave evidence concerning the terrifying events:

> This deponent [witness], perceiving fear of his men and the imminent danger that they stood in, for safeguard of themselves leapt into the *Minion* out of the said *Jesus*, where into he was hardly received, for in that instant was she under sail and departing from on board the *Jesus*.

Another witness at the same hearing, Jean Turren, a French trumpeter, stated:

> The said John Hawkins, Captain and general, tarried so long upon board that said *Jesus*, for the better defence and safety thereof, that he was almost left behind, and hardly came to the *Minion* which was then in shifting to loose and withdrew herself.

With Hawkins and his crew transferred to the *Minion*, the ship made for the harbour entrance. Both the *Minion* and *Judith* were overcrowded with men from the ships that had been sunk or were from the *Jesus*. With *Judith* nearby, *Minion* spent the night just outside the harbour. By morning, and without warning Hawkins of his departure, Drake was gone. For two days *Minion* lay there while her crew repaired the rigging and the hull, waiting for a sight of *Judith*. Hawkins wrote:

> Lo and behold, no *Judith* was to be seen! She had disappeared in the night. For two days the *Minion* lay there and still no sign of the *Judith* … So with the *Minion* only and the *Judith* we escaped, which bark [*Judith*] the same night forsook us in our great misery.

Despite this comment, Hawkins remained on good terms with Drake, but they did not sail together again until the Armada. In his will, dated

3 March 1594, Hawkins bequeathed 'To my very good cousin Sir Francis Drake Knt. My best jewell which is a Cross of "Emorodes" [Emeralds]'. After a voyage lasting some four months, *Judith* reached Plymouth on 22 January 1569. This voyage would normally have taken just thirty days, but no explanation for the delay is recorded and it remained a black mark against Drake's name despite his subsequent heroic exploits.

Hawkins, with few provisions, was unable to feed his overcrowded vessel. The crew subsisted on what they could find: cats, rats in the hold, parrots, monkeys and even hides which they chewed. In adverse weather conditions, it took until November before Hawkins passed through the Florida Channel and into the Atlantic. Instead of sailing direct to England, the *Minion* was blown off course and arrived at Ponteverde north of Vigo on 31 December. The starving crew, overwhelmed by the plentiful food, were unable to control their hunger; forty-five died after eating too much fresh meat. With his manpower severely diminished, Hawkins sailed to Vigo and managed to enlist twelve men from another English ship to help sail the *Minion* back to England. When Hawkins limped into Mount's Bay in Cornwall on 25 January 1569, he had literally a 'skeleton crew', the men barely able to perform their duties. A labourer spotted Hawkins' vessel and travelled to Plymouth with the news. A rescue boat arrived and *Minion* was able to reach her home port. The treasure she was carrying amounted to £13,500, which was a reasonable return for such a disastrous expedition. Within days, Hawkins wrote a report to Lord Burghley in which he declared:

> Our voyage was, although very hardly well achieved and brought to reasonable pass, but now a great part of our treasure, merchandise, shipping and men devoured by treason of the Spaniards. I have not much or anything more to advertise our honour more the rest, because all our business hath had infelicity, misfortune, and an unhappy end, and therefore will trouble neither the Queen's Majesty nor the rest of my good lords with such ill news.

Hawkins wanted to organise another expedition to rescue his men and recoup his losses. The third voyage had been a disaster, not least the destruction of the *Jesus* and the losses to his backers. But his reputation was under a cloud and Hawkins did not undertake any more trans-Atlantic voyages. Lord Burghley was particularly critical as he did not hold with the slave trade and had barely tolerated the piratical adventures of John Hawkins.

Hawkins came up with a plan which did not require him to cross the Spanish Main. He knew when the treasure ships would sail for Spain via the Azores, and on 1 June 1570 he wrote to Robert Dudley, Earl of Leicester, with a proposition to seize the fabulous wealth carried by the *flota*. Dudley heartily supported the plan and put it to the queen, who was agreeable. It was discussed by the Royal Council, which refused to sanction the plan as there were more pressing matters affecting the Crown. Burghley considered that England had enough irons in the fire already without running the risk of irritating Spain.

One major problem was the Ridolfi Plot. Lord Burghley persuaded John Hawkins to act as an *agent provocateur* in uncovering the planned attempt to assassinate Elizabeth or replace her on the throne with her cousin, Mary Queen of Scots. Hawkins was keen to have the Spanish release his captured men and in early 1570 he met with the Spanish ambassador. Whether Hawkins was bitter at his treatment by the ungrateful English government, or whether he was simply misleading the Spanish, Ambassador Don Gueran de Espes reported back to Philip that Hawkins was willing to bring over to Spain his considerable fleet in exchange for his captive crew. To emphasise his willingness to enter Spanish service, he sent his close friend George Fitzwilliam, one of the prisoners, to negotiate with Philip. The king wanted proof of Hawkins' sincerity, and a letter from Mary Queen of Scots explaining what she wanted done would have sealed the matter. Fitzwilliam met with Mary and received the incriminating letter, which was passed not to Philip but to Burghley.

About thirty prisoners had been brought back from the New World to Seville, still facing terrible privation, starvation and even the rack. King Philip, now fully involved, released the surviving captives and even gave them 10 dollars each 'so they would not arrive back in England penniless'. He also sent Hawkins £40,000 for the ships he had promised and bestowed on him an honour, which Lord Burghley contemptuously referred to as 'the very great titles and honours from the King, from which God deliver me'. All this was, of course, a ploy by Burghley to expose the Ridolfi Plot and he used Hawkins as part of his plan. The main instigator was Roberto di Ridolfi, a Florentine banker, who had business connections with London. In 1555 he resided in the capital and became well acquainted with the prominent men of the age, including William Cecil. He began to play an active part among the Catholics and by 1570 he was one of the faction seeking to have Mary Queen of Scots marry the Duke of Norfolk and to place her on the throne of England. He visited – and gained the support of – the Duke of Alva in Brussels, Pope Pius V in

Rome and Philip II in Madrid. By 1571 Elizabeth's intelligence network was sending her information about the plot to assassinate her. With Burghley's connivance, John Hawkins had gained the confidence of Ambassador Don Gueran de Espes, pretending to be supportive of the plotters. Once he had discovered the details of the plot, he passed on the names to Burghley. The ringleaders, including Thomas Howard, Duke of Norfolk, who was regarded as a poor leader and was not even Catholic, were rounded up and executed. Fortunately for Ridolfi, he was out of the country at the time and never returned to England. For Philip this was a costly and humiliating deception and it only added to the increased friction between the two nations.

As Hawkins and Drake arrived back in England, a new band of seafarers had been formed; known as the Beggars of the Sea (Sea Beggars), they were commanded by a Dutchman, Count de la Marck. Comprising Dutch, Huguenot and English privateers, they carried out their own war against the Catholic shipping heading up the English Channel to the new Habsburg province known as the Spanish Netherlands, which was made up of Belgium, Luxembourg, parts of northern France, the southern Netherlands and western Germany. The Duke of Alva's army had occupied the Spanish Netherlands and the duke was in need of money to pay his men and re-equip his force. All reinforcements had to run the gauntlet of the heretic ships that lay in wait in the 'funnel' leading to the Spanish Netherlands. Philip could not produce the enormous sum of money that Alva demanded and turned to the Genoese bankers for a loan. In a rush of arrogance, the Spaniards immediately despatched the bulk of the money in a single merchant ship, escorted by a few unarmed pinnaces carrying the rest.

The Spanish vessels were sighted as they entered the Channel in December 1568, and they were soon scattered. One of the most prominent English seafarers at the time was Sir Arthur Champernowne, another Devonian, who served as Vice-Admiral of the Devonian Coasts. It was a post he held for the most part of his life in which he cooperated with other privateers. He attacked the Spanish ships, which fled for refuge in the ports of southern England. The big Spanish merchantman, carrying fifty-nine chests of coin in her hold, made for the nearest port, Southampton, with six privateers on her heels. When she docked, the officials, backed by the guns in the fort, persuaded the captain to deposit his treasure onshore 'for safe-keeping'. Several pinnaces had taken refuge in Portsmouth, Plymouth and Falmouth harbours, and their captains were 'advised' to deposit their ninety-five boxes into the safe hands of the port authorities.

Champernowne organised the 'acquiring of the bullion' and personally delivered sixty-four boxes weighing 8 tonnes to London. The queen used half of it to fund her Royal Navy, and the rest she sent to the Dutch rebels in Amsterdam. The Spanish ambassador protested that the bullion should be released immediately but the queen procrastinated, refusing to hand it over until it was confirmed that John Hawkins had been killed in the Caribbean. She also demanded an investigation, which further prolonged matters. It was revealed that Spain had borrowed the money and that it was not their property until it was delivered to Antwerp; until then, it still belonged to the Italian bankers. The queen ordered another investigation as to who owned the £100,000 of bullion and the result found in favour of the Italian bankers. Realising that they would lose all their money if they failed to cooperate, they agreed to loan the money to the queen, and so the abandonment of much of the treasure at San Juan de Ulua was redeemed by the convoluted machinations of the queen and her councillors. The loss of so many men and ships to the Spanish increased tensions between England and Spain, the friction only exacerbated by the queen's opportunism.

On 11 October 1573, whilst riding down the Strand, John Hawkins was badly wounded in a botched assassination attempt. Peter Burchett, a Puritan fanatic, mistook the well-dressed Hawkins for Sir Christopher Hatton, Lord Chancellor of England, and a favourite of the queen. Burchett was immediately apprehended and tried. Found guilty, he was hanged near the site of his murder attempt and his hand severed and placed above his head. Such were the summary punishments handed out to miscreants.

In 1577 John Hawkins became co-Treasurer of the Navy with his father-in-law, Benjamin Gonson, with the promise that he would take over when the latter retired. Hawkins did not have to wait long, for Gonson died in 1578. Hawkins knew naval ships intimately and put into effect 'race-built' vessels which were faster and more manoeuvrable. He put all his efforts into making the queen's navy more efficient, despite being opposed by the Council, which largely comprised men who had overseen the building of ships for more than a decade and had grown fat on corruption.

Hawkins investigated the costs for the ships and the dockyards and sent a report to Lord Burghley; he also wrote a document entitled *Abuses in the Admiralty touching Her Majesty's Navy exhibited by Mr Hawkins*. Although he exposed widespread corruption, none of the Board members was replaced. Instead they launched their own criticism of Hawkins, and in 1582 accused him of graft – an accusation that plagued him for some years. The following year a royal investigating commission under Lord Burghley, and including Francis Walsingham, the Lord Admiral, the Lord Chamberlain, the Chancellor of the Exchequer and several sub-commissioners, including Francis Drake, sat to examine the finances of the navy. They concluded that there was no undue corruption and that the queen's navy was in first-rate condition. Burghley suspected Hawkins of fraud but, as he turned out to be an innovative and capable administrator, he absolved him of corruption, along with the rest of the commission. Hawkins, already a confidant of Lord Burghley, frequently wrote to him. In a fit of patriotism, probably a result of the San Juan de Ulea betrayal, he wrote in 1584:

> The Queen can strongly annoy and offend the King of Spain, the mortal enemy of our religion and the present government of our realm of England. When I consider whereunto we are born, not for ourselves but for the defence of the Church of God, or prince and our Country. I do nothing at all doubt of our ability in wealth, for that I am persuaded that the substance of this realm is trebled in value since Her Majesty's reign. God be glorified for it! ... annoy the King of Spain without charge to Her Majesty, which shall also bring great profit to Her Highness and subjects.

Hawkins' Puritanical side increased with age and he launched frequent diatribes against the Catholics. His fervent Puritanism was so marked that on occasion, when he returned from an unsuccessful voyage, the queen upbraided him, commenting 'You went forth a soldier and came home as a divine.'

During the years of his tenure in charge of the navy, Hawkins made great strides in improving the ships, the ordnance and the crews. He upped the pay for crewmen from 6 shillings and 8 pence to 10 shillings per month. This helped to attract to the navy seamen who were more capable than the disinterested men who had previously made up the large crews. He later described how he wanted men 'Such as could make shift for themselves and keep themselves clean without vermin.'

Hawkins advanced from Treasurer to Head of the Navy Council, despite his failing health. He was plagued with malaria, which he had contracted during his visits to the west coast of Africa and the Caribbean. As one of the foremost seamen of the period, he was the chief architect of the Elizabethan navy. He made improvements to the design of naval vessels, introducing his 'race-built' designs which were longer, with the forecastle and aft castle (poop deck) greatly reduced in size. This gave them greater mobility and speed compared with the large lumbering ships of the Spanish navy. He also placed the mainmast further forward, which made the ships more manoeuvrable. He had spent his life on ships and understood their capabilities in sea warfare. By 1587 the English navy included twenty-five of these refurbished galleons and eighteen smaller warships. His designs even influenced the frigates built in the eighteenth century. The generous pay Hawkins introduced helped to muster an international crew: 'They would thus prevent Spain from declaring war on England; since this party not only consists of Englishmen, but rather of French, Flemings, Scots and such like.'

Hawkins had not been to sea for fifteen or so years, spending most of his exertions on improving Elizabeth's navy. His reward was to be appointed rear-admiral for the fight against the Spanish Armada in 1588.

Chapter Four

The Captives

After the débâcle at San Juan de Ulua, Hawkins travelled slowly north along the Mexican coast for two weeks. Aboard the *Minion* were an extra 200 men that he could not house or feed. On 8 October he was forced to put ashore those he had no use for, hoping they would be able to make their own way home. One such, page boy Miles Phillips, just 16 years old at the time, wrote an account of the wretched separation. He eventually managed to return to England fifteen years later:

> First he [Hawkins] made choice of such persons of service and account as were needful to stay: and that being done, of those willing to go, he appointed such as he thought might be best spared, And presently appointed, by the boat, they should be set on shore: our General promising us, that, the next year, he would either come himself, or else send someone to fetch us home. Here again, it would have caused any stony heart to have relented, to have heard the pitiful moan that many did make; and how loath they were to depart.

Another of the seamen put ashore on the Mexican coast, near the mouth of the River Tampico, was Davy Ingram, who was born in Barking, Essex. While the majority chose to head south or west, Ingram, along with Richard Browne and Richard Twyde, headed north; both men were conveniently dead before an account of their journey was written in 1583. They walked some 20 to 30 miles inland from the coast and covered an estimated 3,000 miles in a year. They were picked up at Cap Breton by Captain Champaigne of the merchant ship *Gargarine* from La Havre. Ingram reached England in January 1569 or 1570 and, according to him, was rewarded by John Hawkins. In August and September he was questioned about his extraordinary journey by a group of men headed by Sir Francis Walsingham who were collecting information about North America. They omitted the details of Ingram's lengthy adventure in their report but the tale was evidently believed for it was written down by Walsingham in 1583. That same year Ingram signed on as a crew member with Sir Humphrey Gilbert's voyage to Newfoundland. Richard Hakluyt reprinted Ingram's lurid story in his *Principall Navigations* in 1589, but left him out of the second edition.

There can be little doubt that the three men did cover this huge distance in a year. Ingram made mention of the Indians, who described large ships with sails, and his account is consistent with encountering the Micmac tribe on the Gulf of the St Lawrence river. He also described the buffalo they came across as they travelled across the plains. There is a chance they may have reached the Carolinas, where the French had established settlements, and may have caught a ship back to Europe. Ingram did exaggerated his account but it is probably true that he did cover this great distance before eventually reaching England. Part of his story appears to derive from his experiences in Africa and the Caribbean for he mentions 'elephants', although this term may simply mean 'large beasts'. Another possibility was that he and his companions were picked up by a French ship, possibly a privateer, somewhere along the Mexican coast and dropped at Cap Breton before sailing home to Europe.

To judge by the description of the terrain through which they travelled, they may have passed some way west while heading north. As they reached the eastern seaboard of North America, Ingram recalled seeing a strange bird:

> There is also another kind of fowl in that Country which hunted the rivers near unto the islands; they are of the shape of a goose, but their wings have coloured feathers and cannot fly ... They have white heads, and therefore the Countrymen call them penguins.

Some writers have worked out that the word 'penguin' was first used to describe auks in the northern hemisphere, and not the penguins in the south. The reference to the bird's 'white head' suggests he was describing great auks, which are now extinct but had a white spot on the head. The illiterate and superstitious Ingram always broadcast his experiences verbally. He relied on being questioned about the American coast by Walsingham, John Dee and Sir George Peckham. The result was a confusing account of Ingram's wanderings through North America. Certainly the journey was one of epic proportions, and he and his companions were the first Europeans to have walked across America from south to north. The framework of the tale has some degree of plausibility, even if parts of the story have little coherence. Ingram may have exaggerated, but there is enough substance in his tale to suggest that he did travel up the eastern seaboard, and returned to England thanks to Captain Champaigne of the merchant ship *Gargarine*.

Another survivor, chief gunner Job Hartrop, did not return to England until 1590. He was captured and sentenced to work as a rower on one of the Spanish galley ships. Following many years of misery, the ship in which he was serving a life sentence was captured and he was returned to England. After being deposited ashore from the *Minion*, he was captured by a cannibalistic tribe known as the Chichimec, who 'used to wear their hair long, even down to their knees; they do also colour their faces green, yellow, red and blue, which maketh them seem very ugly and terrible to behold'.

The Chichimec, having initially attacked the fugitives, realised that they were not Spanish and allowed them to depart. Their journey was constantly beset with danger as they were attacked by other tribes and many of the sailors were killed. They were finally captured by the Spanish, roped together and forced to march 180 miles to Mexico City. Here they were herded into a small compound and two months later sent to a grim prison some 20 miles away, where many died. Unable to bear this treatment, the remaining prisoners broke out during a stormy night and found themselves back in Mexico City. The governor decided that the prisoners should be sold to the Spanish colonists as servants, and some became overseers at the silver mines. Many married Mexican women and reverted to Catholicism.

This was a period of reasonable calm before the Inquisition arrived in 1574, at which time orders were sent all over the country for the English to report to Mexico City, where they were again imprisoned. About thirty men were tried by the Inquisition and received various sentences. They were subjected to terrible tortures and even execution by the fanatical Inquisitors, and the surviving captives later wrote of their awful experiences. The boys were spared death but were still tortured. They included David Alexander, Miles Phillips and Paul Hawkins, who had served as pages on the *Jesus* and the *Minion*, 16-year-old John Storey, a 'grumete' (cabin boy) on the *Swallow*, Robert Cooke, a kitchen boy, and Thomas Evans, a servant to the cooper on the *Jesus*. When he escaped to England, Miles Phillips wrote:

> About the space of three months before, they proceeded to their severe judgment against us, we were all racked; and some enforced to utter against themselves, which afterwards cost them their lives.
>
> And having thus got, from our mouths, sufficient for them to proceed to their severe judgment against us; they caused a large scaffold to be made in the midst of the Market Place in Mexico [City], right

over against the Head Church: and fourteen or fifteen days before their day of their judgment, with the sound of trumpet and the noise of the *attabalies* [a kind of drum] they did assemble the people in all parts of the city; before whom it was solemnly proclaimed that,

'Whosoever would, upon such a day, repair to the Market Place, they should hear the sentence of the Holy Inquisition against the English heretics, Lutherans, and also see the same put in execution' ... Which being done, and the time approaching of this cruel judgment; the night before, they came to the prison where we were, with certain Officers of that Holy Hellish House, bringing with them certain fools coats, which they had prepared for us, being in their language, *San Banitos*, which coats were made of yellow cotton, and red crosses upon them both before and behind ...

The next morning being come, there was given to every one of us, for our breakfast, a cup of wine and slice of bread fried in honey; every man alone, in his yellow coat, and a rope about his neck, and a great green wax candle in his hand unlighted ... So coming to the Scaffold, we went up by a pair of stairs, and found seats readymade, and prepared for us to sit down on. Every man in the order as should be called to receive his judgment ... presently the Inquisitors came up another pair of stairs, and then the Viceroy and all the Chief Justices with them ... then came up also a great number of Friars, White, Black and Grey. They being number of 300 persons ... And then they began their severe and cruel judgment.

It must have been a harrowing ordeal for the three teenagers to witness their shipmates' harsh penalties. Miles Phillips' account continued:

The first man that was called, was one Roger, the chief armourer of the *Jesus:* and he had judgment of to have 300 stripes on horseback [he was flogged and then paraded on horseback in front of the population] and after was condemned to the galleys, as a slave, for ten years. After him, were called John Gray, John Browne, John Rider, John Moon, James Collier and Thomas Browne. These were adjudged to have 200 stripes and after to be committed to the galleys for a space of eight years. Then severally called, to the number of fifty-three ... And then I was called, Miles Phillips, and was adjudged to serve in a monastery for five years without any stripes and to wear a fool's coat during all that time.

Which being done, and it now drawing towards night, George Runce, Peter Momfrey and Cornelius the Irishman were called: and had their judgment to be burnt to ashes. And were presently sent away to the place of execution in the Market Place, but little from the Scaffold: where they were quickly burned and consumed.

Among older men, the punishments were extremely severe. One such was Thomas Goodall, aged 30, the brother-in-law of Robert Barrett, who escaped on the *Minion* at San Juan de Ulua. Goodall was tortured at his trial, and received 300 lashes before being sentenced to ten years rowing in the Spanish galleys, as was Job Hartrop. Prisoners over the age of 21 received similar brutal sentences and very few survived. The younger boys were spared death but had to serve for several years in a monastery before being released. Miles Phillips was sent to the order of Black Friars to oversee the Indian workmen building a new church. He learned to speak their language and later wrote that he had 'a great familiarity with many of them', finding them to be 'a courteous and loving kind of people, ingenious and of great understanding, and they hate and abhor the Spaniards with all their hearts'.

Having served their time, Phillips and his companions were free to go anywhere in Mexico to find work. It is of interest that David Alexander and Robert Cooke chose to serve the Inquisitor, who married both of them to two of his black women servants. Richard Williams married a rich widow, while Paul Homewell married a Creole who owned a good house and had a dowry of 4,000 pesos. William Lowe managed to obtain a licence to go to Spain, where he married and settled down. Miles Phillips dared not settle in Mexico with the threat of the Inquisition hanging over him. Instead he paid to train as a weaver and after three years he saw an opportunity to escape.

In 1578 Mexico City was in a panic over the news that an Englishman was marching with a strong force from Acapulco on the west coast to plunder Mexico City. It turned out to be someone the Spanish feared most: 'El Draque', Francis Drake. In fact he had not landed at Acapulco but had sailed north beyond California. Having rounded the southern tip of South America he had raided along the Chilean, Peruvian and Panamanian coasts, causing great panic. Miles Phillips, together with Paul Homewell, was sent by the Viceroy to find out more information. Phillips was appointed interpreter to Captain Don Pedro de Robles, who led 200 men towards Acapulco to try to capture Drake. By the time they reached the port, they found that Drake had sailed a month earlier. Despite this, the Spaniards decided to pursue him. Phillips later wrote that they seemed an unseaman-like lot and Drake would have easily beaten them.

After several attempts to escape from this mission, Phillips made his way to a Guatemalan port and sailed to Cavallos. Here he sold his horse and persuaded the captain of a wine vessel to take him to join a thirty-seven-ship fleet bound from Havana to Spain. He was engaged as a soldier on Admiral Don Pedro de Guzman's ship and it is interesting to read what an Englishman thought of life aboard a Spanish ship:

> Yet to speak truly of what I think, two good tall ships of war would have made a foul spoil amongst them, For in all this fleet there were not any that were strong or warlike appointed, saving only the Admiral and Vice-Admiral; and again over and besides the weakness and the ill furnishings of the rest, they were all so deeply laden, that they had not been able to have held out any long fight. This unseaworthy fleet did, after a long and tiresome voyage of three months, arrive intact at San Lucar.

Phillips was then recognised by a seaman who informed the captain, and there was no doubt that the captain would have handed him over to the Inquisition in Seville. But on arrival at San Lucar on 10 September 1581, Phillips managed to escape in a rowing boat, and then made his way on foot to Cadiz. Reverting to his role as a weaver, he kept a low profile until he had saved some money. Walking back to San Lucar, he tried to persuade an English captain to take him back to England, but failed. Instead, he pretended to be a soldier and managed to get a passage on an English merchantman, returning to Poole in February 1582. Phillips wrote a damning account of his adventures and persecution at the hands of the Spanish, which only inflamed the public in their hatred of Spain and the Catholic religion.

Another seaman who sailed with Drake in his circumnavigation of the world was Peter Carder from St Verian in Cornwall. He was aboard the *Marigold*, a 5-ton eight-oared pinnace which became separated from Drake's fleet after sailing through the Straits of Magellan from the Atlantic to the Southern Sea. When a strong storm drove them southwards, Drake ordered the *Marigold* to look for the *Elizabeth* in the Strait. For fifteen days they searched but could not find the ship. Abandoning the search they attempted to return to Drake, but were unable to locate the *Golden Hind*. Carder later wrote that they once again sailed back through the Strait and then up the east coast of South America until they reached the Rio de la Plata. Coming ashore, they were attacked by Indians and only Carder and William Pitcher managed to get away in the pinnace. They sailed to an offshore island, where the *Marigold* was wrecked. Here they managed to exist on fruit and shellfish for two months. During that time they were able to fashion a crude raft to take them back to the mainland, a journey that took them three days. They soon found fresh water, but Pitcher was so thirsty that he 'over drank' and died. Carder buried him, and set off along the Brazilian coast until he was taken prisoner by the Portuguese and set to work as an overseer in a sugar plantation. As he was an experienced sailor, his Portuguese master signed him on to work on a small barque. Warned that a ship would arrive soon to take him back to Portugal as a prisoner, his master gave him the boat to escape to Pernambuco, where he hid for some months. He then signed on with a merchant ship and sailed for Europe. At the Azores the Portuguese vessel was attacked by two English ships and Carder was taken aboard. He arrived at Chichester in late November 1586, nine years after his parting from Drake's fleet. He told his story to Charles Howard, the Lord High Admiral, who took him before the queen at Whitehall, where he recounted his adventure and

Where it pleased her to talk with me a long hour's space in my travails and wonderful escape, and among other things of the manner of M. Doughty's execution; and afterward bestowed twenty-two angels on me, willing my Lord to have consideration of me; with many gracious words I was dismissed; humbly thanking the Almighty for my miraculous preservation, and safe return into my native country.

Chapter Five

Francis Drake

Francis Drake was the eldest of eleven sons born to Edmund and Lizabeth (née Mylwaye). His early life is obscure, and even the date of his birth (?February/March 1540) is not definite, although the general consensus is that he was born between 1540 and 1542. His grandfather held a lease to Crowndale Farm near the river Tavy, south-west of Tavistock in Devon, where he made a secure if unspectacular living. His landlord was Lord Francis Russell, 2nd Earl of Bedford. The Drakes stood in good stead with the Russells, sufficiently so for the new baby to be named Francis, and for Russell to act as his godfather. Infant mortality hit the Drake family hard, and Francis lost four brothers – Edward, John, Thomas and Joseph – and his sister Elizabeth. Edmund Drake was referred to as a 'farmer/preacher' and was a staunch Protestant, a religion his offspring followed.

Edmund may have been a sailor in his youth but the Lay Subsidy Rolls of 1544 show he derived a living from working as a shear man. This involved the use of large hand-shears to remove the raised nap of the cloth made in Tavistock. It was a skilful job but monotonous. Around Tavistock, weaving was often combined with farming, usually on a small scale. It was intermittent work and one that Edmund disliked. Using a nearby corn mill on the river Tavy that had been converted into a fulling mill, Edmund operated the hammers that beat the rough-spun kersey cloth into a finer material.

Originally Edmund had been a Catholic but after the changes wrought during King Henry's reign, he had converted to Protestantism. The abbey at Tavistock was dissolved by Henry in 1539 and all the lands and properties were given to the Russell family. Now vehemently anti-Catholic, Edmund applied to be ordained as a deacon but it is not known if he was accepted. In 1539, as a Protestant and a lay-preacher in the area, he was able to marry. King Henry still continued the Catholic traditions in church services and favoured priests who were unmarried and celibate. Under Henry, the new Church of England had severed ties with Rome and services were conducted in English instead of Latin. It was a time of religious intolerance when families were split between the two religions. The

Drakes, like many living in the area, embraced Protestantism and rejected Catholicism.

Barely able to scrape a living, Edmund turned to crime, either as a way of making money or as an anti-Catholic statement. According to the 1548 administrative records known as patent rolls, on 16 April at the nearby Dartmoor village of Peter Tavy, Edmund Drake and William Master, a former priest, together with an unknown person, accosted wealthy land-owner Roger Langisford. It was not a chance meeting, and it seems likely that the three men were there to collect a debt. Langisford probably disputed it, so the three men laid into him with a stave and the flat of their swords. Snatching Langisford's purse containing 21*s*/7*d* (£674 in today's currency), they made their way back to Tavistock.

Nine days later Drake and another man named John Hawkins (no relation to the famous Hawkins family) returned to Peter Tavy and attacked another landowner named John Harte and stole his horse worth £3. These crimes were not hushed up, but were well known in the area. Despite this, and after a period of nearly nine months, the robbers had not been apprehended for their crimes. The robberies may have had their cause in the intense religious ferment that was prevalent in the West Country and Edmund's acts may simply have been crimes against the Catholics. In the event, Drake and his fellow criminals were pardoned, largely thanks to Edmund's father borrowing a significant amount of money from the deposed Abbot of Tavistock to pay Lord Francis Russell to plead his son's case and ask for clemency.

The Fitz family lived next-door to Crowndale Farm and also owned land by the river Medway in Kent. Edmund and his family were now targets for the angry Catholics in the region, and sought to leave the area. Previously, Edmund had taken his family to Plymouth, where they stayed with their wealthy relations, the Hawkins. This coincided with the so-called Prayer Book Rebellion of 1549, when Catholics in the West Country rose up against its enforcement through an Act of Uniformity. This time the Drakes went further east. Richard Drake of nearby Whitchurch, who may have been a relation, owned a small barque called *The English Galley*, on which he carried Edmund Drake and his family to the river Medway, far from the turbulent events in the West Country. After the long journey to Gillingham in Kent, near the shipbuilding town of Chatham, the family took up residence in an abandoned ship's hulk on the banks of the Medway. The land here probably belonged to their former neighbours, the Fitz family. Edmund made a scant living as a prayer reader to the sailors and shipwrights at Chatham, and the family were forced to live a hand-to-mouth existence during Mary Tudor's Catholic reign. One of their near neighbours was an old bachelor who owned a small barque, and at this point Francis Drake enters the story. In William Camden's *History of the Reign of Elizabeth*, he remarked:

> His father by reason of his poverty put his son [Francis] to the master of a barque, his neighbour, who held him hard to his business in the barque, with which he used to coast along the shore, and sometimes carry merchandise to Zealand [the Netherlands] and France. The youth, being painful and diligent, so pleased the old man by his industry, that, being a bachelor, at his death he bequeathed the barque unto him by will and testament.

Edmund later applied to the Church authorities at Canterbury to become the vicar in the parish of Upchurch on the Medway's opposite bank. Despite his shady past, he was accepted and took up the position in 1560. In 1564 Spain seized every English ship she could find and the cross-Channel trade stopped. Francis's trading was impaired and he was forced to sell his vessel. Only after the death of Mary Tudor was it safe for Francis to return to the West Country to serve with his cousin, John Hawkins.

Drake was described as shorter than the average male, but well built, with a ruddy complexion, beard and fair hair. He was a natural working sailor, a skilled navigator and a born commander. By turns, he was puritanical, genial, obstinate and strict, but he was always protective of his crews. He treated his Spanish prisoners courteously and would either release them on an island or a remote beach with food and water. He was the very antithesis of a pirate, although the Spanish regarded his plundering as piracy.

By 1558 Drake was serving on a Hawkins ship that plied its trade between England and the Bay of Biscay area, and quite possibly also sailed to the Canary Islands. Hawkins had learned in the Canaries of the need for slaves in the Caribbean, where so many Carib natives were dying of smallpox and bubonic plague that the Spanish colonists were running out of manpower to work their plantations and mines.

The 'heretic' Protestant nations at this time were denied trading rights in the New World by Catholic Spain, and the English, Dutch and French relied on something akin to piracy for their riches; for decades they raided the large Spanish treasure vessels, plundering their cargoes to fill their coffers. Inheriting an impoverished exchequer from Mary Tudor, Queen

Elizabeth was forced to turn to partnerships with privateers like Drake and Hawkins to help boost the country's finances. John Hawkins was keen to launch a third expedition but protests from the Spanish authorities persuaded the British government to block him. Instead, in the summer of 1566 a Hawkins-sponsored voyage under Captain John Lovell, a friend and experienced captain, set out for the 'triangular trade route'. Among his crew was Francis Drake, who gained his first taste of action near the Cape Verde Islands off present-day Senegal. Rather than land, they attacked and plundered five Portuguese merchant ships and stole their cargo of slaves. These they took across the Atlantic to sell to the Spanish colonists, ignoring the embargo on non-Catholic ships trading slaves with the Caribbean. Despite using the same mercantile tactics as John Hawkins had done, Lovell lacked his mentor's charm, which had won him many friends among the colonial Spanish.

When Lovell landed on Hispaniola, he allowed his men to go raiding without control. This did not realise any profit, but instilled a greater fear of the English throughout the Caribbean. He cooperated with the French privateer Jean Bontemps in a raid on the island of Margarita off the Venezuelan coast. This show of force paid off and Lovell was able to sell some slaves. Still frustrated in his efforts to exchange slaves for treasure, Lovell was compelled to drop ninety infirm slaves on the river bank opposite Rio de la Hacha. His expedition proved to be a financial disaster, mainly because his crew was too small and unruly to force the Spaniards to trade with him. Within a year the expedition returned to Plymouth.

Three weeks later Drake was elevated to third officer on the *Jesus of Lübeck*, rented to Hawkins by the queen. After the disappointment of Lovell's expedition, the queen granted Hawkins another chance to sail to the Caribbean. As his fleet lay in Plymouth harbour, seven armed ships flying the Spanish royal standard entered the Sound. Their commander, the Flemish admiral Alphonse de Bourgogne, omitted to dip his flag and strike his topsails to the queen's ships at their anchorage. This was regarded as a flagrant discourtesy and Hawkins fired his culverins (simple hand-held smoothbore guns firing lead bullets) at the newcomers until the customary salutes were made.

About the same time a Spanish galleass anchored off Plymouth. On board were some Flemish prisoners who had been condemned to row on King Philip's galleys until they died. During the night masked men boarded the ship, overcame the crew and freed the prisoners. De Bourgogne protested, but Hawkins said it was more likely that Flemings from one of the Spanish ships had sprung the captives. The privy council considered this business and concluded that the Flemish admiral was correct, although this was not the time to pick a fight with Spain.

On 2 October 1567 the *Jesus of Lübeck*, bearing the green and white colours of a queen's ship, led Hawkins' six vessels out of Plymouth Sound and set sail for Tenerife. Here Drake would have sensed the hostility of the Spaniards and probably witnessed the confrontation between Hawkins and the Earl of Leicester. Drake was serving on the obsolete *Jesus* as she lumbered through a storm off Cape Finisterre, which caused the planking to separate and flood the bilges. When they were ready to cross to the Caribbean, the *Jesus* pitched and rolled to the great discomfort of the crew. It must have been with some relief that Drake was put in command of the 50-ton *Judith* some months later.

After selling their slaves in exchange for treasure, Hawkins' fleet was forced back into the Gulf of Mexico by a hurricane, the ships seeking shelter in the only port on the Mexican east coast, San Juan de Ulua, where they could make repairs. Having promised not to seek plunder, Hawkins began to repair his vessels, but a Spanish assault caught the English unawares at their mooring and they suffered several hundred dead and lost most of their ships, including the *Jesus*. Hawkins on the *Minion* and Drake's *Judith* were the only ships to escape. Overloaded with men from the other ships, the *Minion* and *Judith* spent the night among the reefs and sandbanks outside the harbour. Sometime during the night the two ships lost sight of each other. Drake may have misinterpreted Hawkins' order to sail clear of the obstacles and, with a storm blowing, navigated away. By the morning he no longer could see the *Minion*. Although his critics accused him of abandoning Hawkins, his cousin bore him no grudge. For decades to come the battle of San Juan de Ulua would haunt Drake. Returning to Plymouth after a four-month voyage (the details of which are not known), Drake arrived home a month before the *Minion*.

Having escaped from San Juan de Ulua, Drake for ever harboured a hatred of Catholic Spain and now began his twenty-year campaign against the Spanish. Drake had been well-taught by his Puritan father and Protestant zeal burned within him. His enemies, including the Spanish, made sure to remind everyone of his disgrace in abandoning John Hawkins at San Juan de Ulua, but Hawkins readily forgave his cousin and even left him a gift in his will. There is speculation that Drake undertook a voyage to Hamburg in early April 1569 as part of the seven-ship escort accompanying a wool flotilla. This may have been to escape the recriminations over his abandonment of John Hawkins. The new mission was a combination of trade and a show of support for their religious allies, who were being pressed by the Habsburg-Spanish in the Netherlands.

During the months that followed Drake married Mary Newman on 4 July 1569 at St Budeaux Church just north of Plymouth. Little is known of Mary, and Drake was at sea for most of the next decade. In the West Country piracy was partly legitimised by support from the gentry. Wealthy men like John Hawkins, Francis Drake and Walter Raleigh not only added support but actively took part in expeditions to the Spanish Main to raid supply routes and capture Spanish treasure ships to satisfy their backers as well as to increase their own wealth. The Spanish Main was a disease-infested wilderness which was home to deadly snakes, scorpions and insects. It was rare that a seaman did not catch malaria, yellow fever or dysentery, and effective medical treatment was still centuries away. Scurvy, the plague of the sea, was the most common sickness and it too was not treatable until much later, when lime juice or sauerkraut was carried as an antidote – hence the epithet 'Limey' used by the Americans.

On 24 May 1572 Francis Drake went on another expedition to the Spanish Main with two small vessels, the 70-ton *Pasco* and the *Swan*, 25 tons. The *Pasco* had a crew of forty-seven, the *Swan* just twenty-six, and they had provisions to last a year. Stowed away in the vessels were three dismantled pinnaces, which could be reassembled if necessary. The ships headed to a small hidden cove that Drake named Port Pheasant, which he had found on a previous trip. They entered the narrow entrance between the reefs, which Drake refers to in his account. Here they found a beach about a mile in length, with a water depth of 7 fathoms. Drake noticed a thin column of smoke rising from the trees that fringed the anchorage. Rowing ashore, he found a lead plate with a message scratched on its surface. It read:

> Captain Drake, if you fortune to come to this port make haste away, for the Spaniards which you had with you here last year have betrayed the place and taken away all that you left here. I departed from hence this present 7 of July 1572.
>
> Your loving friend, John Garret.

Garret was known to Drake from a previous voyage and it was he who had set a tree alight as a warning and then sailed away five days before Drake arrived. As the nearest Spanish port was 100 miles away, Drake thought he would be safe in this haven. He must have been alarmed when the next day a barque was seen entering the anchorage, but it was captained by James

Ranse, whom he knew from the ill-fated San Juan de Ulua fight. The two men agreed to join forces, with Drake in command, and to launch an attack on Nombre de Dios. To this end, the carpenters began assembling the pinnaces, including one from Ranse's ship. Five days later Drake and Ranse sailed for Nombre de Dios, towing the five pinnaces.

Some eighty years before, a number of black slaves had escaped their captors and fled into the jungle-clad mountains. They intermarried with the local Indians and became known as Cimarrons. As their numbers increased over the years they became a constant threat to the Spanish in the Panama region. The Bishop of Panama wrote to King Philip explaining that for every 1,000 slaves landed, 300 managed to escape and join the Cimarrons.

Six weeks before Drake's arrival, the Cimarrons had almost taken Nombre de Dios in a surprise attack. Drake made contact with them at the Islas de Las Palmas and, despite the English being involved in the transporting of slaves, they became allies. Under cover of darkness, Drake led his men into Nombre de Dios bay. The town was quite small but it was an important port for the Spanish treasure ships. Silver and gold from Bolivia and Peru were shipped to Panama on the south of the isthmus and then carried by mule-train north to Nombre de Dios for onward shipment. According to Michael Turner's book, *In Drake's Wake – the Early Voyages*, it is unlikely that a huge amount of silver would have been stored there awaiting the arrival of the treasure flotilla, which was not due for another three months. It was more likely that once the fleet arrived, a mule-train would bring the treasure from Panama to be loaded directly onto the waiting ships. Turner estimates that this probably happened in early January, the beginning of the dry season, to make the mule-train's journey easier.

As the pinnaces entered the port, they came under fire from the townspeople. One of the bullets struck Drake in the leg; although initially he made light of it, he soon fainted from loss of blood. His collapse coincided with a sudden violent rainstorm which drenched the crew's match and gunpowder, rendering the English weapons useless. Although some of his men had taken control of the town, and found some silver bars in the governor's house, when Drake came round he ordered his men to return to the pinnaces and retreat westwards to Isla Bastimentos. The attack had been a failure through faulty intelligence, but Drake had an alternative plan in mind to steal the treasure from the mule-train.

Drake quickly recovered from his wound, but he was left with a limp. Seeking to divert attention away from Nombre de Dios, he led a raid on

Cartagena, some 500 miles away. Under cover of darkness, and knowing that the port was well defended, Drake used three pinnaces to seize a merchant ship, the *Pasha*, which had just unloaded supplies. Locking the Spanish crew below deck, he sailed back to the San Bernados Islands, where he released the crew on one of the islands.

Drake now had a problem. Having captured the Spanish merchantman, one of his own ships, the *Swan*, captained by his brother John, was surplus to requirements. That night he secretly instructed Thomas Moone, the *Swan*'s carpenter, to bore three holes near her keel. Moone was aghast, but Drake talked him around. The next morning Drake invited his brother to accompany him on a fishing trip, and pointed out that John's ship was riding low in the water. John yelled to a crew member to check the water level. When he was told it was filling up, Francis persuaded John to leave the crew to pump the water out and to enjoy a day's fishing. When they returned, it was obvious that the *Swan* was sinking, despite the use of the pumps. The crew were instructed to grab their belongings and set fire to the ship. John was distraught until Francis appointed him captain of the *Pasha*. Drake then sailed for the Gulf of Darien and hid the *Pasha* in an inlet. He then set about building a small village and resting his crew.

From this remote bay, Drake made several minor raids on Spanish supply vessels, which yielded foodstuffs that kept his men fit and healthy. It also alerted the Spanish to the fact that Drake was attacking vessels on the east coast of the Panama isthmus. The diverted a number of their ships to either kill or capture him, but Drake managed to elude them all. His next big raid was against the mule-train travelling from Panama City to Nombre de Dios. He was dealt a heavy blow when his brother John was killed during a raid on a heavily defended frigate. This was followed up in January 1573 when Joseph, his younger brother, died of yellow fever after being bitten by a mosquito. In a rather ghoulish exercise, Drake, determined to discover what had killed Joseph, ordered the doctor to perform an autopsy. Nothing was found that pointed to yellow fever. Nevertheless, the doctor mixed a powerful antidote, which he hoped would save other crew members; in testing its efficacy on himself, the doctor also died. Although he mourned the loss of his brothers, Drake was still determined to carry out the raid on the mule-train.

On 1 February 1573 he led forty-eight men, including eighteen young crew members, inland to ambush the expected mule-train from Panama City, accompanied by their new-found allies, the Cimarrons. The trek through the steaming jungle was made worse as they had to climb over the ridge of mountains known as the Cordilleras. As they approached the high-point of the ridge, Pedro Mandingo, the Cimarron chief, took Drake's hand and led him to a tall tree. Steps had been cut into the trunk leading up to a wooden platform large enough to accommodate about a dozen men. From here Drake could look to the east and see the Caribbean and to the west the Southern or Secret Sea, renamed earlier by Magellan as the Pacific Ocean. Drake was the first Englishman to observe both oceans, although Vasco Nunez de Balboa had climbed the same tree in 1513 and saw the same vistas.

Falling to his knees, Drake thanked God for showing him the Southern Sea and declared that one day he would sail upon these new waters. Drake was intensely Christian, and even described himself as a Puritan, but rather than the dour and strict edicts of the Puritans, Drake enjoyed hearty good humour and childish jokes. He held prayers for his crew at mid-day and in the evening, and he could be boastful, though he was always conscious of his lowly origins. When he attained the formal trappings of nobility he became something of a snob, and was aware that members of the Elizabethan court were waiting to bring him down. Despite this, he was regarded by the wider English population as a great hero.

Drake chose an ambush position a few miles from Venta Cruces on the Chagres river. Here he positioned half his men in the long grass about fifty paces from the trail. On the other side, John Oxenham hid his men, all dressed in white shirts so they could be recognised in the dark. Soon they heard the jingle of the harnesses as the mule-train approached. Suddenly, Drake suffered a stroke of bad luck when a mounted Spaniard coming from Venta Cruces spotted a drunken sailor trying to get closer to the track. Spurring his horse, he galloped off to warn the mule-train that Drake was lying an ambush. The leader of the mule-train cunningly decided to try to fool the English by allowing a few mules loaded with silver and food to carry on to Venta Cruces. Drake's men duly seized the silver and retreated to Venta Cruces, which they easily occupied. Here Drake again demonstrated his humanitarian side by stressing the need for his men to act in a Christian manner:

> Of all the men taken, we never offered any kind of violence to any, after they once came under our power, but either presently dismissed them in safety or [kept] them with us some longer time. We always provided for their sustenance as for ourselves, and secured them from the rage of the Cimarrons.

Finally the whole party retreated to the coast to meet up with the two pinnaces. Although the raid had been a fiasco, Drake was planning another. On 23 March he was sailing a pinnace named the *Bear* off Cativas Island when he spotted a sail. It was a Huguenot ship, the *Havre*, captained by Guillaume Le Testu, a well known navigator and cartographer who knew the Caribbean well. They joined forces and again attempted the mule-train robbery. This time it was to take place near Nombre de Dios, where it was hoped the Spanish would relax their vigilance. Drake instructed his pinnaces to return to the Francisca river on 3 April to collect his men and the treasure. Sailing to the west of the town, the landing party faced a difficult march of some 20 miles through dense jungle. It took them two days. The following morning scouts reported 190 mules were approaching, guarded by forty-five armed soldiers. Drake held his men back until he judged it right to attack.

By 1 April Drake's men were hidden just a mile from Nombre de Dios. When the attack was launched, it was short and sharp, with the first and last mules captured. A haquebus was fired, badly wounding le Testu in the stomach. The Anglo-French corsairs descended on the mule-train and were amazed at the wealth they found. It was impossible to carry it all away and some was buried. In all, some £40,000 worth of silver was taken. Le Testu was left with two of his men in the hopes that he would be able to follow. But, unable to move, he was killed and beheaded by the Spanish.

Drake's men spent two days staggering over difficult terrain and through a heavy storm, laden with booty, until they reached the mouth of the Francisca river. There were no ships to meet them and it seemed as though their luck had run out. Instead of abandoning the treasure, Drake ordered a crude raft be built. Trees that had been toppled by the storm were hauled into place and roped together, and a mast with a makeshift sail installed. Carrying only four men, including Drake, it was launched into the heavy swell; barely afloat, they managed to sail some 12 miles until they spotted the two pinnaces. The two vessels had been beaten off by a strong westerly wind and could not reach the Francisca river. The crews had given up hope of seeing their captain again. The raft was beached on a nearby island and the treasure and the four men transferred to the boats. Making their way back, they collected the rest of the crew and what remained of the treasure, and the spoils were divided.

Having replenished his food stocks and careened his vessels, Drake set sail for Magdalena, where he guessed he would find a Spanish supply ship. The only problem was that he would have to sail past Cartagena, where a number of ships lay at anchor. Instead of trying creep past the port, he had his ship ostentatiously draped in colourful silks and flew the Cross of St George from the maintop. Perhaps the Spanish deliberately chose not to spot him, but they did not attempt to pursue him. The next morning Drake spotted a supply ship which satisfied his crew's needs, and he returned before a fair wind to Plymouth.

The Spanish branded the upstart English pirate *Draq*, *El Daque* or *El Draco* ('the dragon'). The Panamanian Municipal Council wrote to King Philip complaining about the recent attacks:

> The realm is at the present moment so terrified, and the spirits of all so disturbed, that we know not in what way to emphasise to your Majesty the solicitude we make in this dispatch, for we certainly believe that if remedial action be delayed, disaster is imminent. These English have so shamelessly opened the door and a way by which, with impunity, whatever they desire, they will attack the pack-trains travelling overland by this highway.

Chapter Six

Drake's Circumnavigation (1): The Doughty Incident

On 9 July 1577 Francis Drake wrote to the government claiming the royal bounty for construction of his new ship, the 150-ton *Pelican of Plymouth*. She was about 100ft in length and some 20ft in beam, and had the appearance of a typical merchantman, but she had been built to suit Drake's purposes, with a capacious hold and a double-planked hull. She also carried four pre-fabricated pinnaces. Fully laden, she drew 13ft, which enabled her to operate in shallow coastal waters. Importantly, she also carried fourteen cannon – the slender, long-range demi-culverins – and a range of smaller ordnance, as well as an armoury of other weapons. Accompanying her was the queen's 80-ton barque *Elizabeth* and the 30-ton *Marigold*, with the 15-ton *Swan* as a victualling vessel.

The peace between England and Spain was now over and yet more conspiracies against the queen were exposed by agents working for Francis Walsingham. One was a plot to have Philip's half-brother, Don John of Austria, invade England with 10,000 men, depose Elizabeth and install Mary Stuart on the throne. Don John would then marry Mary and together they would rule England. Even Lord Burghley, as always seeking peace with Spain, had to admit that Philip had undermined the peace process. Spain's diplomatic agent in London, Antonio de Guaras, realised something significant was happening but reported back that Drake was preparing to go to Scotland on a royal mission.

Lord Burghley was suspicious and employed Thomas Doughty to report to him about Drake's intentions. Drake was worried by the rumours about Doughty's meeting with Burghley but accepted the explanation that he had been offered the job of Burghley's private secretary. Drake made scrupulous preparations for his voyage to the South Sea and consulted both England's foremost navigator and geographer Dr John Dee and instrument-maker William Bourne. Supplied with the latest navigation aids, plus a map of the world (which was not accurate), Drake's flotilla left Plymouth on 15 November 1577. Almost immediately they ran into a terrible storm, which drove the ships into Falmouth harbour. When the storm abated after two days, the battered ships returned to Plymouth for repairs. Finally they were ready to depart again on 13 December. Once out of sight of land, Drake issued his sailing orders: they were bound not for the Mediterranean, as expected, but for the island of Mogador off Morocco.

Drake was accompanied by representatives of his backers, young high-born gentlemen who contributed little to the running of the ships. One was Thomas Doughty, whom Drake had befriended during his brief service in the Irish wars. Doughty had been a courier for the Earl of Essex but had been dismissed for some infringement. A plausible personality whom Drake liked, he stirred up a rift between Essex and the Earl of Leicester, which was patched up by Lord Burghley. Doughty was elegantly dressed and highly educated. He had been a lawyer at the Temple in London and was a scholar of Ancient Greek and Hebrew. At that time he was employed by Sir Christopher Hatton, one of Drake's principal backers, as his private secretary. However, for all his apparent friendliness, Doughty began to subtly undermine Drake's authority.

Only when they sighted Africa did Drake reveal to his crews the real purpose of the voyage: they were going to the Southern Sea to raid the unprepared Spanish. Most accepted this, although some of the crew who were expecting to travel to Alexandria felt they had been misled. There was one subject that particularly riled the seamen, and that was the gentle-men representatives who refused to do any work. The all-too-evident class distinction was having a corrosive effect on the crews.

On 27 December the small fleet anchored at Mogador, a barren island standing about a mile from the mainland. A group of Berber tribesmen arrived on the beach and Drake sent a boat to meet them. The following day a larger group appeared and John Fry, one of the crewmen, was sent to parley with them. Instead, they captured him. It seemed he had got caught up in the civil war currently raging in that area. Taken to the rebels' head-quarters, Fry explained that the seamen were English, and this seemed to pacify them. He was given presents and told to return to Mogador, only to find the fleet had already sailed away. Eventually Fry did manage to return to England on a merchant ship.

En route to Cap de Guerre, Drake captured three Portuguese fishing vessels off the Guinea coast and seized their catch. He retained one of the fishing vessels and named her the *Christopher*, in honour of Sir Christopher Hatton. He then sailed to Cape Verde, where they took the provisions from two smaller merchant ships. As they approached the island's principal port, Santiago, they spotted a ship making for the harbour and gave chase. It turned out to be a Portuguese merchant ship named the *Santa Maria*, captained by Nuno da Silva, a 60-year-old man sporting a long white beard. Drake renamed the ship *Mary* and added her to his small fleet, under the command of Thomas Doughty; he also took along the experienced Nuno da Silva and was delighted to discover that da Silva had frequently sailed to Brazil and carried new charts of the new continent. As they left Cape Verde they passed the island of Fogo and witnessed the eruption of her volcano. The last island they visited was Brava, where they stocked up with fruit, vegetables and fresh water. Drake also released his Portuguese prisoners, letting them have one of his pinnaces to reach Santiago.

During the crossing to Brazil some of the crew returned from the *Mary* and reported to Drake that Doughty had stolen items from the ship. Drake crossed to the *Mary* and confronted Doughty with the pilfering, but the young man shifted the blame onto Thomas, Drake's youngest brother. Drake sent Doughty back to the *Pelican*, while he himself remained on the *Mary*. The voyage across the Atlantic was not straightforward. They lay in the doldrums for days before sudden cloudbursts drenched the crews. Finally they found a steady wind that blew them to Brazil.

Meanwhile, Thomas Doughty's aim was to break away from Drake. Doughty's younger brother John allegedly told the crew that they possessed powers of witchcraft and could call up the Devil and inflict spells on their enemies. This was a period when the population was superstitious and believed in witchcraft, and nowhere was more susceptible than the close confines onboard ship. When Drake sent his messenger over to the *Pelican* on an errand, Thomas Doughty seized him, bent him over a barrel and invited the crew to administer a sound beating. When Drake learned of this, he summoned Doughty and humiliated him by sending him to the provision ship, *Swan*. He put his brother Thomas in charge of the *Mary* and took da Silva over to the *Pelican*.

On 5 April, fifty-four days after leaving the Cape Verde islands, the Portuguese navigator advised that they should not sail close to Brazil as there were ships patrolling the coastline. Drake took his advice and turned to port. But soon they were engulfed by a storm coming up from the south, during which the *Pelican* lost contact with the *Christopher*. Battling their way down the coast, they made landfall near latitude 32 degrees south. This put them at the mouth of the Rio de la Plata, where they rested. Two days later *Christopher* arrived and together they journeyed upriver to replenish their water barrels and depleted provisions.

On 27 April 1578 they left the river estuary and soon ran into another southerly storm, this time losing contact with the *Mary* and *Swan*. After a fruitless search for them, Drake continued down the coast of Patagonia until he reached a cape at longitude 47 degrees south, which he named Cape Hope. Another storm scattered the fleet and Drake instructed signal fires to be lit on the beach to guide the missing ships into the anchorage, but to no avail. Drake then sailed 30 miles further south to a more suitable bay which he named Port Desire. He sent the *Elizabeth* further south, while he searched for the missing ships to the north. While the search was being made, Doughty was openly defying Drake's orders and claiming that it was he who was in charge of the expedition. He boasted that he had been approached by Lord Burghley to be his secretary and confidant. Annoyed at the young man's arrogance, the master of the *Swan*, John Saracold, took issue with him and the two came to blows.

The *Swan* was eventually found by the *Pelican* and joined the other ships at Port Desire. Trying to keep so many ships together was almost impossible, so Drake ordered that the provisions be removed from the *Swan*, and the ship was then beached and burned. The antics of the English intrigued the local native tribe and eventually they met and exchanged presents. The natives began to dance and Drake ordered the *Pelican*'s musicians ashore to play for them. After a while the natives dispensed with exchanging presents and began stealing. One native even snatched Drake's red sea-cap off his head but he advised the crew to let it go. This cap was possibly the one that Queen Elizabeth had given Drake before he left Plymouth.

After two weeks at Port Desire, Drake prepared to continue his voyage. Having seen Doughty in quiet conversations with the officers and crew of the *Pelican*, Drake confronted him; in the heated exchange that followed, Drake struck Doughty and ordered him to be tied to the mainmast. He was left tied up for two days, after which Drake ordered him to board the *Christopher*; Doughty objected to this, claiming that he would be killed. Once again, storms separated the ships and *Christopher* had disappeared. Drake searched for four days and found her in a bay. Aware that he could not keep looking for missing ships, he ordered the vessel to be stripped of all useful material before being set on fire. He then went on board the *Elizabeth* and told the crew that he was sending two mutinous men who were stirring up discontent, and warning them that if anyone spoke with them they would be regarded as enemies of the voyage.

On 14 June they sailed south for three days, heading for a bay named Port St Julian, which lay within 100 miles of Magellan's Strait. Drake was worried about his brother on the *Mary* as she had not been seen since Rio

de la Plata two months before. Finally they spotted the ship on 19 June and brought her into the bay. She was in poor condition and leaking badly as a result of continual battering from the storms. Caulking and general refurbishment restored the *Mary*, leaving her in better condition to face the Magellan Strait. Drake's ships were now not far from Magellan's sheltered bay, Port St Julian, the last refuge before they entered the Straits. On 20 June the diminished fleet entered Port St Julian. There was a low sandy island which was an ideal place to careen their vessels before attempting the passage through the Straits. The next day Drake rowed ashore with a few men to look for fresh water and game. He took along with him the surgeon Richard Winterhay with his longbow and a master gunner named Oliver, armed with a harquebus, and a small party of men. Going ashore, they met two Indians armed with small bows. Winterhay indicated that he could fire further, and they competed against each other until his bowstring broke. Just then an older Indian arrived and began making hostile gestures at the Englishmen. As Drake's party withdrew to their boat, one of the Indians fired an arrow at Winterhay, wounding him in the arm. The native fired again, and this time the arrow punctured Winterhay's lung. Oliver aimed his harquebus at the assailant but it failed to fire. Another Indian fired; his arrow hit Oliver in the chest and pierced him through, killing him. As Drake ordered the men to retreat to the boat, he picked up the harquebus, reprimed it, aimed and fired it at the Indian. It caught him in the stomach, which caused the other natives to flee. Winterhay, barely alive, was carried to the ship, where he lingered for two days before dying. He was buried with Oliver in a common grave. Although Port St Julian was a sheltered haven, it had an atmosphere of doom. Back in 1526 Magellan had executed Gasper Quesada and Luis de Mendoza here, and left two more mutineers marooned on the desolate coast. Magellan's gibbet was found and the ship's carpenter used the wood to make drinking tankards.

By this time Drake had become deeply suspicious of Thomas Doughty and was aware that he was plotting against his plans to reach the Southern Sea. Despite being several thousand miles from England, Drake was determined to put Doughty on trial. However, Doughty had about thirty supporters who would rather abandon this whole venture and return home. Drake was worried about Doughty's attempts to undermine his command and was determined to resolve the problem before he led his ships through the Magellan Straits. He was also worried about the queen's reaction to the trial of one of her courtiers, and Sir Christopher Hatton's response to the behaviour of his representative. On 30 June Drake assembled the entire company on the shore of a small island in the bay and delivered the charges against Doughty:

> Thomas Doughty, you have here sought by diverse means, in as much as you may, to discredit me to the greater hindrance and over- throw of this voyage, besides other great matters wherewith I have to charge you withal, the which if you can clear yourself of, you and I shall be very good friends, where to the contrary you have deserved death.

Drake ordered the accused to be bound, while Doughty denied all allega- tions of flagrant action against Drake. The jury, numbering forty gentle- men and seamen, listened while Captain John Winter, the jury's foreman, read out the statements made by several witnesses, which cast Doughty in a bad light. One of the witnesses, Edward Bright, had been present in Drake's garden in Plymouth when he overheard Doughty declaring that the queen and her Council could be corrupted with money. Doughty tried to deny the accusations and let slip that he had revealed the route of the voyage to Lord Burghley, who was completely set against it. Drake was furious; the queen had been at pains to keep Burghley completely in the dark as he was opposed to any mission that might upset the Spanish. Leonard Vicary, Doughty's lawyer friend, declared the trial illegal and Drake's reaction was to declare that he would 'have nothing to do with you crafty lawyers, neither care I for the law, but I know what I will do. You shall not have to do with his life, let me alone for that. You are but to see whether he be guilty in these articles.'

Another accusation was made by Doughty's brother, with Doughty's support, about the use of witchcraft in conjuring up storms and adverse winds. It was all too plausible to the simple seamen and a phenomenon they could all understand. Drake then asked the jury to deliver their verdict. After deliberation the forty members of the jury returned a verdict of guilty. After the sentence of death was pronounced, Doughty asked to be put ashore at Peru but Drake refused. Captain Winter offered to take Doughty back to England but was met with a chorus of objections from his crew. Finally, Drake told Doughty to prepare for his execution in two days' time. He was asked how he would prefer to meet his end and he chose to die under the axe.

On 2 July Drake and Doughty behaved with a certain cold-blooded display of mock friendship. Doughty asked to receive the sacrament from Chaplain Fletcher and Drake offered to accompany him. Drake then invited Doughty to lunch with him in his tent and they toasted each other.

At the conclusion of the meal, Doughty was led out to the place of execution in front of the whole company. Kneeling before the block, Doughty prayed for the queen before lowering his head upon the block. The executioner raised his axe and severed Doughty's head. Calling for the severed head to be held up, Drake declared, 'Lo! This is the end for all traitors.' He followed this with a warning that if there was any more sign of mutiny, then he would not hesitate to execute the offender. Thomas Doughty's body was buried next to the graves of Winterhay and Oliver. The bones found at the foot of the gibbet were gathered together and interred with the bodies of the Englishmen.

A month was spent careening the hulls of the three ships and preparing for the passage through the Magellan Strait. On 11 August Drake ordered the entire company ashore, where he delivered a speech that was part sermon, part pep-talk. To his crews' delight, he finished with the words, 'The gentlemen in the future must haul and draw with the mariner, and the mariner with the gentlemen.' He then told the ships' officers that they were demoted to ordinary seamen, which elicited shouts of anger. Having won the argument, he then restored the officers to their former rank; there would be no further dissent. Drake then ordered that the *Mary* should be burned and her crew divided amongst the three remaining ships. Finally, on 17 August, they weighed anchor and headed south to the Magellan Strait.

Doughty's death played on Drake's mind for the rest of the voyage. On 21 August 1578 he held a small ceremony in the lee of a headland to change the name of his ship, the *Pelican*, to the *Golden Hind*, after Sir Christopher Hatton's coat of arms, perhaps in an attempt to curry favour with Hatton, whose representative was Thomas Doughty. Either way, the Doughty incident was soon overtaken by the adventures and riches that were to come.

Chapter Seven

Drake's Circumnavigation (2): Drake's Fortune

After three days the ships entered the Magellan Straits. August was not the best time of year for such a voyage. For one thing the winds were against them and they often strayed into landlocked inlets; for another, the charts they had were unreliable. Onshore they could see the fires of the natives who lived in this harsh environment. Magellan had seen the same thing and named this land Tierra del Fuego – 'the land of fires'. The Strait – the only way to reach the Southern Sea – was 363 miles long and it took Drake's fleet from 21 August to 6 September to pass through it. It was not a straightforward east–west journey; instead they headed south down Broad Reach before making a sharp turn to the north-west, travelling through a narrow passage some 2–3 miles wide, until they reached Cape Deseado. Here they finally entered the Southern Sea.

On 24 August they anchored close to three small islands at the beginning of Broad Reach. Landing on the largest of them, Drake named it Elizabeth Island. He had one of the trees felled and the trunk placed in the hold for presentation to the queen. Elizabeth Island was estimated by Nuno da Silva as being at 57 degrees south but it has since disappeared. It was probably a volcanic or a sunken island that over the centuries has disappeared beneath the waves. The other islands he named St George and St Bartholomew. There he found 'fowls that could not fly, bigger than a mallard, short and thick set together, having no feathers but instead thereof, a certain hard and matted down . . . their feeding and provision is in the sea'. These birds were later identified as penguins. As they had no fear of humans, the crews caught them easily, gutting them and salting the meat in barrels.

Passing Cape Forward at the end of Broad Reach, they entered the most daunting phase of their journey. Now heading north-west, they were dwarfed by the beginning of the Andes Mountains, which stretched right the way up South America. The Strait narrowed to 2–3 miles wide and the mariners felt a sense of being hemmed in by the height of the mountains.

The ships struggled for three days to make any headway and found they had only travelled 30 miles. Drake also discovered that he could not anchor his ships as the water was so deep. After three days they did find an anchorage and Drake went ashore. Here he found a variety of herbs and other strange plants which helped supplement their diet. The only natives Drake came across were in a canoe made of bark, their only tools hatchets and knives made from giant mussel shells.

Finally the three ships emerged into the Southern Sea at Cape Deseado. The wind was favourable and they made 150 miles in two days. Then the wind direction changed and they ran into a series of storms, which blew them back past Cape Deseado. Remarkably the three ships stayed together. The storms finally abated on the night of 28 September, with high seas pounding the tip of South America. At this point Drake lost sight of the *Marigold* and was fearful she had foundered. As the wind grew stronger, the *Golden Hind* and *Elizabeth* tried to reach safety in a rock-strewn bay just north of Cape Deseado but the *Golden Hind* was unable to drop its anchor and had to put to sea. Francis Fletcher recorded the great storm:

> Where coming to anchor, within small time (being night), we had like entertainment from the hills as we had before from the mountains, and with greater and more dangerous violence our cables broke, our anchors came home, our ships were separated, and our spirits fainted as with the last gasp unto death.

Drake had left instructions that the two ships should rendezvous at latitude 30 degrees off the coast of Chile. The following day Captain Winter, suffering from considerable stress and without bothering to look for Drake's ship, waited just three days before making for the Magellan Strait. Most of the crew on the *Elizabeth* wished to continue the voyage with Drake but Winter was adamant that they should turn about and set sail for England. Eight months later he arrived off the Devon coast. He wrote to the privy council defending his decision to turn back and including details of Thomas Doughty's trial and execution.

Meanwhile a series of storms drove the *Golden Hind* further along the south coast of Cape Deseado until they died down. Drake was able to exchange gifts with some natives in canoes and rested up for five days. Again the storms returned; again their cable parted and they lost another anchor. They were driven further and further south until 24 October, when the weather turned calm and bright. It had been fifty-two days since they had emerged from the Strait, during which time they had been in a constant battle with the terrible storms. Finally, on 1 November, the

Golden Hind set a course to the north by north-west and headed for the Chilean coast. This time they were able to sail for some 1,200 miles without stopping.

They anchored at the island of Mocha, about 18 miles from the coast. Initial communications with the natives were amicable but the next day they met an entirely different reception. As Thomas Brewer and Thomas Flood set about filling their casks with fresh water, about a hundred natives charged at them, firing arrows. The rest of the shore party rushed back to the boat, various of them being hit by the arrows, including Drake, who was hit twice, once under his right eye and the other creasing his scalp. Somehow the boat managed to get free. Francis Fletcher wrote in his journal:

> Not any one person escaped without some grievous wounds, and most had so many that their bodies were loaden with arrows ... at whose departure arrows were sent to them so thick as gnats in the sun, and the sides of the boat within and without stuck so full of them ...

Another boat quickly left the *Golden Hind* to try to rescue Brewer and Flood, but they arrived too late to save them being butchered. The other members of the shore party had all suffered wounds but the arrowheads were small enough to be extracted and only one man died. The men were all for firing their cannon at the crowds of natives but Drake refused, on the grounds that 'they were English and not Spanish as the Indians believed them to be'. He then ordered his crew to set sail and, after a 350-mile voyage, they reached the Bay of Quintero.

An Indian fisherman explained that they had missed the entrance to Valparaiso, the port of Santiago. Turning about, the *Golden Hind* entered the harbour and captured the *Los Reyes*, renamed the *Capitana*, the only ship at anchor. Besides finding a cargo of wine, they also found four chests each containing 75lb of gold. Sailing north again, they reached the beginning of the Atacama Desert, one of the driest deserts in the world, and one where water was non-existent. Fortunately, before they reached the sandy wastes, they found fresh-water springs and a herd of llamas, which fascinated the crew.

On the border between Chile and Bolivia lay the small coastal village of Tarapaza. Here they found a slumbering Spaniard on the beach, alongside 13 bars of silver. Quietly they took the silver and left the snoring man asleep. After sailing another 500 miles north, they reached the verdant valley housing the small port of Arica, from where most of the silver was collected by ships for onward shipment to Panama. It was Drake's bad luck to discover that the two barques present were empty, but they learned from a slave that a ship had not long since departed from Arica carrying gold and silver to the port of Chule, 50 miles up the coast. Once again, they were too late to capture this rich haul as the ship had been unloaded and there was a military presence in the town which Drake was loath to confront. Sailing north for 450 miles, Drake came in sight of Callao, the port of Lima. Situated about 6 miles inland from the coast, Lima was the centre of Spain's southern colonial area. With the coming of night, the *Golden Hind* managed to slip into the harbour, where there were seventeen ships at anchor. Once again Drake's timing was off as the ships had not yet been loaded. Once their presence was discovered by the harbour master, Drake's crew cut the anchor cables of the Spanish ships and de-masted two of the largest vessels. The *Golden Hind* captured the newly arrived *San Cristobal* but had to relinquish her when she became becalmed outside the harbour. Instead, Drake concentrated on catching up with the treasure ship *Nuestra Senora de la Conception*, irreverently referred to by the Spaniards as the *Cacafuego* ('Shitfire'), which had sailed nine days earlier. Realising the treasure ship would call at several ports along the way, Drake was sure he had the speed to overtake her.

On the way, he captured a barque which he relieved of 18,000 gold and silver pesos. From her crew he learned of the deaths in Europe of King Sebastian of Portugal, the Pope, the King of France and Philip's half-brother, Don John of Austria. Sensing that they were closing in on the *Cacafuego*, Drake offered a gold chain reward to the man who first spotted their prey. Soon there came a cry from the crow's nest that sails had been spotted 12 miles to the leeward and Drake's young brother John claimed the reward. To conceal the fact that the *Golden Hind* was a heavily laden merchantman, the sails were furled and she trailed strings of wine jars to slow her progress. The ship's captain, San Juan de Anton, later recalled Drake boarding his vessel at about nine o'clock at night off Cape San Francisco:

> When they heard this, a whistle sounded in the English ship and a trumpet responded. At once, they discharged what seemed to be about sixty arquebuses, and then many arrows which struck the side of my ship. Shortly, a heavy gun was fired with chain-balls which carried away the mizzen-mast into the sea with the sail and the yard. Another heavy gun was fired, someone saying I should strike. At this point, the launch came alongside on the port side with a matter of some forty arquebusiers, who climbed up the channels to which the

shrouds are fastened and came aboard my ship. The English ship lay alongside on the starboard and thus made me strike sail ... I saw the Corsair, Francis Drake, armed with a coat of mail and a helmet, already disarming himself. He embraced me, saying, 'Have patience, such is the custom of war' ...

Moving out of sight of land, the two vessels remained locked together. The following morning Drake inspected the treasure. In the *Cacafuego*'s hold were 1,300 bars of silver weighing 26 tons, as well as thirteen chests filled with 400,000 pesos of silver and gold, and 80lb of gold. On 3 March Drake's crew began to transfer the treasure to the *Golden Hind*. It took three days to replace the ship's ballast with silver and to balance her equilibrium, during which time Captain de Anton dined with Drake, where he learned that neither Hawkins nor Drake could forget the treachery at San Juan de Ulua, and that Drake had come to raid the Southern Sea to compensate for this outrageous act. Despite Drake's bitterness, he gave de Anton a gilt silver bowl, a harquebus and a silver breastplate. To his passengers and crew he gave 30 or 40 pesos each. Finally leaving the stripped *Cacafuego*, Drake sailed 600 miles further north to the shores of Costa Rica, where he stopped and took the provisions from a barque captained by Rodrigo Tello. He also found that the vessel was carrying navigational charts for the Philippines, which interested him. He captured another barque and then entered the harbour at Guatulco, a small port on the southern coast of Mexico. Little was found in the village except for a chest of coins and other valuables, which was naturally lifted aboard the *Golden Hind* to join the rest of the haul. The released captives, including Nuno da Silva, gave evidence to the Inquisition that Drake would not return down the west coast of South America, nor attempt the perilous route via the East Indies and the Cape of Good Hope. Instead they thought he would attempt to return to England via the legendary North West Passage.

Chapter Eight

Drake's Circumnavigation (3): The East Indies and Home

News of Drake's raiding in the Southern Sea had a mixed reception in London. The backers who had invested in the expedition were absolutely delighted with the profits they expected to make. The merchants, on the other hand, depended on trade with Spain and the inevitable repercussions would lead them to ruin. As the months passed, and with no sign of Drake's ships returning home, the backers began to worry that Drake had met with disaster, while the merchants continued their trade with Spain and became less alarmed. Nuno da Silva, the Portuguese pilot who had been released by Drake, was interrogated by the Inquisition. Falling into Drake's hands did not make things easier for the unfortunate navigator, especially as Philip had seized the Portuguese throne on the death of the king. Nuno da Silva described Francis Drake to the Inquisition in Mexico:

> This Englishman calls himself Francis Drake and is a man aged 38. He may be two years more or less. He is low in stature, thick-set, and very robust. He had a fine countenance, is ruddy of complexion and had a fair beard and hair.

For Drake, meanwhile, the raiding was over. He had seized a vast amount of treasure and could not accommodate any more. Leaving Guatulco, he sailed west for 1,500 miles before he turned north and followed the Californian coast. By this time the Spaniards had lost all contact with him and assumed he was on his way back to England. By June he had reached 42 degrees north, approximately in line with the border between California and Oregon. It was here that the fair weather changed and the temperature plummeted. Still travelling north, the ship encountered bitter squalls and fog, and the rigging grew stiff with frost. She reached 48 degrees north, just south of Vancouver Island, although some thought they had travelled further north. The bad weather, bitter cold and poor visibility persuaded

Drake that trying to find the North West Passage would be impossible. He wrote:

> We found the air so cold, that our men being grievously pinched with the same, complained of the extremity thereof, and the further we went, the more the cold increased upon us. Whereupon we thought it best for that time to seek the land, and did so, finding it not mountainous, but low plain land, till we came within 38 degrees towards the line. In which height it pleased God to send us into a fair and good bay, with a good wind to enter the same.

To the relief of his crew, Drake's decision to turn south to careen his ship, and then take the route back to England through the Spice Islands and around the Cape of Good Hope, was welcomed. After turning south and sailing for 600 miles, he found a haven inside Point Reynes which he named Drake's Bay. It was just north of the present-day city of San Francisco, although an alternative location may be just north of Point Loma (present-day San Diego), which was the northernmost extent of Spain's reach.

The *Golden Hind* had sprung a leak, and her hull was covered in weed and in need of cleaning before she set off across the Southern Sea. The crew built a small fort in which to store the treasure they had amassed, and then began to clear and caulk the hull. They were visited by friendly, if mystified, native Indians, who later crowned Drake with a headdress of feathers. Drake also planted a small brass plate proclaiming the country as New Albion and a new dominion for Queen Elizabeth. After four weeks they were ready to sail. It is worth noting that there had been no sickness on the *Golden Hind* since departing Plymouth.

Drake's ship caught the north-east trade winds which blew her along for sixty-eight days without incident, until they reached the Palau Islands, about 500 miles east of the Philippines. Here Drake paused for a day, but the crew found themselves threatened by the natives, who stole all they could, including the knives from the sailors' belts. With some effort, the crew managed to eject them from the ship, only for the natives to unleash a hail of stones from their slings. With some relief, Drake sailed on to Mindanao in the Philippines, where they refilled their water butts. Using the crude maps Drake had collected in Lisbon, he steered south to the Spice Islands. In November 1579 he met a Portuguese galleon, which he hailed and asked for food in exchange for goods. Without stopping, the galleon fled into shallow water where Drake could not reach her.

Sailing on, they came to an island where two fishermen agreed to guide them to the island of Ternate. Spotting a line of conical mountains in the distance, Drake caught the aroma of nutmeg, mace and cloves from the fabled Spice Islands or Moluccas. These islands were situated between the Celebes and New Guinea. The people of the islands had been ill-treated by the Portuguese and Spanish, and as a consequence were only too pleased to welcome these English travellers. They were not the only Englishmen to venture this far: a few merchantmen had previously visited the islands, trading cloth for spices. The Portuguese had occupied one island in the Moluccas, where they had two warships; the rest of the islands were ruled over by Sultan Babu. Anchoring off the island of Ternate, Drake was greeted by one of the Sultan's rajahs.

The next day four war canoes carrying important officials announced that Sultan Babu himself was on his way to welcome the emissary from the Queen of England. With much pomp, the war canoes towed the *Golden Hind* into the port of Ternate, accompanied by the royal barge. Drake and his officers changed into their finest clothes in order to meet the Sultan, and Drake ordered the crew to fire the ship's cannon in salute and then his small orchestra began to play, which enthralled the potentate. In this amiable atmosphere, gifts and food were exchanged. This changed when Drake expressed an interest in acquiring cloves but balked at paying the duty levied by the Sultan. It escalated so far that Drake was in danger of being killed, but a further exchange of gifts smoothed things over. Despite the threat to Drake's life, the gentlemen and crew were invited to the royal compound. Francis Fletcher described the visit to Babu:

> From the waist to the ground was all cloth of gold, and that very rich; his legs were bare, but on his feet a pair of shoes of leather dyed red; the attire of his head were finely wreathed in diverse rings of plated gold ... about his neck he had a chain of perfect gold, the links very great and one fold double; on his left hand was a diamond, an emerald, a ruby and a turquoise, four very fair and perfect jewels, on his right hand, in one ring, a big and perfect turquoise, and in another ring many diamonds of a smaller size. As thus he sat in his chair of state, at his right side there stood a page with a very costly fan, richly embroidered and beset with sapphires breathing and gathering the air to refresh the king, the place being very hot.

The Sultan expressed his desire that the Portuguese should be expelled from his islands, and a trade in the supply of cloves was approved between England and the Spice Islands. The Sultan agreed to supply Drake with

6 tons of cloves, and gave him a ring to present to the queen. Word had reached the Portuguese of the new arrival, and before the *Golden Hind* departed Ternate two Portuguese officials visited Drake's ship, thinking she was a Spanish vessel. The two men were surprised to find it was Drake's ship, and Drake told them that he had ten ships all visiting different places. He also told the astonished visitors that their king had died in Morocco.

After two days, the *Golden Hind* reached a small island in the Banggai Archipelago off the Celebes, and the crew found a beach suitable for careening, scraping away the weed, caulking and coating the ship with pitch. After four weeks on the island, they set sail once again. They made good headway, but on 9 January 1580 they came to a juddering halt as the vessel struck a submerged reef. Stranded on the coral, they could do little to refloat her. Drake's resident chaplain, Francis Fletcher, who was considered to be rather an obstruction than a spiritual leader for the crew, delivered an alarming sermon in which he said that Thomas Doughty's execution had caused the *Golden Hind* to founder and that the crew must bear the guilt of his death. The morale of the crew plummeted. Drake was furious with Fletcher and had him excommunicated and kept below deck. He also made him wear a label reading: 'Francis Fletcher the falsest knave that liveth.' The following morning Drake ordered eight cannon and 3 tons of cloves to be ditched over the side. With the rising of the tide, the ship suddenly refloated and slid off the reef into deep water.

As they rounded the south-east tip of the Celebes, they met contrary winds which blew them eastwards towards Timor. According to Samuel Bawll's book *The Secret Voyage of Sir Francis Drake*, when the Dutch arrived on Timor in 1587 they found that Francis Drake had got there before them:

> A ship had anchored in that same place with people who were in some respects like us – fair complexioned and bearded ... Among them were some who knew how to divide a rope into five or six parts and then make the rope whole again.

With a change of wind, and after a voyage of two months, Drake was able to reach Java, anchoring at the port of Cilacap on the south coast. Drake sent gifts to the local rajah, who reciprocated by sending him rice, coconuts and some hens. Drake even sent his musicians to entertain their host and for the next two weeks visited a succession of chiefs. The next morning, March 1580, the *Golden Hind* departed, heading across the Indian Ocean to the Cape of Good Hope. Little of note happened during that leg of the voyage, but after rounding the Cape, they narrowly escaped being wrecked on the Skeleton Coast. They were running low on water, but in the end they spread their sails over the decks and collected enough rain-water to keep them going.

A month later they reached Sierra Leone and replenished their water and foodstuffs. They then set out for La Rochelle on the coast of France, where Drake could again careen his vessel. He also wanted to find out if it was safe to return to England, as he had received no word as to the state of his country. There are some contrary versions of what happened next. His brother John wrote later:

> On reaching Plymouth they inquired from some fishermen 'How was the Queen?' and learnt that she was in good health, but that there was much pestilence in Plymouth. So they did not land, but Captain Drake's wife and the Mayor of the port came to see him on the ship. He dispatched a messenger to the queen who was in London, which was sixty leagues distant, apprising her of his arrival, and he wrote to other persons at Court who informed him that he was in Her Majesty's bad graces because she already heard, by way of Peru and Spain, of the robberies that he had committed ...
>
> Thereupon Drake left the port of Plymouth with the ship and, lying behind an island, waited until the queen sent him word.

There is no doubt that Elizabeth was apprehensive about the Spanish preparations for an invasion and she wanted Drake to lie low for a while. Walsingham and Leicester counselled that since Drake had arrived carrying a fortune in treasure, he should be welcomed. So, on 26 September 1580 Drake and his fifty-nine remaining crewmen once again entered Plymouth harbour to a rapturous reception. While Drake awaited a summons from Elizabeth, he put his treasure into temporary storage in Tremonton Castle near Plymouth. While he waited, he received news that a small force of Spanish troops, backed by Pope Gregory, had landed at Munster to shore up the Irish rebellion against the English. Drake was ordered to sail to Ireland to assist in expelling the Spanish soldiers. In a brief action, the English defeated the invasion force, massacring the survivors. This half-hearted Spanish incursion helped to make up the queen's mind and she invited Drake to Richmond Palace, her favourite residence, with 'some samples of his labours'.

Drake loaded about £326,580-worth of treasure and coin onto a train of horses accompanied by guards, and they made their way to Richmond. By the time the treasure was transferred to the Tower of London, it had diminished to £264,000-worth. It is probable that £100,000 was secretly handed to the queen, which further sweetened her regard for Drake. The secret was kept by Elizabeth and Francis Drake for two years. The queen invited Drake to accept £10,000 for himself and an additional £14,000 to be distributed among his crew as a bonus. At the queen's invitation, Drake then sailed the *Golden Hind* from Plymouth to Deptford on the river Thames, where it was put on display.

On 4 April 1581 Elizabeth travelled in state to Deptford and ate a sumptuous lunch aboard the ship. When the meal was finished, she took her golden sword and handed it to the French ambassador, asking him to knight the master mariner. She also gave Drake his official coat of arms and ordered the *Golden Hind* to be taken on land as a permanent memorial. Drake gave Elizabeth a jewelled token commemorating his circumnavigation; made of enamelled gold, it was set with an African diamond and bore a ship with an ebony hull. Over the following century the *Golden Hind* fell victim to dry rot and gradually fell apart. Any wood that was salvaged from her was used to fashion furniture.

Sir Francis Drake was now the most famous celebrity in the Western world. He had sailed around the world and survived – a feat that Magellan, who had died en route, had failed to achieve. He also brought home most of his crew. It was the beginning of Spain's decline and England's birth as a naval power. Perhaps mindful of his modest beginnings, Drake could not resist bragging about his accomplishments and revelled in his fame. He sat for portraits and began to invest heavily in property. He purchased manors at Yarcombe (near Honiton) and Sampford Spiney (Tavistock), as well as many properties in Plymouth, making him the second biggest landlord in the town. His main place of residence would be Buckland Abbey, which had been refurbished by his arch-enemy, Richard Grenville. To Grenville's dismay, Drake bought Buckland Abbey using his intermediaries, Christopher Harris and John Hele; he knew Grenville would never have sold it to him. It was purchased for £3,200, with the proviso that if Drake did not want it after three years, Sir Richard would buy it back.

In 1581 Sir Francis Drake was elected Lord Mayor of Plymouth and he proved to be an excellent administrator. He took up residence in a large house in Looe Street, before moving to Buckland Abbey in 1582. He took up the plans to have a leat or canal dug from Dartmoor to Plymouth, a distance of 17 miles, thus bringing fresh water into the town. The leat was completed in the 1590s, and Drake had a number of water-mills built along its length. With the assistance of his god-father, Francis Russell, Earl of Bedford, he was elected Member of Parliament for Bossiney, North Cornwall. Brief as it was, his time in the House of Commons widened his circle of influential friends, and brought potential investors for future voyages.

Following the death of his wife Mary in 1583, he married Elizabeth Sydenham in 1585. She was entirely different from Mary, who came from the same level of society as Drake himself. Elizabeth was the only daughter and heiress of Sir George Sydenham, Sheriff of Somerset, one of the richest men in the West Country. Drake was very differently regarded by many of his great contemporaries. Well-born men like Richard Grenville and explorer Martin Frobisher disliked him intensely. He was a *parvenu*, a rich but common upstart with West Country manners and accent, with none of the courtier's graces.

Sir William Cecil, Lord Burghley, who ever sought peace between England and Spain, never approved of Drake. He was for ever advising Queen Elizabeth to distance herself from such a 'war-monger', who was sure to provoke Spain into a war with an unprepared England, commenting, 'Sir Francis Drake is a fearful man to the King of Spain.' When Drake set out to raid on the Pacific side of Spain's New World, Elizabeth concealed the information from Cecil until Drake's small fleet had left English waters. One can get a description of Drake from the various observations of the man. He was short, stocky, bearded and florid-faced; he also had a spark in his temper and suffered black moods. He could be abrupt, and boastful of his skill as a mariner but he was feared and obeyed by his men. He was swift to punish, restless, ambitious but generous and liberal. He was not a cruel man, and inspired loyalty and affection among most men. He was a master of detail and planned his operations with meticulous thoroughness. Unlike most of his fellow mariners, he treated his captives with fairness, discovering valuable intelligence from them. Drake was a solitary man who had few close friends. Even aboard ship, as with most captains, he was isolated by his position and was rarely close with fellow officers and gentleman adventurers, with the exception of his brothers.

Chapter Nine

Thomas Cavendish

The second Englishman to circumnavigate the world was Thomas Cavendish. Born on 19 September 1560 at Grimston Hall, Trimley St Martin, near Ipswich, he was the son of William Cavendish and Mary (Wentworth); his father was a descendant of Roger Cavendish, brother of Sir John Cavendish, from whom the Dukes of Devonshire and Dukes of Newcastle derive their family name of Cavendish. Thomas was related by marriage to the Cecil, Frobisher, Brandon, Seckford, Tollemache, Wingfield and Wentworth families. His own sister, named Duglesse, married the Elizabethan writer Richard Hakluyt, who wrote extensively about the Golden Age.

Thomas had several older brothers but they all died young. When their father died in 1572, Thomas, aged 12, inherited a fortune and Thomas and his mother went to live with her brother, Lord Wentworth, at Nettleshead in Suffolk. When he reached 15, he attended Corpus Christi College in Cambridge for two years but he did not take a degree. In 1580 he was sent to Elizabeth's court, where his sister Anne was one of the queen's ladies-in-waiting. As a young man, he had easy access to many of the courtiers, including George Clifford, Earl of Cumberland, and George Carey, the son of Lord Hunsdon, the Lord Chamberlain.

In 1584 Cavendish became Member of Parliament for Shaftesbury, Dorset, but it was a short-lived role and the following year he sailed from Plymouth on 9 April 1585 with Sir Richard Grenville to Roanoke Island, Virginia. Off the coast of Portugal their ships ran into a violent storm, which sank one of the pinnaces and scattered the rest of the fleet. Grenville sailed on to Puerto Rico, where he constructed a fort and built a new pinnace. Thomas Cavendish, by skilful navigation, sailed his ship and found Grenville. Once established in Puerto Rico, he took part in attacking and boarding Spanish ships but gained little profit.

On 26 June they were sailing near the Outer Banks off Virginia. Three days later Grenville's ship, the *Tiger*, ran aground, with the loss of most of the supplies. Despite this setback, they continued to explore the area and visited three Indian villages. Grenville, who had a violent temper, was overcome with rage when a silver cup went missing. Unable to retrieve it, he burned down the village, which soured relations between the Indians and the English colonists. The following year Cavendish returned to Roanoke Island with Grenville, who later complained about the behaviour of his fellow courtier. Unfortunately Cavendish lost money on his investments in this colony, which disappeared after a few years. On his return to England, he was appointed Member of Parliament for Wilton, Dorset, in the same year that Spain and England declared war.

Cavendish wanted to repeat Francis Drake's circumnavigation of the globe, as well as seizing treasure from Spanish vessels. After obtaining permission from the queen to make personal raids, Cavendish ordered the construction of a new 120-ton sailing ship, the *Desire*, to be armed with eighteen cannon. In company with the 60-ton *Content* and the 40-ton *Hugh Gallant*, with a total crew of 123 men, the *Desire* left Plymouth on 21 July 1586. Five days later they were involved in a skirmish with five Spanish ships off Cape Finisterre. Passing the Canaries, they reached the coast of Guinea on 21 August, where they captured a Portuguese ship and attempted to burn a native village.

Leaving Guinea in September, Cavendish reached Brazil, where he took on water and provisions and built a pinnace. The small fleet turned south and by 17 December had reached Port Desire, near the tip of South America. Here they celebrated Christmas and met some of the local natives, who chose to fire arrows at the crews, wounding some of them. After careening his ships, Cavendish entered the Straits of Magellan on 6 January 1587 and anchored at the island of Santa Magdalena near present-day Punta Arenas. With plenty of tame penguins about, they filled two barrels with salted penguin meat.

To protect against English depredations, two large settlements – Rey Don Felipe and Nombre de Jesus – had been founded on Tierra del Fuego. When Cavendish landed at the former, he found only ruins. The other settlement was equally grim; driven out by the harsh climate, the settlers and soldiers of Nombre de Jesus had travelled along the narrow coast looking for Rey Don Felipe. Many of them starved, and the sole survivor was picked up by the *Desire*. Cavendish named the area Port Famine. The three ships explored the many inlets and channels and the weather-beaten islands of Tierra del Fuego until they reached the Pacific on 24 February and headed north along the coast of South America. Along the way, they captured and sank nine Spanish ships and looted several settlements. They also careened *Desire* and *Content* but set fire to *Hugh Gallant* as by now they lacked the men to sail her.

Travelling as far north as the Baja California Peninsula, they captured a Spanish pilot, who revealed that a treasure galleon from Manila was due to call at Cape San Lucas before sailing on to Acapulco. The Manila galleons were restricted to one or two voyages a year. In 1587 two Manila vessels, the *San Francisco* and *Santa Anna*, were due to reach Mexico but as they passed Japan they were hit by a typhoon and were wrecked on the coast. Only the 700-ton *Santa Anna* was salvageable; after making repairs, she continued her voyage.

Reaching the Gulf of California, Cavendish careened his ships and made general repairs while waiting for the *Santa Anna*. They then sailed to where they hoped *Santa Anna* would appear. Finally, on 4 November 1587, the Manila ship was spotted and Cavendish gave chase. After several hours the English ships overhauled the Spaniard. Like most treasure ships she carried no cannon, allowing more space for the cargo, although there were 200 men on board. Following several hours of fighting, during which the English ships pounded the *Santa Anna*, she surrendered. Because of the great disparity in size, Cavendish and the crew had to choose which treasures to transfer to their ships. They loaded about 122,000 pesos' worth of gold, silks, damask, spices, wines and provisions.

Finally, the *Santa Anna*'s crew were given food and water and told to head for the Baya Peninsula. Cavendish kept back two Japanese sailors, three boys from Manila, a Portuguese traveller familiar with China and a Spanish navigator. As *Desire* and *Content* sailed away on 17 November to cross the Pacific Ocean, *Santa Anna* was set on fire. As she burned, the treasure ship drifted onto the coast, where the survivors put out the flames, patched up the hull and limped into Acapulco. According to a claim by the Spanish authorities, Cavendish had overlooked a substantial proportion of the cargo, worth some 2 million pesos.

As they headed for the Philippines, *Desire* lost sight of the *Content*, which was never seen again. On 3 January 1588 Cavendish arrived on the island of Guam. Here he traded iron tools for fresh supplies, water and wood. Avoiding all conflict, Cavendish traded with the Philippine Islands, the Moluccas and Java. He also collected information about the Chinese and Japanese coasts, which he hoped to investigate when he next undertook a voyage. By now his crew had shrunk to forty-eight, and their clothes were little more than rags. Cavendish ordered new uniforms to be made for them from the silken damask they had captured. Leaving the East Indies, they sailed across the Indian Ocean to the Cape of Good Hope. Rounding the Cape, they sailed on to St Helena in mid-Atlantic, and took on fresh supplies.

On 9 September 1588 the *Desire* arrived back in Plymouth. Cavendish had secured enough treasure to make the circumnavigation worthwhile. A little while later *Desire* sailed up the Thames, displaying her new sails of blue damask. The voyage had been a great success and had beaten Drake's voyage by nine months (although this did not take into account Drake's efforts to find a North-West Passage, or the weeks spent careening and reprovisioning his ship on the coast of California). Cavendish learned that the Armada had been defeated and that he had probably crossed its survivors as they limped back to Spain. Thomas Cavendish was knighted by Elizabeth, who was invited aboard the *Desire*. The year 1588 was a good one for England: the Armada had been defeated and Cavendish had sailed round the world. In August 1591 he sailed again, this time commanding the *Leicester Galleon* and accompanied by the *Desire* and the *Black Pinnace*. He was joined by one of the great Elizabethan navigators, John Davis, and his friend Adrian Gilbert, a corpulent man who spoke his mind; both had been born at Sandridge near Dartmouth.

Davis was left to explore the Straits of Magellan but was defeated by foul weather. He sailed east and discovered the Falkland Islands, before returning home with only fourteen crew left alive. He had an adventurous life, which came to an unpleasant end in 1604 off Bitan Island near Singapore; he had seized a pirate ship and captured several 'Japanese pirates', but they managed to make a surprise attack in which Davis was 'dragged back, hacked and slashed and thrust out again'. He did not survive.

Meanwhile Cavendish's aim was to discover the North-West Passage 'upon the back parts of America' – in other words, to try to find the Passage from the western entrance. They went south to the Magellan Straits, where the weather was stormy and supplies were running short. Cavendish quarrelled with his subordinates, behaving in such an 'unbalanced way' that it was thought 'his mind was becoming deranged'. Losing touch with the other ships, Cavendish returned to Brazil, where his men raided the towns of Santos and Sao Vicente. They also got into a fight with the Portuguese at the village of Victoria, where he lost most of his crew.

At this time Anthony Knyvett, who had contracted frostbite during his time in the Straits of Magellan, was left with nineteen other sick and mutinous men on the remote island of Ilhabela. It took some years before Knyvett escaped from South America and in 1601 he returned to England.

In May or June 1592 Cavendish, his expedition in tatters, sailed for St Helena. Off Ascension Island he died; the cause was unknown, but it may have been the result of a brain tumor. A few days before his death he wrote a letter to Tristram Gorges, his executor, in which he accused John

Davis of being a 'villain' and causing the whole expedition 'to decay'. He also wrote:

> Every adventurer receive proportionally to his adventure ... I left none in England whom I have loved half as well as yourself. I have no more to say, but take this last farewell, that you have lost the lovingest friend that has lost by any.

Chapter Ten

The Military Elizabethans

To the many readers of books about the Elizabethan age of maritime exploits, it may appear that Hawkins and Drake were the only seamen to have explored, plundered and antagonised the Spanish. This was not so, for there were many who followed in their footsteps and helped to make England a leading maritime nation. The following privateers/explorers were among the many seamen who were driven either by religion or by a thirst for finding out what lay over the horizon, or were just plain mercenary.

John Oxenham

John Oxenham, Drake's friend and captain, left Plymouth on 9 April 1576 with a vessel, name unknown, and fifty-seven men, some of whom were veterans of Drake's expeditions to the Caribbean. Oxenham had been captivated by the vision of the Southern Sea from the platform built in the tall tree on the Cordilleras. He shared the view with Drake, and vowed that he would be the first Englishman to sail that ocean. He departed from England without the support of the government or backers hoping to capture Spanish treasure. In the late summer his pinnaces captured a Spanish frigate. He hid both of these pinnaces on the Isla de Pinos but in August the Spanish discovered them, leaving Oxenham with just two pinnaces.

Ten months later, having established good relations with the Cimarrons, Oxenham depended on their assistance to capture and hold the Panama Isthmus. During the winter Oxenham's crew and their Cimarron allies cut down cedar trees to build a 45ft boat, powered by twenty-four oars, to sail up the Chucunaque and Tuire rivers in eastern Panama. The boat carried fifty Englishmen and ten Cimarron allies, and reached the Gulf of San Miguel by February 1577. Oxenham had realised his dream: he became the first English captain to sail the Pacific. Here he was able to loot without the risk of Spanish ships appearing. Although Francis Drake would later follow, it was Oxenham who first caused problems for the Spanish around the Panama area. Some 30 miles off Panama City, Oxenham found the Pearl Islands, a chain of some 200 islands. He and his men spent three weeks pillaging and stealing pearls on the main island, before boarding and seizing two ships bound for Panama City. To their delight they found the ships were transporting gold and silver to the value of 160,000 pesos from Peru. Like Drake, he later released the prisoners, who alerted the Panamanian authorities.

Satisfied with their haul, Oxenham and his crew sailed up the Tuire river and made camp. Unfortunately, they were lax enough to leave a trail of chicken feathers scattered in the river, which the Spanish pursuers followed. When the camp was attacked, many of Oxenham's men were killed and the treasure was recaptured. Oxenham and some of his men disappeared into the jungle and probably stayed with the Cimarrons.

Nine months after his February raids, Oxenham and his companions were captured in a banana grove near the Rio Banique. Imprisoned and tortured, John Butler, Thomas Sherwell and John Oxenham were sent to Lima in Peru, where they faced the *auto-da-fe* of the Inquisition. It took three years of wretched incarceration before a verdict was delivered. The result was not in doubt and all three men were hanged for piracy in October 1580.

Richard Grenville

Another West Countryman was Richard Grenville, born on 15 June 1542 at Clifton House in Devon, about 7 miles upriver from Buckland Abbey. His father, Sir Roger Grenville, captained King Henry's great ship, the *Mary Rose*. On 19 July 1545, in her haste to confront the French in Portsmouth Harbour, the *Mary Rose* turned too sharply, flooding the lower decks with water. Sir Roger was among the many who drowned as she sank. Grenville's cousins included Walter Raleigh and the explorer Humphrey Gilbert. When he attained the age of 17, he was sent to study law at the Inner Temple in London but after two years' study, he did not sit a degree and returned to Devon.

Thanks to his noble family, the 20-year-old Grenville was elected to Parliament for Dunheved, Launceston, serving in the role from 1562 to 1563. He was described as a man with a short fuse, and historian A.L. Rowse wrote that Grenville had a 'harsh domineering note ... betraying signs of overstrain and unbalance'. He also had a 'new and active strain of immense and passionate energy', which was displayed on 19 November 1562 when he became involved in a fight in the Strand in London. He was in the company of his cousin Nicholas Specott and their two attendants when they encountered Sir Edmound Unton, step-brother of the Ambassador to France, Fulke Grenville, Robert Bannister and Thomas Allen, with their servants. All were armed. In the confrontation Richard Grenville ran Bannister through with his sword and left him to die. Grenville and his companions were outlawed for three months for 'public duelling and manslaughter' before being pardoned. The Elizabethan playwright William Shakespeare alludes to this type of conflict in two of his plays, *Romeo and Juliet* and *Hamlet*. With so many noblemen carrying swords and daggers, it was little surprise that there was so much blood-letting.

When Grenville reached the age of 21, he inherited his grandfather's estates at Stowe in Cornwall, Biddeford and Buckland Abbey. In 1565 he married Mary St Leger, the daughter of Sir Warham St Leger, a wealthy Devon landowner. In the same year Grenville joined in the petitioning of Queen Elizabeth for service abroad. In 1566 he joined with his West Country cousins, the Godolphins, Carews, Killigrews, Champernownes and Basets, to travel to Hungary to fight the Turks. Little is known about their participation; the only major battle was the siege of Szigetvar, which took place in that year and ended in a bloody victory for the Ottoman army.

On his return to England, Grenville became involved in the Irish wars, courtesy of his father-in-law Sir Warham St Leger. In 1568 he put down an Irish rebellion and in return was appointed High Sheriff of Cork. Grenville seized lands to the west of Cork for colonisation. This landgrab led to bitter disputes with the Irish, which escalated into the first of the Desmond rebellions. (The word 'Desmond' derived from the Irish *Deasmumhain*, meaning South Munster.) Grenville saw the attack on the English garrison at Tracton and witnessed the massacre that followed. James Fitzmaurice, camped outside the walls of Waterford, demanded the surrender of Grenville's wife. In the event, reinforcements arrived and drove away Fitzmaurice's men, thus saving Mary St Leger. Grenville lost his investment in the plantations that he had hoped to develop and did not visit Ireland for another twenty years.

In 1571 Grenville was elected Member of Parliament for Cornwall and in 1576 was appointed High Sheriff of the same county. The following year he arrested the Catholic priest, Cuthbert Mayne, at his house near Probus. On gaining entry to the house, Grenville found a devotional *Agnus Dei* around Mayne's neck, together with other books and papers. Mayne was imprisoned in Launceston Castle, and at his trial he was sentenced to be hanged, drawn and quartered. Mayne's death caused the English government to fear the possibility of papal agents arriving in the country to foment rebellion among the population against Elizabeth. In his role as High Sheriff, Grenville hunted down Catholic dissidents in Cornwall for the government. This religious persecution helped to bring about harsher legislation against Catholicism in England, leading to war between England and Spain.

Grenville's adventures until now had largely been ashore, but he wished to emulate the exploits of Hawkins and Drake and return with much plunder. In 1574 he submitted a proposal to the privy council to take his single ship, the *Castle of Comfort*, to attack Spanish treasure ships in the Pacific and to establish colonies in South America. After a considerable delay a licence was granted, only for the queen to withdraw it, on grounds that England's relationship with Spain had improved considerably. Had it gone ahead, Grenville would perhaps have been the first Englishman to sail through the Straits of Magellan and into the Southern Sea. Although Drake was not directly involved with Grenville's plans, there can be no doubt that he was conversant with the voyage from the information he received from his friend John Oxenham.

By the end of 1575 Elizabeth was increasingly disturbed by the events in the Netherlands and began to have second thoughts about a peaceful relationship with Spain. The Spanish Netherlands was a refuge for English Catholics, who supported Mary Queen of Scots and continued to plot against Elizabeth. Thanks to support from Essex and Walsingham, Drake was able to plan for a fleet to enter the Southern Sea via the Straits of Magellan, while Grenville was resigned to abandoning his proposed voyage. This increased the bad blood between the two men, and Grenville refused ever to serve with Francis Drake.

In 1575 Sir Richard was back in his home at Biddeford, his plans for a privateering adventure scuppered. By this time he and Mary had six children. Nearby Buckland Abbey was deemed a more suitable place to bring up his children and, in the absence of any more sea adventures, he set about converting the former abbey into a comfortable family home. Grenville appeared to have settled for a quiet retirement. He decorated the great hall with a plaster frieze depicting skulls set below a tangled vine, upon which a weary soldier hung his shield and his warhorse was turned to pasture. The ceiling plasterwork was decorated with navigational themes, and the Grenville coat of arms was depicted above the mantelpieces.

That same year Grenville was thanked by the privy council and the Earl of Bedford, then Lord Lieutenant of Cornwall, for raising troops to fight Sir Thomas Stukeley, who had named himself the Duke of Ireland. Stukeley was the youngest son of Sir Hugh Stukeley, lord of the manor of

Affeton in Devon. Ten years later, in May 1585, Grenville was called to command a fleet of seven ships which were to sail from England for the colonisation of Virginia. On his return in October that year Grenville was attacked by a Spanish ship, homeward bound from St Domingo, but Grenville got the better of things. Having no pinnace to board the Spanish ship, he had a raft hastily made from some old chests but as the raft approached the Spanish vessel, it fell to pieces and the ship escaped. Enraged, Grenville landed at the Azores, where he went on the rampage and pillaged the town, grabbing anything of value. At about this time, the Spanish captives described Grenville's eccentric behaviour:

> He would carouse three or four glasses of wine and in bravery take the glasses between his teeth and crush them to pieces and swallow them down, so that often the blood ran out of his mouth without harm at all unto him.

In 1586 Grenville returned to Virginia with stores for the colonists but found that his arch-nemesis, Francis Drake, had already rescued the colonists, who were on the point of starvation. Unloading the provisions, Grenville left fifteen of his men to defend his cousin's New World territory. He brought back with him a Native American whom he named Raleigh, who subsequently converted to Christianity. Sadly, on 27 March 1588 Raleigh died of influenza while staying at Grenville's house. He was buried at St Mary the Virgin Church alongside Grenville's young daughter Rebecca, who had also succumbed to the influenza.

In 1583 and 1584 Grenville had been employed as a commissioner for the works at Dover Harbour, and in 1587 he became actively engaged in the defence of the ports of Devon, Cornwall and Dorset. He was also given the task of repairing the fortifications at the Cinque Ports in Sussex and Kent, as well as Boscastle Harbour. In anticipation of the arrival of the Spanish Armada, Grenville equipped five ships that left Biddeford for Plymouth. Although he himself did not take part in fighting the Armada, he was commissioned to keep watch at sea on the western approaches to the Bristol Channel, in case the Spanish fleet returned.

In the summer of 1591 Grenville was appointed vice-admiral under Admiral Thomas Howard, 1st Earl of Suffolk, who was sent with a squadron of sixteen ships to the Azores to waylay the two Spanish treasure ships on their twice yearly voyage from the Spanish Main. One treasure ship had already reached Spain before the fleet arrived, but the other was expected in September. Howard decided to anchor his fleet on the north side of Flores Island, which was 30 miles long and 9 broad, and to intercept the treasure ship as she approached from the west. Grenville anchored his ship, the *Revenge*, some way off. Half of the English crews were suffering from fever and scurvy, and were taken ashore, while the rest were busy looking for water onshore. The *Revenge* was a state-of-the-art ship which, coincidentally, had been Drake's ship during his battle against the Armada three years before. Unbeknown to Howard, the Spanish King had dispatched about fifty-three ships from Ferrol to accompany the treasure ship from the Azores.

George Clifford, Earl of Cumberland, was cruising off the Portuguese coast when he spotted the Spanish fleet heading for the Azores. He quickly launched a pinnace, the *Moonshine*, to warn Howard of the enemy's approach. The *Moonshine* kept pace with the Spanish fleet for three days, en route to the Azores. Counting the number of ships, Captain Middleton then made haste to bring the startling intelligence to Admiral Howard. On 31 August the pinnace reached the *Defiance*, but Howard had scarcely heard the news before the Spanish fleet was in sight. Realising he was outnumbered, he called for his sick crewmen and the water-gatherers to return to their ships and depart as quickly as possible. With all his men aboard, the fleet weighed anchor and stood out to sea.

Grenville, either not knowing or not believing Captain Middleton's report, was convinced that the ships coming round the western point were the long-awaited treasure ships, and he refused to follow Howard. This seems to have been the opinion of an officer, William Monson, and Jan Huyghen van Linschoten, a Dutch trader. On the other hand, Grenville was delayed in getting his sick men brought on board, but the other ships also had to get their sick men on board, and sickly as the *Revenge* was, she was no worse off than her consorts.

By the time the *Revenge* was ready to leave her anchorage, the Spanish ships had cut her off from the rest of the squadron. An English merchant ship, the *George Noble*, was fired at, but her captain bravely asked Grenville if he could help. In his usual brusque manner, Grenville told the merchantman to leave him to fight his own battle. Grenville had never seen action at sea before and he made some glaring errors, not least sailing into the midst of the Spanish ships. He would not let his pilot steer the ship with the stern facing toward the enemy. Coming under the lee of some of the Spanish galleons, *Revenge* was becalmed, making her an easy target for the Spanish ships.

From three in the afternoon until dawn the next day, the *Revenge* took on fifteen of the largest Spanish ships, sinking four of them and badly damaging several others, despite being fatally outnumbered. She was boarded fifteen times but each time the *Revenge*'s seamen repulsed the Spanish. The pick of the Spanish vessels came alongside but were pounded by the *Revenge's* cannon and haquebuses. Finally, after twelve hours of continuous fighting, Grenville's ship was down to its last keg of powder; demasted and battered, she was finally captured. Grenville had been wounded early in the fighting, and again later on. While being attended to by the ship's surgeon, he was shot in the head with the same ball that killed the surgeon.

Their swords broken and their pikes splintered, the English crew surrendered. As he lay dying, Grenville urged his crew 'to destroy the ship with themselves – to die, rather than to yield to the enemy'. In his ill-tempered manner, he called them cowards, which they were certainly not. During the battle the *Revenge* had received some 800 cannon shot and 10,000 bullets from hand weapons. She was badly damaged but still afloat, and five days later her new Spanish crew set out for Spain. On the way they encountered a storm that sank the *Revenge* as well as several damaged Spanish ships. Grenville was taken aboard the Spanish admiral's ship *San Pablo*, where he died a few days afterwards. He was eventually buried at St James the Great Churchyard, Kilkhampton, Cornwall.

Thomas Stukeley

Thomas Stukeley was one of the most colourful characters of the Elizabethan age. His exploits brought him fame and notoriety throughout Europe. He was variously quixotic, opportunistic, prone to swapping sides, extremely lucky and very brave. Born in 1520, he was the younger son of Sir Hugh Stukeley, Lord of Affeton Manor near Crediton, Devon. His father served King Henry VIII as a Knight of the Body, and in 1545 was appointed Sheriff of Devon. His mother was Jane Pollard, the daughter of Sir Lewis Pollard, Lord of King's Nympton Manor in Devon. There is no documentation to support the story that Jane Pollard was King Henry's mistress, but during his lifetime Stukeley played on the 'fact' that his father was Henry VIII, which helped to smooth his way through life. In this world of tangled relationships, this meant he was also Queen Elizabeth's half-brother.

England had to fight France on three occasions, in 1526, 1544 and 1547, and Stukeley's military talents were noted during the 1544–45 siege of Boulogne. He was also appointed standard-bearer in the service of Edward Seymour, 1st Duke of Somerset and Protector of Edward VI. In 1549 Seymour was accused of felony, arrested and taken to the Tower. He was replaced by the Duke of Northumberland, who tried to put his daughter-in-law, Lady Jane Grey, on the throne instead of Mary Tudor. But the coup quickly faded and Northumberland was arrested and later executed. It was a turbulent time, with Mary trying reinstate Roman Catholicism and the nobility fighting amongst themselves.

As he was one of Somerset's close companions, a warrant was issued for Stukeley's arrest but he managed to escape to France, where he served in the French army. When Henry VI of France entrusted Stukeley with a letter for the teenaged Edward VI, Stukeley, looking for the main chance, revealed to John Dudley, Duke of Northumberland, the French plans to capture Calais. But Stukeley was refused a reward. Falling into debt, he was imprisoned in the Tower of London. Released in 1553, he settled on becoming a soldier of fortune. (This was not his only financial difficulty, nor was it his only spell in the Tower; he was later arrested for breaking into a late relative's house and searching for money. About the same time he also was arrested for robbing an Irishman and sent to the Tower.)

Released from the Tower, Stukeley returned to France and joined the service of Emmanuel Philibert, Duke of Savoy – a man anxious to expand his realm. With the help of the Duke of Suffolk, Stukeley returned to England in December 1554 after obtaining an amnesty with his creditors. His situation improved upon his marriage to Anne Curtis, the heiress of Sir Thomas Curtis, but he still managed to squander £100 each day. Within a few months another warrant for his arrest was issued, this time on a charge of 'uttering false money'. In 1557 he deserted his wife and again entered the service of the Duke of Savoy, taking part in Savoy's victorious battle at St Quentin.

The following year he returned to England, only to be summoned before the privy council on a charge of piracy. Yet again he was let off, owing to insufficient evidence. On the death of his wife's grandfather he inherited a small fortune and was restored to wealth. He joined the Protestant movement and become a supporter of Robert Dudley, Earl of Leicester. In 1561, as a token of friendship, he was appointed Captain at the fortress at Berwick on the Scottish border. Reverting to his sumptuous lifestyle, he became firm friends with the Ulster nobleman Shane O'Neill. He managed to obtain a warrant permitting O'Neill to bring French ships into English ports to trade, even though England and France were on the brink of war.

Stukeley later devised a plan to found a colony in Florida, which was being contested by Spanish and French settlers. He managed to persuade the queen to supply him with a ship and to supplement another five vessels. In June 1563, having staged a naval pageant before the queen on

Drake's birthplace: Crowndale Farm.

A portrait of Sir Francis Drake, Anglo-Dutch school, late sixteenth century.

John Hawkins.

Hawkins' coat of arms.

Cavendish, Drake and Hawkins.

THE MARINERS MIRROVR

Wherin may playnly be seen the courses, heights, distances, depths, soundings, flouds and ebs, risings of lands, rocks, sands and shoalds, with the marks for then trings of the Harbouroughs, Havens and Ports of the greatest part of Europe: their seueral traficks and commodities Together w.th the Rules and instrumēts of NAVIGATION.

First made &Set forth in diuers exact Sea-Charts, by that famous Nauigator LVKE WAGENAR of Enchuisen And now sitted with necessarie additions for the use of Englishmen by ANTHONY ASHLEY.

Herein also may be understod the exploits lately atchiued by the right Honorable the L. Admiral of England with her Ma.tie Nauie and som famer seruices don by the worshy Knyghtt St FRANC DRAKE,

The Mariners Mirror.

A typical Elizabethan warship.

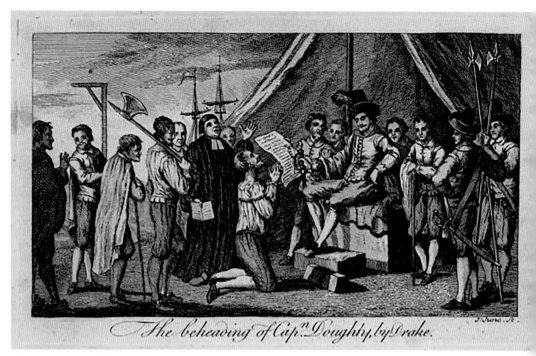

The beheading of Cap.ⁿ Doughty, by Drake.

The execution of Thomas Doughty.

Lord Burghley.

Sir Francis Walsingham.

Richard Grenville.

Martin Frobisher.

Thomas Cavendish.

John Norreys.

Christopher Carleill.

A replica of the *Golden Hind*.

Buckland Abbey.

The execution of Mary Queen of Scots.

Fotheringhay Castle.

Above) Queen Elizabeth knighting Francis Drake. (*Below*) Drake's sword and drum.

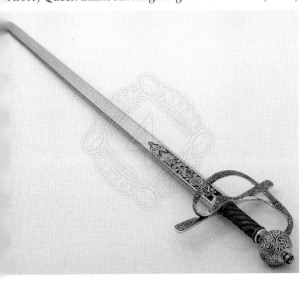

ATLANTIC OCEAN

Rathlin I.

55   55

The Route

Swilly

L. Foyle

Derry

O'DONNELL

TYRCONNELL

DOGHERTY

O'CAHAN

CLANDEBOYE

O'NEILL

Belfast

R. Bann

L. Neagh

R. Loggan

Dungannon

T Y R O N E

ULSTER

U L S T E R

MAC ARTANE

L. Erne

MAGUIRE

MACMAHON

O'HANLON

MAGENNIS

Ards

O'ROURKE

Newry

O'REILLY

Dundalk

Burkes and Barretts

O'CONNOR Sligo

MAC DERMOT

O'CONNOR

FARREL

54   54

C O N N A U G H T

Roscommon

DELVIN

R. Boyne

Drogheda

O'Navan

Trim

O'MALLEY

O'FLAHERTY

Athlone

R. Liffey

Dublin

Galway

EARLDOM OF CLANRICARDE

KINGS COUNTY

L E I N S T E R

Ballymore Eustace

Naas

Kildare

Philipstown

CARROLL

53   53

THOMOND

Maryborough

O'BYRNE

O'BRIEN

Neagh

O'Dempsey-Ossory

QUEENS COUNTY

Carlow

Arklow

O'Ryan

O'Ryan

Leighlin Bridge

Limerick

O' DWYER

Kilkenny

KAVANAGHS

R. Shannon

L. Gur

Kilmallock

Caspel

R. Nore

R. Barrow

R. Slaney

Lixnaw

Clonmel

Carrick

Wexford

O R M O N D

R. Suir

Tralee

Mallow

Lismore

Waterford

Dingle

R. Blackwater

DECIES

Dingle Bay

O'SULLIVANS

MACCARTHIES

MUSKERRY

Cork

Dungarvan

52

Kenmare Bay

R. Lee

Youghal

Kinsale

Bantry Bay

CARBERY

IRELAND

ABOUT 1570.

The red lines indicate the extent
of Desmond influence; the blue
lines that of the Ormonde family.

London: Longmans & Co.   Edwd Weller lith

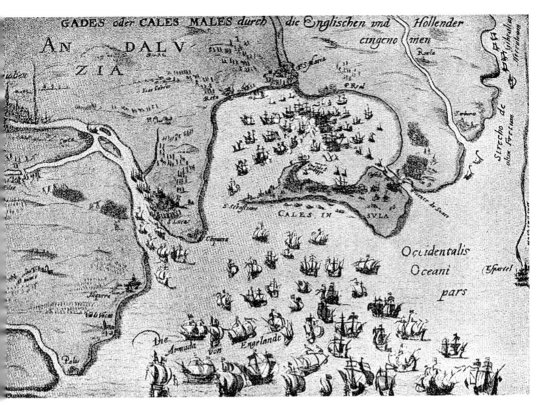

Map of Cadiz.

William Cecil, Queen
Elizabeth and Francis
Walsingham.

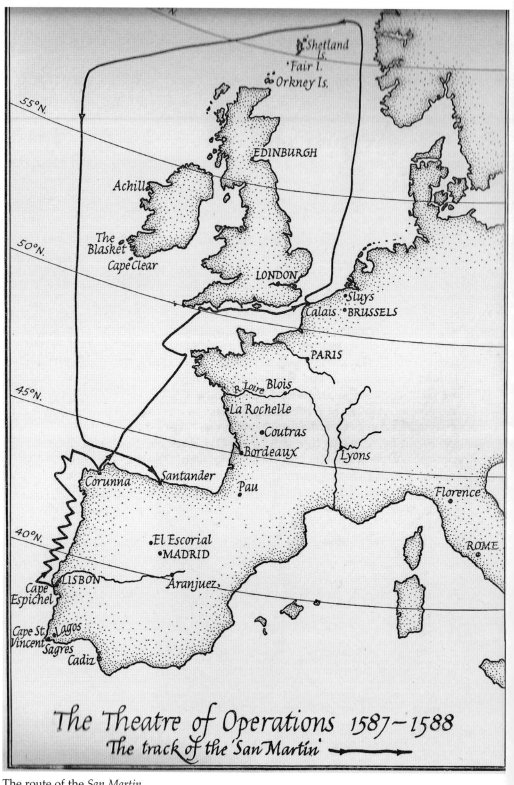

The route of the *San Martin*.

Queen Elizabeth
(the 'Armada portrait').

Phillip II of Spain,
by Antonio Moro.

The Spanish Armada in formation in the English Channel.

The Armada at Calais.

The Armada approaching Scotland. The crew on the ship in the foreground are throwing all the horses overboard.

The Armada Medal.

Queen Elizabeth at Tilbury.

Drake's funeral off Porto Bello.

the Thames, he sailed his fleet to Munster in Ireland. From here, he began a period of piracy against Spain, Portugal and France. After repeated objections about his activities, the queen sent a naval force against him and he was arrested in Cork and accused of piracy. Thanks to his friend Shane O'Neill, who pleaded his case through diplomatic channels, he was again released.

His association with Shane O'Neill extended Stukeley's interest in Irish affairs. Thanks to his tenuous connection with the queen, he was recommended as an intermediary in an effort to induce his friend to enter negotiations with the government. O'Neill used Stukeley as a go-between with the Lord Lieutenant, Sir Henry Sidney. In the outbreak of fighting against the Scots, Sidney recommended Stukeley for service, as he had military experience. Later, Sidney sought permission for Stukeley to purchase an estate in the east of Ulster worth £3,000, but the queen refused the transaction as these lands were in Scottish-Norman possession and were constantly being fought over by the Irish and Scots. Within a decade these lands were seized by the English and used as a base for the colonial plantations.

In June 1569 Stukeley was incarcerated in Dublin Castle for eighteen weeks on the grounds that he used 'coarse language against the queen and supported certain rebels'. In his usual devious manner, he had swung back to the Catholic faith, but in October that year he was again acquitted, despite being suspected of proposing an invasion of Ireland by the Spanish king. With a great show of piety, he returned to Waterford and proceeded through the streets of the town on his knees as he offered himself up to God. It was, of course a sham: all the time he was scheming to find a route to wealth.

Devising another plan to colonise Florida, he persuaded Elizabeth to fund a ship. This time, instead of sailing from Ireland to London, he headed for Vimeiro, north of Lisbon. Philip II invited Stukeley to Madrid, where he was flattered with honours, and he was known at the Spanish court as the Duke of Ireland. Philip's efforts to deflect Elizabeth's attention away from the threat of an invasion of Ireland caused her to increase her support of the Dutch rebels in the Spanish Netherlands. The invasion of Ireland was never wholeheartedly supported by the Spanish, who had other European problems to contend with. Stukeley was playing a very dangerous game; not only was he behind the proposed attack on Ireland to help along the Ridolfi Plot, he also became embroiled in a planned invasion of England from the Spanish Netherlands. The Irish invasion was to be 'aided' by Sir John Hawkins, working as an agent of Lord Burghley.

When Hawkins revealed to the privy council that Thomas Howard, 4th Duke of Norfolk, was heavily involved in the plot, he was arrested, incarcerated and finally executed in 1572.

On 12 February 1571 Philip was informed by the Spanish ambassador that London had received news from France that Pope Pius had excommunicated Elizabeth and ceded the English throne to Philip. It was rumoured that Stukeley was to be sent to England with fifteen companies of troops to help the Duke of Alba in the Spanish Netherlands. But all this was pie in the sky, and nothing came of it. There was much in-fighting amongst the Catholics, particularly involving the Archbishop of Cashel, Maurice Fitzgibbon, who discredited Stukeley's plans and requested the appointment of Philip's brother, Don John, as King of Ireland. Sir Francis Walsingham, the English ambassador in France, interrogated Fitzgibbon about Stukeley's aspirations to make Ireland a vassal state of Spain. In this world of murky religious planning and counter-planning, much was debated but little was acted upon. Elizabeth was well aware of Stukeley's machinations and demanded that he should be dismissed from the Spanish court. Though he played many roles – pirate, spy, mercenary, counterfeiter, deceiver and scoundrel – he was a colourful enough character to intrigue Europe's population. While his confederates faced execution, he somehow evaded death.

Now, once again, he was on the move, this time to Rome. Finding favour with Pope Pius V, he was given command of three galleys. On 7 October 1571 he participated in the Battle of Lepanto in the Ionian Sea, the largest naval battle ever seen in the west, involving more than 400 warships. Once again, Stukeley displayed great valour during the battle. The Holy League's victory over the Ottoman Empire at Lepanto allowed Spain to devote more resources to the Spanish Netherlands. Stukeley was welcomed back to Seville in March 1572 and the court offered him a fleet of twenty ships to oppose the English in the Narrow Seas (the English Channel) between the Netherlands and England. Tiring of Philip's lengthy procrastination, Stukeley allied himself with the new Pope, Gregory XIII, who had aspirations of appointing his son, Giacomo Boncampagni, the King of Ireland, thus isolating England between two Catholic countries to east and west.

At the papal court James Fitzmaurice met Thomas Stukeley and together they persuaded Pope Gregory to fund the cost of supplying 1,000 troops, 600 of them Italian mercenaries, for the invasion of Ireland. Rather flatteringly, Stukeley had been granted a new title, Marquis of Leinster, by the papal court. With the Pope's financial and military help,

Stukeley set sail from Italy on 2 February 1578 on a ship carrying provisions for 3,000 men. The vessel was in very poor condition and took two months to reach Cadiz, a journey that a seaworthy vessel could have made in just two weeks. On board were the 600 Italian mercenaries who were later to be joined by Irish rebels in Cadiz for the long-planned invasion.

By the time Stukeley's ship anchored off Cadiz, his Italians were on the verge of mutiny. Stukeley's enthusiasm for the Ireland invasion was waning, and when he received a message from King Philip asking him to join Sebastian at Lisbon and take command of part of the army for the young Portuguese king's invasion of Morocco, he jumped at the chance to swap horses. Once again Stukeley had changed his mind, abandoning the occupation of Ireland in favour of a better offer from the Portuguese king. He also said of Ireland that 'there were only to be got there hunger and lice'. The rebel members of the Irish invasion were forced to return to Rome, the ill-fated invasion now deprived of most of its money, its troops and Stukeley himself.

Stukeley's change of mind concerning the restoration of Ireland to Catholicism rankled with Pope Gregory, who had instructed him to 'do all the mischief that [he] may to that wicked woman', referring to Queen Elizabeth. Yet by that summer Sebastian's invasion of Morocco had received Gregory's blessing after the Portuguese king had committed his vast treasury to the campaign. He had no military experience but lived in a world of knightly valour, which connected him to the vast army under his command. His forces included 9,000 raw peasant levies armed with pikes, 1,500 Portuguese nobles who paid their own way, 1,000 cavalry and 5,500 foreign mercenaries, including Stukeley's Italians. The latter were still resentful that they had been tricked into serving under a foreign ruler, and had to forage for their provisions. Along with a similar number of camp-followers, they were conveyed to the Moroccan coast in 500 ships, landing at Asilah on the Atlantic coast.

On 29 July 1578, in the heat of summer, the army left their camp and the cumbersome cavalcade marched to meet the enemy at Ksar-el-Kebir. They were soon short of water and food, despite their extensive baggage train. Heedless of the dangers of supply problems and the inhospitable terrain, Sebastian refused all advice. After six days his army had only covered 33 miles. On the night of 3 August Moulay Mohammed joined forces with Sebastian's men and advised them to delay their attack until late the following day. During a council of war Sebastian refused to listen to the more experienced military men and ordered an attack to be launched right away.

Stukeley was on the left wing with his Italians and some Spanish. On the other wing were mercenaries from Germany, Spain and the Spanish Netherlands. The pikemen, conscripted peasants, were stationed behind the foreign mercenaries, with the musketeers in the rear. Opposing Sebastian was Abdelmalek's army of some 60,000 men, well supported by artillery and cavalry. Sebastian, confident that his plans could not fail, led his army straight at the Moorish centre without any thought of attacks from the flanks.

The battle commenced on 4 August and lasted six hours, with the Portuguese army almost beaten before it began. The numbers soon told and Sebastian's army was on the back-foot with little artillery and weak cavalry support. By the end of the fighting, the Portuguese army had lost 8,000 men, with another 15,000 captured; in contrast, the Moors lost 4,000 killed. The three rulers, Sebastian, Moulay Mohammed and Abdelmalek, were among the dead, as was Thomas Stukeley.

There are two versions about how Stukeley died. One says that he again fought with great courage but was killed early in the battle when a cannonball severed his legs and he bled to death. The other version says that he was killed by his own disgruntled Italian mercenaries after the Portuguese were defeated. Although Stukeley remains virtually unknown today, he made a considerable impression on his contemporaries, and his death attracted as much speculation and gossip as his life had done.

John Norreys

Perhaps the most acclaimed English soldier of the Elizabethan period, John Norreys (Norris) was born in 1547 at Yattendon Castle, a fortified manor house in Berkshire, the son of Henry Norreys, 1st Baron Norreys, and his wife Marjorie (née Williams). The family had close links to the tempestuous world of nobility and politics, for John Norreys' paternal grandfather was one of the men found guilty of committing adultery with Anne Boleyn, the mother of Queen Elizabeth, and executed. His maternal grandfather, Lord Williams of Thame, had been the guardian of the young Elizabeth and she was well acquainted with the family. She was great friends with Marjorie, whom she nicknamed 'Black Crow' on account of her jet-black hair.

Norreys attended Magdalen College, Oxford, but did not sit his degree, as many of the nobility chose not to do. In later years, however, Norreys was presented with the degree of Master of Arts. In 1566 his father was posted as English ambassador to France, and he took his family with him. John and his brother William travelled to watch the Battle of St Denis just outside Paris in November 1567, and John drew a map that formed part of the report sent to the queen. When his father returned to England in 1571, John Norreys stayed behind and developed a friendship with the new ambassador to France, Sir Francis Walsingham. Norreys had decided that he would like to become a soldier and he volunteered to fight with the Huguenots in the French Wars of Religion.

Two years later Norreys became an officer in Elizabeth's army. In October 1574 he was in Ireland as a captain under the command of Sir Walter Devereux, 1st Earl of Essex. When Essex issued an invitation to bring peace to the province, a banquet was held in Belfast for the O'Neill family. It was part of a ruse, which saw the O'Neills and their attendants slain, and Norreys was pleased to take part in the massacre.

Another bloody massacre occurred on 26 July 1575 at Rathlin Island off the north coast of Ireland. Acting on instructions from Sir Henry Sidney, Essex instructed Norreys to take a company of soldiers and reduce the castle by storm. Norreys used cannon to pound the castle into submission. The garrison surrendered, but 200 soldiers and 400 civilian men, women and children were killed; only the constable, his family and one of the hostages were spared. The entire family of Sorley Boy MacDonnell were slain while the chieftain watched on helplessly from the mainland, 'like to run mad from sorrow'. It was a grim start to Norreys' military career.

The Dutch Revolt started in the Low Countries against the rule of the Habsburg King Philip of Spain, the hereditary ruler of the provinces. This was an area that Philip was not remotely interested in; in fact he only once briefly visited it. The northern provinces gradually separated from the southern provinces, which continued under Habsburg Spanish rule until 1714. Queen Elizabeth favoured the Protestant Calvinists and gave her support for English soldiers to fight on the rebel side. With regard to the Dutch rebels, she offered very limited aid to foreign Protestants and failed to provide sufficient funds for her commanders to make a difference. Even so, in 1577 Norreys led a force of English mercenary volunteers to the Netherlands to fight for the States General in their rebellion against the Spanish at the beginning of the Eighty Years War. Although the sea route was faster, it was fraught with danger, with ships coming under attack from English and French corsairs, so Spain did not convey her troops by sea but sent them along 'le chemin des Espagnols' ('the Spanish Road'), marching 620 miles from Milan to Flanders.

Norreys' first battle was at the village of Rijmenam on 2 August 1578. Don John of Austria attacked what he thought was the rebels' front line, drawn up in front of the village. After three hours he ordered troops and cavalry to enter the village from the rear but Norreys' men blocked the attack. Norreys then set fire to a few houses, which the Spanish mistook for the firing of the baggage train. In the thick of the battle, Norreys had three horses shot from under him. Thinking the Dutch were retreating, the Spanish pressed home their attack, only to find they had walked into a trap. It turned out that the States Army had positioned some of their men in front of the village, leaving the bulk of the force behind the village, complete with cannon and numerical superiority. Some 500 Scottish soldiers, stripped to the waist and singing psalms, attacked the trapped Spanish. At the same time the artillery opened fire and the Spanish seemed to be on the point of annihilation. Fortunately for them, Alexander Farnese, Duke of Parma, managed to lead the trapped troops to safety by way of a covered path. By the end of the battle the Spanish had lost around 1,000 men.

The next battle Norreys' men took part in ended in defeat. At the village of Borgerhout near Antwerp on 2 March 1579 the Spanish army under Alexander Farnese managed to cross the many ditches that were scattered about the area and breached the rampart. Inside the village the French commander, Francois de la Noue, and John Norreys managed to reorganise their men to disrupt the advance in the barricaded streets. Nevertheless, with the Spanish looking like the victors, the Dutch and English soldiers retreated behind the walls of Antwerp. The mercenaries, who had not been paid, kidnapped the abbot of St Michael's Abbey and demanded their back pay.

On 9 April 1580 the city of Mechelen was easily captured by the Anglo-Dutch forces but there followed periods of pillaging during which more than sixty civilians were killed. This killing spree became known as the 'English Fury', and may have had a lot to do with the failure to pay the English mercenaries. They plundered homes, churches and monasteries looking for riches. Among the many instances of murder, John Norreys himself killed a monk with his bare hands. In the chaos the Catholic archbishop hid in a cupboard, before leaving the city dressed as a peasant. By this time John Norreys had become famous among the English and was regarded as their pre-eminent soldier. He had gained a reputation for aggressive leadership and was forceful in obtaining payment for his men. But instead of making Norreys the army commander, the queen appointed to the post her favourite Robert Dudley, Earl of Leicester, a man with no experience of warfare.

Norreys was ordered to go the city of Grave, which was being besieged by Alexander Farnese. The city was the only obstacle preventing the

Spanish army from advancing into the northern provinces. Norreys joined forces with the city's Dutch commander, Count Hohenlohe, and in the desperate encounter with the Spanish that ensued, Norreys suffered a pike wound in the chest. The relieving army managed to force back the Spanish, and Grave was relieved. It was only a brief respite, however, as the Spanish were soon admitted to the city through the treachery of its governor, Baron van Hemart. Leicester ordered that Hemart be executed, while Norreys urged a milder measure, not least because he had fallen in love with Hemart's aunt. Despite the disagreement, Leicester was won over and, during a great feast he gave at Utrecht, he knighted Norreys and two of his brothers, Edward and Henry. The harmony did not last long, for the English camp was soon torn apart by dissension. Leicester wrote to Francis Walsingham, complaining that:

> Norreys habitually treated him with disrespect and matched the late Earl of Sussex [his old enemy in court]. He will dissemble, so crouch and so cunningly carry his doings as no man living would imagine that there were half the malice or vindictive mind that doth plainly his deeds prove to be … Since the loss of Grave he is as coy and as strange to give any council or any advice as if he were a mere stranger to us.

Despite the uncongenial atmosphere, Norreys played a prominent part in the skirmish near Zutphen. One casualty was Sir Philip Sidney, the gifted poet and writer, who was shot in the thigh and twenty-six days later died of gangrene. At the end of the year Norreys was recalled to England, despite the protests of the States General who wanted him to stay. At court he had to endure the disdain of the queen, still indulging her favorite courtier, Leicester.

In July 1584 Norreys was sent to Ireland, a situation he found miserable. Two months later he marched into Ulster with the Lord Deputy of Ireland, Sir John Perrot, to dislodge the Scots. He helped capture a huge herd of cattle from the Glenconkyne Woods, so depriving the enemy of their food supplies. The campaign was not entirely successful, for the Scots retreated across the Irish Sea to Kintyre, where they regrouped and waited. When they saw the English had retired, they re-occupied Ulster.

In 1587 Norreys was recalled to London, where he found that Leicester had been replaced by Lord Willoughby and the queen's attitude towards him had greatly improved. He prepared for another campaign in the Low Countries, and recruited some 4,000 men and 400 cavalry. The queen was wavering between establishing peace with Spain or helping the Dutch.

While she hesitated, Norreys led an attack on a fort at Arnhem, which upset her as she had hoped for less aggressive activity to placate the Spanish king. Her attitude toward Spain was mercurial, sometimes pacific and other times aggressive. The problem for Norreys was the queen's half-hearted response to the Dutch war. It was now mid-winter and Norreys' troops were without adequate supplies of clothing, food and money. The high mortality rate amongst his men was alarming but his desperate appeals for aid were ignored. Despite their wretched condition, his troops still managed to repulse the Prince of Parma in a day-long fight at Aarshot.

The declaration of war between England and Spain changed Elizabeth's attitude. Norreys was recalled from the Low Countries and appointed Marshal of the Camp at West Tilbury. Ahead of Elizabeth's visit, he prepared pavilions decked with flags and pennants for the nobility and ranks of green booths for the common soldiery. There was no risk; the Armada had already been scattered and its surviving ships were by now probably approaching the Shetland Islands. Norreys stage-managed the whole event. The queen arrived by royal barge and was escorted along a raised causeway across the marshes to the camp. Flanked by the Earls of Essex and Leicester, with John Norreys bringing up the rear, she wore a plumed helmet, and a steel cuirass over a white velvet gown; mounted on a white horse, she carried a gold and silver baton. Riding to every part of the camp so all her soldiers should see her, she stated that she was ready to fight alongside her people.

Afterwards, a coach conveyed her to a nearby manor, Arden Hall, where she would spend the night. On 9 August 1588, still wearing a half-suit of armour, she delivered her famous speech to the 16,500 troops who were to defend her realm against the threat of a Spanish invasion. According to Neil Hanson's book, *The Confident Hope of a Miracle*, the speech was pure theatre and clearly intended for a far wider audience than the ranks of soldiers at Tilbury. It seems likely that it was subsequently rewritten, polished and distributed in pamphlet form. It was stirring stuff:

> I know I have the body but of a weak and feeble woman, but I have the heart and stomach of a king and a king of England too – and think foul scorn that Parma or any prince of Europe should dare to invade the borders of my realm ... I know that already for your forwardness you have deserved rewards and crowns, and I assure you in the word of a prince you shall not fail of them.

In October 1588 Norreys was again ordered to the Low Countries as an ambassador to the States General to thank them for their efforts in thwarting the Armada. Lord Willoughby, despite some friction between them, was requested to give Norreys all possible assistance. Willoughby wrote, perhaps with some sarcasm, 'but he is so sufficient to debate in this cause as my councils are but drops in the sea'.

The next campaign for John Norreys was to reimpose a Portuguese monarch following the Spanish takeover of the country. Antonio, Prior of Crato, had only a weak claim to the throne but Philip II had managed to persuade the Portuguese nobility to support him as a personal union with Spain would be highly profitable for Portugal at a time when the state finances were suffering. In 1589 Norreys began planning an invasion that would encompass the destruction of the survivors of the Armada in the Spanish ports and the establishment of Don Antonio on Portugal's throne. A fleet of some 146 ships, including Dutch vessels, was assembled and under the joint command of Sir Francis Drake and Sir John Norreys a strong expeditionary force of some 23,000 men, which included 19,000 troops, was sent to the Iberian Peninsula. This expedition excited as much enthusiasm in England as the Armada had done. Unfortunately, despite the able leadership of the country's most prominent commanders and the huge force of soldiers, the expedition was a failure.

It started well, with Norreys landing near Corunna in northern Spain. His men surprised and burnt the lower part of the town and beat off a Spanish force of some 8,000 troops. Taking to the sea, Norreys directed an attack on Lisbon, an awkward port to reach, but the Spanish declined to fight. Having advanced with one of the greatest fleets and biggest armies ever assembled, Drake and Norreys had little alternative but to return to Plymouth without a decisive outcome.

In April 1591 English forces went to Brittany to aid Henry IV of France's campaign against the forces of the Catholic League. Landing at St Malo on 5 May, Norreys joined up with the army of Prince Dombes. On 24 May they besieged the town of Guingamp, which surrendered after a brief fight, and the French king wrote to Elizabeth describing Norrey's bravery. On 11 June Norreys defeated a combined army of Spanish and French troops at Chateau Lauren. Shortly afterwards, 600 of his soldiers were transferred to Normandy, where the Earl of Essex was fighting around Rouen. After a long lull in the conflict, Norreys returned home.

In September 1593 he was again summoned back to Brittany, where he joined forces with the Duc D'Aumont to capture the fortress of Crozon, which defended Brest. In the fierce fighting Norreys was again wounded. In May 1594 he was recalled to England, as there was dissension between Norreys and his French allies. By this time John Norreys was approaching

50 and was beginning to feel the effects of his many wounds. In 1595 he was sent to Ireland, where he acted more as a diplomat than as a soldier. During the two years he was there, he fell out with the Lord Deputy, Sir William Russell, Lord Borough and Sir Richard Bingham. Norreys wrote to Sir Richard Cecil, Lord Burghley's son, requesting that he be allowed to return to England.

By 1597 he was back in England with his health in decline. Queen Elizabeth seemed to disregard his twenty-six years of service, which greatly depressed him. He later stated that 'he had lost more blood in Her Majesty's service than any he knew … yet was he trodden to the ground with bitter disgrace'. He died on 3 July that year in the arms of his brother Thomas, in the latter's house in Marlow. His body was taken home and buried in the graveyard of Yattendon Church. A letter of condolence from the queen was all that the family received, and thus the most successful soldier of the Golden Age died largely forgotten in a parish churchyard. Later a monument was erected in Westminster Abbey to the Norreys family, which included John Norreys and his siblings.

Christopher Carleill

Christopher Carleill was born around 1551, the second son of Alexander Carleill and his wife Anne (née Barnes). Alexander died in 1560, and two years later Anne married Sir Francis Walsingham. The family were close-knit and prominent: Anne's father was Lord Mayor of London (1552–53), and both he and her first husband were members of the Muscovy Company, which traded with Russia. Anne's daughter married trader Christopher Hoddesdon, who informed Walsingham on ship movements and dissident Catholics. In 1564 Anne died, but Walsingham continued to support his stepson in his military career in the Netherlands.

Christopher Carleill was militarily skilful and travelled to Flushing (Vlissingen). He was present at the siege of Middelburg at the mouth of the river Scheldt, where the rebels invested the Spanish-held fortress for two years before it surrendered. Despite his youth, his talent was held in high esteem by Lodewijk van Boisot, the Dutch admiral, so that any plans the Dutch had were referred to Carleill before being put into execution. Later, he took two ships and sailed to La Rochelle to serve under Prince Henry of Conde. Given Henry's lack of military knowledge, the command devolved on Carleill, who sailed to Brouage, a port on the west coast of France, which was being invested by Duke Charles of Mayenne to little effect. When Carleill's ships appeared they were perceived as too well armed, and the Royalists withdrew.

Carleill was next sent to Steenwijk, which was being besieged by the Spanish, and was given command of the English troops at the fortress of Zwarte Sluis. While leading his men there, they were surprised by a large body of the enemy consisting of 2,000 infantry and 600 cavalry. He manoeuvred his men skilfully and inflicted heavy losses on the enemy. Once again he was given command in preference to the Prince van Oranje, and managed to raise the siege. He was on the point of returning to England when the Prince made him commander of the Anglo-Dutch army, a role he maintained until Sir John Norreys arrived to share the command with him. Altogether Carleill served the Prince for five years but did not receive any pay. The war had now reached a stalemate, so Carleill, having fulfilled his duty, returned to England.

In 1582 Carleill escorted a group of English merchants to Russia, despite the war that had broken out between Denmark and Russia. The Danish fleet met them in the Baltic, but did not engage his squadron of eleven ships. Carleill collected a Russian envoy and took him to London to discuss a possible settlement in America. The Russians proposed to send about 100 men to settle on the coast south-west of Cape Breton, but in the event the project was unsuccessful.

In 1584 Carleill was sent to Ireland and appointed commander of the garrison at Coleraine. Within a short time he fell out with Sir John Perrot, Lord Lieutenant of Ireland, who accused him of piracy and he quickly returned to England. Walsingham was instrumental in the elevation of his step-son to the rank of lieutenant general of land troops in the expedition to Santo Domingo. The queen, through Walsingham, ordered Sir Francis Drake to lead a large fleet consisting of twenty-one ships. Drake himself sailed in the queen's ship, the 600-ton *Elizabeth Bonaventure*, a new, fast, race-built galleon built by John Hawkins. As second-in-command, Christopher Carleill was given command of the 160-ton *Tiger*. Other vessels in the fleet included the *Golden Lion*, *Francis*, *Bark Bonner*, *Bark Benjamin*, *Hope and Duck*, *Aid* and *Galleon Leicester*, plus some pinnaces. War had just been declared between England and Spain, and the English ships were quickly off the mark with a pre-emptive strike on Spain's New World capital city, Santo Domingo. Lord Burghley declared: 'England was about to sustain a greater war than ever in any memory of man it hath done.' He was always of the opinion that England should not go to war with Spain.

Drake's force made their first halt at Vigo on the north-west coast of Spain to release the merchants who had been imprisoned. They also set about destroying Spanish ships and 'liberating' any treasure they came upon. The Spanish made a great display of waving flags and beating drums, but Carleill ignored them. He led his 700 men ashore and parlayed with the council, who told him that the English merchants had already been released. He asked for food, and the council agreed to supply victuals but procrastinated. Drake grew impatient and landed his men to destroy a chapel, having first removed a few papist treasures, including a magnificent silver cross. The fleet remained in Vigo for a week to refit and re-victual, and sank about twenty ships. Drake referred to this expedition as 'singeing the King of Spain's beard'.

Leaving Vigo, the set sail for the Canary Islands, and Drake was greatly annoyed to learn that they had missed intercepting one of the most valuable of Spain's treasure ships. They sailed on to the Cape Verde Islands and on 11 November captured the largest island, Santiago. With Carleill's help, the port town of Cidade Velha was sacked, as were Sao Domingos and Praia. In an effort to wreak as much damage as possible on the Spanish at the start of the war, the fleet headed west to the Caribbean and Hispaniola. At the uninhabited island of St Kitts they landed the fevered and sick patients. Drake sent pinnaces to scout the area around Santo Domingo and found the landward side had a city wall with some artillery, with the defences manned by about 2,000 soldiers. Drake and Carleill sailed 10 miles to the west and found a good place for the soldiers to land. During the night Carleill's troops disembarked and began to make their way through the jungle to the landward side of the city. At daybreak, the people of Santo Domingo awoke to find a large flotilla at the harbour entrance. They were just in range of the Spanish guns and so they began an artillery bombardment. Drake moved in closer to distract the Spanish. Around noon Careill appeared with his 700 men. Drake then sent some more men in boats to land and confront the Spanish. Meanwhile, Carleill's men swept out of the jungle, formed up into two columns and, with standards flying and music playing, appeared on the right flank of the town.

Carleill had placed his pikemen and musketeers on both sides, and they began to force the Spanish back. Within half an hour the landing party had reached the western walls and the Spanish troops were put to flight. Scarcely 300 Spaniards were left at the two gates, most of whom had no firearms. Carleill ordered Captain Anthony Powell to attack one gate while he assaulted the other. Both columns broke into a run and in the brief hand-to-hand combat that ensued, they overwhelmed the Spaniards. Moving forward, the storming parties met up with Drake's men in the market square. Barely stopping, Carleill's troops then headed towards the

Fortaleza Ozama, the main fortress. With artillery bombarding the walls until nightfall, the remaining Spaniards slipped away under cover of darkness. In the morning the English flag was flying from the fortress. The battle was over and the Spanish capital was now in their hands. Carleill had lost only seven of his men killed, with around twenty wounded. The English sailors and soldiers went on a looting spree, with churches especially singled out. Ornaments were stolen, statues and windows smashed, tapestries and altars desecrated. Public buildings and private homes were all looted as the English took what they could.

Drake knew the Spanish would negotiate a ransom in return for saving their town. They would also release the prisoners and galley slaves who had been captured in previous raids. Drake demanded 1 million ducats, but the Spanish could not come up with that amount. The destruction of the city continued until a more realistic amount could be agreed upon: 25,000 ducats. On 1 February Drake sailed away, having occupied the city for a month. More than twenty ships in the harbour had been burned or sunk, and Drake had commandeered three vessels to replace his unseaworthy ships, *Hope, Benjamin* and *Scout.* One of the biggest captured ships was renamed *New Years Gift* and scores of liberated galley slaves were recruited to sail her. Garcia Fernandez de Torrequemada was philosophical about the destruction, remarking 'this thing must have had divine sanction, as punishment for the people's sins'. He may have been referring to the genocide inflicted by the Spanish over the past decades, when they slaughtered 1.6 million Native Americans.

Drake's next target was the port city of Cartagena in present-day Columbia. The town was more easily defended but it received the same rough treatment as Santo Domingo. Under cover of darkness Carleill led 600 troops to secure the narrow spit of land that separated the outer harbour from the sea. They then stormed the outer defences and forced their way into the city against fierce opposition. After hand-to-hand fighting, the Spaniards gave way and the city fell to the English. Grabbing what treasure was available – some 107,000 ducats – and dozens of bronze guns, which was less than they anticipated, the fleet headed north through the Caribbean and attacked St Augustine on the eastern seaboard of Florida. This was soon captured and burned to the ground, so alleviating any threat to the English colony at Roanoke in Virginia.

On 26 July 1588 Carleill was appointed constable of Carrickfergus in County Antrim, and also served as governor of Ulster in the same year. He displayed his merciful nature when he sent to Scotland those Spaniards who were shipwrecked on the Irish coast, paying for their transport out of his own pocket. Christopher Carleill served in the English army until 1593. He died in London on 11 November 1593 at the age of 41.

Walter Raleigh

Walter Raleigh was one of Queen Elizabeth's most interesting and enigmatic courtiers, and he can be presented as either a hero or a scoundrel. A talented poet and writer (he wrote *A Historie of the World*), he served as a soldier and politician, and was one of the queen's favourites at court; he was also at various times a spy and explorer. He is credited with popularising tobacco and bringing the potato to England. He is believed to have been born on 22 January 1552 at Hayes Barton, East Budleigh in Devon. His father was also named Walter Raleigh, and his mother was Walter senior's third wife Katherine Champernowne, the fourth daughter of Sir Philip Champernowne of the manor of Modbury in Devon. Raleigh's maternal uncle was Sir Arthur Champernowne, Member of Parliament for Devon and Admiral of the West Coast; Richard Grenville was a cousin, and his older step-brother was Humphrey Gilbert. Along with Francis Drake and William Shakespeare, he was the one of the most notable figures of the Elizabethan era.

Raleigh's family were fanatical Protestants who needed to keep a low profile through the reign of Mary Tudor – his father narrowly avoided arrest and execution in 1549 during the western rebellion, hiding in a tower to avoid the men searching for him. Under Elizabeth, in 1561, he became the churchwarden in East Budleigh. When he was only 17, young Raleigh went to France to serve with the Huguenots, in what became the second deadliest religious war fought between 1569 and 1598. He returned in 1572 and registered as an undergraduate at Oriel College, Oxford, but left without a degree. This was not unusual as formal qualifications were generally for those seeking a career in the Church. He then finished his education at the Middle Temple, in the Inns of Court, before returning to France.

Little is known about his life between 1569 and 1575, although he did witness the battle of Moncontour, fought on 3 October 1569 between the Catholic forces of King Charles IX and the Huguenots commanded by Gaspard de Coligny, which saw some 9,000 men killed and many more wounded. Around 1575 he came back to England and took an interest in Ireland. Between 1579 and 1583 he took part in the Desmond Rebellions and participated in the siege of Smerwick, held by a mixture of Spanish and Irish. When the castle fell to the Anglo-Irish army, Raleigh led a party that decapitated some 600 Spanish and Italian soldiers. As a reward,

Raleigh received 40,000 acres from the rebels; this made him one of the principal landowners in Munster. Despite this tremendous accumulation of land, he had limited success in finding tenants to settle on his estates. For seventeen years he made Ireland his occasional home and was made Mayor of Westmeath from 1588 to 1589. By 1602, unable to turn a profit from his lands, he sold them to the Earl of Cork.

Despairing of Ireland, he turned his attention to North America and organised a settlement on Roanoke Island off the coast of Virginia. After several years all attempts to supply the colonists failed. There was a three year-gap, during which the colony received no supplies, and the settlement disappeared; it is known as 'the lost colony of Roanoke island'. Raleigh returned from Ireland having disbanded his company, but he had helped to establish the Protestant Church there. He became a favourite of Queen Elizabeth, who knighted him and made him Warden of the Stanneries (tin mines) in Cornwall and Devon, Lord Lieutenant of Cornwall and Vice-Admiral of both counties. His participation in the Armada was marginal and he was involved in a purely defensive role against the Spanish in the West Country.

As the queen's favourite, Raleigh received many rewards, including Durham House on the Strand and an estate at Sherborne in Dorset. Unfortunately he made a catastrophic error by falling in love with Bess Throckmorton, one of the queen's ladies-in-waiting. Without Elizabeth's consent, they married in 1591 and had a child, who died of the plague the following year. By 1593 the marriage was discovered and Raleigh and Bess were imprisoned in the Tower of London. They were not thrown into the dungeons but lived in a suite of rooms which they were not allowed to leave. They were only incarcerated for a matter of months before being released. The queen had relented, largely in order to enable Raleigh to manage the huge treasure captured from the *Madre de Deus* in the Azores. Having divided the spoils, Raleigh was sent back to the Tower, where he remained until early 1593. On release, he was elected a Member of Parliament, and spoke on religious and naval subjects. In 1596 he was one of the commanders of the 150-vessel fleet that captured Cadiz. The fleet was divided into four squadrons, commanded by Lord Thomas Howard on the *Arc Royal*, Sir Walter Raleigh on the *Warspite*, Sir Francis Vere commanding the *Rainbow* and Sir George Carew on the *Mary Rose*. The capture of Cadiz netted more than 20 million ducats and over 100 brass cannon.

For a man who had not sailed very far, he now found a subject that captivated him: the fabled city of El Dorado. He had read a Spanish account that told of a great golden city at the headwaters of the Orinoco and Coroni rivers in Guyana and eastern Venezuela. Raleigh and his step-brother, Sir John Gilbert, put together an expedition of five ships and on 6 February 1595 set sail from England. His second-in-command was his friend Lawrence Kemys, captaining a small Spanish prize named *Gallego*. Reaching Trinidad, they attacked and captured San Jose. Leaving his ships, Raleigh took 100 men to the mainland and sailed up the Orinoco. Following the river upstream with a collection of rafts and a pinnace, they reached a large lake. Crossing the lake, they continued on the Orinoco, but the current made progress very slow. They came upon a river-side village, where they were welcomed, and the chief told Raleigh of a 'rich culture in the mountains', which Raleigh convinced himself was an off-shoot of the Inca kingdom. He sent out parties to search for the fabled gold, and they found gold-bearing rocks. With the rains increasing, and the Orinoco in spate, Raleigh decided to return to England, confident that the rocks would provide sufficient evidence to convince investors to back another expedition that would surely find gold. The journey downstream was far easier and he was relieved to find the ships still safely anchored off Trinidad.

The following year Raleigh sent Kemys, commanding the *Darling*, to explore the Guyanan coast. Kemys returned with glowing accounts of the wealth of the country and urged Raleigh to persuade the queen to take possession of it. While there, Kemys mapped geographical and geological features and compiled botanical reports about the country. He also travelled inland towards the large lake previously encountered, where he hoped to find the mythological city of Manoa – City of Gold. Sadly he failed to find anything resembling a city.

Raleigh was chosen as Member of Parliament for Dorset in 1597 and for Cornwall in 1601. From 1600 to 1603 he was Governor of Jersey and constructed a new fort at St Helier. Once again he fell into royal disfavour, this time with the new king, James I. In 1603 he was accused of taking part in a plot devised by courtiers to remove James from the throne and replace him with his cousin, Lady Arabella Stuart. While Raleigh was in Jersey, Lord Brooke had collected enough money, £160,000, to stage the *coup d'état*, returning to England via Jersey. The plot was soon exposed and Raleigh and his friend Kemys were implicated in the conspiracy and imprisoned in the Tower. Kemys was released soon after and acted as bailiff and agent for his friend, who remained in the Tower for fourteen years.

In 1617 Raleigh was pardoned by the king, and Kemys persuaded him to visit Guyana to search for El Dorado. Raleigh set out with Kemys, hoping to buy himself back into royal favour by discovering gold, but the king was adamant that they should not attack any Spanish towns or ships. Raleigh took along his young son Walter, who joined Kemys in a disastrous attack on a Spanish outpost, Santo Tome de Guayana, on the Orinoco river. During the fight Walter was killed by a musket ball. It is unlikely that Kemys issued an order to attack, for the Spaniards quickly fled. After twenty-nine days of fruitless searching for gold, Kemys returned to the ships and reported to Raleigh that his son had been killed. Raleigh refused to accept Kemys' apology and in a fit of remorse Kemys went to his cabin and shot himself in the chest. The wound was not fatal, however, so he picked up a dagger and stabbed himself in the heart. As Raleigh had been under a suspended death sentence since 1603, he could hardly expect a royal welcome when he reached Plymouth.

The Spanish ambassador demanded that Raleigh's death sentence be reinstated, and King James had little choice but to comply. Sir Lewis Stukeley, whose great-uncle was the mercenary Thomas Stukeley, was sent to bring Raleigh back to London. Stukeley had been told to make the journey easy for Raleigh as he was not in good health. At Salisbury one of Stukeley's entourage, a French doctor named Guillaume Manoury, connived with the sickness Raleigh said he had, and by the time they reached Andover Stukeley was convinced that Raleigh was on the point of escaping, so he doubled the guards. When they reached London on 7 August, Raleigh attempted to escape down the Thames on a wherry (a rowing boat that carries freight). He managed to get past Woolwich but was intercepted by a larger wherry. He was returned to Greenwich where Stukeley re-arrested him. He was finally executed in Old Palace Yard at the Palace of Westminster, the same place where he had witnessed the execution of his bitter rival, Robert Devereux, Earl of Essex. On 29 October 1618 Raleigh made a speech from the scaffold in which he forgave Lewis Stukeley and declared that he was not scared to meet his Maker, further commenting 'Let us dispatch. At this hour my ague comes upon me; I would not have my enemies think I quaked from fear.'

Plenty of people thought Walter Raleigh should not have been put to death and they blamed Lewis Stukeley. The Earl of Nottingham even threatened to take a cudgel to Stukeley, to which King James responded: 'On my soul, if I should hang all that speak ill of thee [Stukeley], all the trees in the country would not suffice.' The king officially pardoned Stukeley but popular hatred pursued him back to his manor at Affeton.

He then fled to the island of Lundy in the Bristol Channel, where he went mad and died in 1620.

Humphrey Gilbert

Born in 1539, the fifth son of Otho Gilbert of Compton near Brixham, Devon, Humphrey Gilbert was related to some outstanding figures. His step-brothers were Carew Raleigh and Sir Walter Raleigh, his cousin was Richard Grenville and his mother was Catherine Champernowne, the niece of Kat Ashley, Queen Elizabeth's governess. As the youngest son, his education was funded but after that he had to make his own way. He attended Eton College and Oxford University, and then resided at the Inns of Chancery between 1559 and 1561.

Gilbert's first foray into soldiering was as part of the garrison of Le Havre. After what turned out to be only a short siege (from 22 May to 31 July 1563), the superior French force expelled the English from the port. The English commander was the Earl of Warwick, with 5,000 men who were short of supplies and infected with the plague. The port was in a very poor condition and only the surrounding marshland and sea gave any protection. During June, Gilbert was wounded during the French artillery barrage, and in the following month the English withdrew. By 1566 he was serving in Ireland under the command of Sir Henry Sidney. Sent home with dispatches for the queen, he took the opportunity to present her with his account, *A Discourse of a Discoverie for a New Passage to Cataia*. Although he had not sailed across the Atlantic, he was convinced that there was a shortcut to China by way of North America.

In 1567 Gilbert was appointed Governor of Ulster and served as a Member of the Irish Parliament, but returned to England 'for the recovery of his eyes'. After several months he had recovered sufficiently to return to Ireland. The historian A.L. Rowse wrote of him in his *Elizabethan Age*:

> Gilbert was certainly an interesting psychological case, with the symptoms of disturbed personality that often go with men of mark, not at all the simple Elizabethan seaman ... He was passionate and impulsive, a nature liable to violence and cruelty – as came out in his savage repression of rebels in Ireland – but also intellectual and visionary, a questing and original mind, with the personal magnetism that went with it. People were apt to be both attracted and repelled by him, to follow his leadership and yet be mistrustful of him.

In April 1569 Gilbert proposed an extensive settlement in southern County Cork and also a large plantation in Ulster for 'Devonshire gentlemen'. That summer he pushed westward with his forces and invaded Leinster and Munster, only to be opposed by the Geraldines of Desmond (a royal dynasty), led by James Fitzmaurice. The Geraldines were driven out but returned to lay siege to Kilmallock. Gilbert rallied his men and rode out against the Geraldines' more numerous army. During the fighting Gilbert's horse was shot from under him and his buckler (a small round shield) was transfixed with a spear. Despite his numerical disadvantage, Gilbert succeeded in driving off the Geraldines, and then marched unopposed through Kerry and Connello. During the three weeks of this campaign, the Irish were harshly treated and even women and children did not escape. It was during this period that Gilbert showed his violent nature:

> The heads of all those which were killed in the day, should be cut off from their bodies and brought to the place where he encamped at night, and should be laid on the ground by each side of the way leading into his own tent so that none could come into his tent for any cause but commonly he must pass through a lane of heads ...
> It brought great terror to the people when they saw the heads of their dead fathers, brothers, children, kinsfolk and friends . . .

Gilbert's feeling towards the Irish was summed up in his comment: 'The people are headstrong and if they feel the curb loosened but one link they will with bit in the teeth in one month run further out of the career of good order than they will be brought back in three months.'

In December 1569, after one of the rebel chiefs surrendered, Gilbert was knighted by Sir Henry Sidney in the ruins of Fitzmaurice's camp amongst the heaps of dead gallowglass (mercenary warriors). A month after Gilbert returned to England, Fitzmaurice retook Kilmallock and sacked the town for three days, leaving it in his words 'the abode of wolves'. Three years later Fitzmaurice surrendered. Gilbert married Anne Ager and they had six sons and a daughter. He was elected to Parliament for Plymouth and in 1572 for Queenborough in Kent. In 1579 he was once again fighting in Ireland. In October Gilbert sailed into the port of Cobh in Cork and again displayed his short temper, delivering a terrible beating to a local man, battering him about the head with his sword. He then had a terrible row with a local merchant, whom he murdered on the dockside.

Turning his attention to alchemy, Gilbert worked to turn iron into copper and lead into mercury. Both failed. He persisted with his theory that the North West Passage was the way to reach China, and his fervour drummed up support and money. Martin Frobisher was appointed captain and sailed for the frozen and fog-bound areas of northern Canada. Despite months of exploring the innumerable inlets in Baffin Bay, he could not find a clear passage to the west and was forced to return home with a cargo of worthless black stone and an Inuit. His crew had suffered the cruelties of an Arctic winter and were almost numb with the cold. Like many of his contemporaries, Gilbert believed that the New World would open the door to untold wealth, which he wished to exploit before others beat him to it.

Gilbert had not yet given up on the colonisation of North America and in 1583 he had raised sufficient funds from English Catholic investors. Constrained by penal laws in their own country, and loath to seek sanctuary in Europe, the prospect of a free future in an American settlement appealed to them. Gilbert had earmarked what was to become New England and proposed to seize some 9 million acres for settlement. At around this time the privy council imposed a recusancy fine on Catholics who refused to attend Anglican services. Without Catholic financing, Gilbert decided to set sail anyway on 11 June 1583. Queen Elizabeth advised him not to undertake such an expedition, saying, 'he was a man noted of not good happ by sea', not least because his previous attempt to reach the New World had ended in disaster when a storm hit his fleet when it was barely out of sight of the English shore. Eventually the queen gave her blessing and the ill-prepared fleet set sail.

One of the ships, Walter Raleigh's *Bark Raleigh*, turned back when disease broke out, while another became separated by fog. Very quickly arguments broke out among the remainder as to which route to take. Some favoured going south, hoping for good weather and fair winds. Others wanted to turn north and try to discover the North West Passage. Finally they agreed to make for Newfoundland, hoping to encounter fishing vessels to boost their inadequate food supplies. They met with thirty-six ships outside the port of St John's. Gilbert hoped to make a grand entrance and claim Newfoundland for Her Majesty, but unfortunately his ship ran aground on rocks at the entrance to the bay and had to be towed off by the fishing boats he had intended to overawe. Once he was able to land, Gilbert set up a tent on a hill overlooking the bay and provided provisions for a celebratory banquet. The fishermen, who came from France, Spain and Portugal, were not impressed by Gilbert's attitude, especially when he dug a turf and declared that he was taking 'possession of the said land in the right of the crown of England by digging of a turf and receiving the same ... delivered unto him after the manner of the law and custom of England'.

Gilbert went on to proclaim that the new colony was to be ruled under the royal charter of England, that its religion was to be Anglican and that treason would be punished by death. His gentlemen passengers were not at all impressed with the terrain of Newfoundland and told Gilbert that they would go in search of a better land further south. Gilbert had no alternative but to go along with the settlers. Almost immediately they ran into fog and storms. The *Delight*, the largest ship and the one carrying most of the supplies, ran aground on a sand bar off Sable Island. The ship's captain, Richard Clarke, had told Gilbert that they could not sail close to the island but Gilbert, no seaman, stubbornly ordered Clarke to take the *Delight* closer. Stuck on the sand bar, the ship was broken apart by the pounding surf. Captain Clarke managed to escape the wreck with sixteen men in a small lifeboat, but eighty-five settlers and the expedition's supplies were lost.

With the storms battering his diminished fleet, Gilbert had no alternative but to return to England. He was now in command of the smallest ship in the fleet, the 10-ton frigate *Squirrel*. By 9 September they had reached the Azores, but ran into another storm. In the rough seas the *Squirrel* was taking on more water than her pumps could handle. Gilbert was seen reading a book in the stern, and called out to the nearby *Golden Hind*, 'We are as near to Heaven by sea as by land!' Around midnight, the small ship's lights suddenly went out as she was overwhelmed by the sea. Gilbert drowned, along with the other ten crew. He was an unpleasant man but a driven one, determined to found an overseas colony for England. He was part visionary and part pirate; both brave and cruel, as witness his treatment of the Irish. He is acknowledged as the founder of a settlement in North America, but in reality he did not follow it up and his efforts are largely forgotten.

Michael Geare

Michael Geare was born around 1565 in the merchant port of Limehouse on the river Thames. He came reportedly from a poor cockney family background but rose to become an excellent seaman. In his youth he served on ships captained by Sir George Carew and was recognised as a skilful navigator. He was also supported by John Watts, a merchant and ship owner, who had a vessel named *Little John* paid for by the City of London. Watts also financed Geare's subsequent privateering exploits and in 1592 he set up a partnership with him. Gaining considerable wealth from

Geare, Watts renamed his ship the *Michael and John*. He even served her as a volunteer and took part in the action against the Spanish Armada. Watts was also one of the founders of the East India Company, formed in 1599, and served as Lord Mayor of London.

In the spring of 1591 Geare took the *Michael and John* to the Caribbean as part of a five-ship flotilla. After catching a Spanish ship, they learned that a treasure fleet was approaching western Cuba, and they sailed to take up positions off Cape Corrientes to await its arrival. The treasure fleet was protected by a number of Spanish naval vessels, but disregarding the danger, Geare and Lane attacked ten ships, including one very rich prize. Their efforts resulted in one of the most successful attacks of Elizabeth's reign, and added considerably to the national exchequer. Geare and Lane had been supported by a large financial investment from John Watts, Walter Raleigh and Francis Drake, among others, and as anticipated they captured and boarded a number of Spanish ships.

In 1595 Geare tried to board a Spanish galleon, but fifty of his crew were lost in the skirmishing and he was forced to withdraw. To make up for this defeat, he successfully captured another Spanish ship and recouped his losses. In 1596 he commanded the *Neptune* and sailed her pinnace with John Rilesden and Christopher Newport to capture several Spanish vessels in the Caribbean. Geare then returned to Jamaica to join a privateering expedition to Honduras led by Sir Anthony Shirley and William Parker. Having failed to capture Trujillo, they sailed to Puerto Caballos, which they sacked but found little of value. Geare then parted company with Shirley and Parker, who crossed the highlands of Guatemala and reached the Southern Sea.

In the West Indies during 1601 Geare commanded the *Archangel* and her pinnace *James*. He captured three ships, although he lost contact with one. This ship finally managed to sail to Morocco, where it was sold. The following year Geare teamed up with Christopher Newport and they captured two Spanish warships and several merchant vessels. On 24 January 1603 Newport and Geare combined forces with some French ships, and landed crews and soldiers near Santiago, Cuba. Their advance was halted by two unusual deterrents: a single cannon and a stampeding herd of cattle. The danger from the charging animals forced the attackers to break off and retreat to their boats. A consultation between Geare and Newport revealed that two galleons were unloading their goods at Puerto Caballos. Sailing east, they were able to attack the port and board the Spanish ships, burning one and capturing the other. The cargo taken was considerable, and was split between the English and French. Michael Geare's portion was enough for him to retire. He bought a house in Stepney and hung a small dagger outside, which gained some notoriety in his later years. Having submitted some of the financial wealth to the Crown, Elizabeth rewarded him with a knighthood. Before his death, he gave an annual subscription of £5 to be shared among the families of those lost at sea and the seafarers of Limehouse.

Interestingly, an archaeological dig around Narrow Lane in the Limehouse area revealed some interesting artefacts, including Oriental china and Mexican coins. There can be little doubt these came from the following seamen, who lived in the area: Michael Geare, William Bushell, Christopher Newport and Captain Paramour.

Christopher Newport

Born around 1561, Christopher Newport was brought up in Limehouse, an important port on the river Thames. He was the son of a ship's master, also named Christopher Newport, who plied his trade up the east coast of England. Young Christopher may have been born on his father's ship, for he was christened at Harwich on 29 December. He went to sea in 1580 and quickly acquired the skills of a master mariner. On 19 October 1584 he married Katherine Proctor, another native of Harwich.

Following the outbreak of war between England and Spain, he took to raiding the Spanish Main in a variety of ships, including the *Little John*, the *Margaret* and the *Golden Dragon*. During one expedition to the Caribbean, he captured a galleon but was so badly wounded during the fighting that he lost his right hand. Fitted with a prosthesis including a hook, he carried on raiding for another twenty years.

In 1592 an English squadron of six ships waited in the Azores to intercept a Portuguese treasure ship, the *Madre de Deus*, which was expected to call there before going on to Lisbon. After a fierce day-long fight near Flores Island, during which many Portuguese sailors were killed, the English, including Christopher Newport, were finally able to board her and seized the greatest amount of plunder taken from a single vessel in the sixteenth century. The quantity of riches was breathtaking: countless chests filled with jewels, pearls, and gold and silver coins, as well as ambergris, richly woven cloth, tapestries, 425 tons of cloves, 35 tons of cinnamon, 3 tons each of mace, nutmeg and balsamic resin, 25 tons of cochineal and 15 tons of ebony. In total, the *Madre de Deus* was carrying cargo valued at £500,000 pounds. Fortunately for the privateers, the six ships were able to accommodate this vast fortune and bring it back to England.

Newport's last raid took place in 1603 when he accompanied Michael Geare in the failed attack on Puerto Caballos. Nevertheless, he managed to bring back to England two baby crocodiles and a wild boar, which he presented to the delighted new king. Newport now settled into a life of exploration and supply. In 1606 he was hired by the Virginia Company of London to establish a settlement in Virginia. He took charge of the company's ship, the *Susan Constant*, and carried across the Atlantic seventy-one male colonists, including John Smith. (During the war between Transylvania and the Ottoman Empire, Smith had reputedly killed and beheaded three Ottoman challengers in single combat. For this he was knighted by the Prince of Transylvania, and given a horse and a coat of arms displaying three Turks' heads. Between 1602 and 1604 he was held by the Turks as a slave but managed to escape via Muscovy.)

Clearly a volatile character, during the voyage Smith was charged with mutiny and was held under arrest for the rest of the voyage. Newport made plans for his execution but relented when it was revealed in a private letter that the Virginia Company had appointed John Smith as one of the leaders of the new colony. On 29 April they reached Virginia, and sailed into a bay which they named Cape Henry, and Newport erected a cross at the mouth of the bay. In the days that followed they sailed miles up the James river seeking a suitable location for their settlement. In 1607 a fort was completed at Jamestown and Newport sailed back to England to collect more colonists and supplies. When he returned on 8 January 1608, he found that more than half of the colonists had died during the freezing winter. He had brought two ships this time, the *John and Francis* and the *Phoenix*, bringing an additional 120 men. They wasted much of the three months spent there loading the ships with iron pyrite – fool's gold – which turned out to be worthless.

Newport returned to England with him a Powhatan tribesman named Namontack, who stayed for three months. In September 1608 Newport went back to Virginia with seventy passengers, including 'a gentle woman and her servant'. He also carried a list of the Company's counterfeit orders, which greatly angered Smith, much to Newport's glee. One of the orders was to make the native leader emperor and give him a comfortable bedstead. The Company also demanded that Smith pay for Newport's voyage with pitch, tar, wood and glass. Whether this was part of the fake letter is not known. Smith also threatened the natives with military force unless they supplied food, which was in short supply, and apparently discovered that the settlers were planning to murder him. Although he exaggerated his experiences, Smith did explore the eastern seaboard of

America and is credited with discovering New England. Although he had many scrapes, he died at the age of 51 in London.

The third supply trip was the biggest, bringing 500 to 600 colonists. A fleet of seven ships, including the company's new vessel, the *Sea Venture*, set out in June 1609 under Newport's command. On 24 July they ran into a hurricane that raged for three days. The caulking on the new ship separated and its commander, George Somers, was forced to run aground on a reef at Bermuda. The survivors of the disaster – 150 settlers, crew members and a dog – set about building two smaller ships from the wreck, plus wood from the island. Somers and the settlers remained on Bermuda, where they found ample supplies of food and water. This was the incident that inspired William Shakespeare to write *The Tempest*. During their time on the island they built a church and houses, so founding the first colony on the island.

Thomas Gates was to be the new governor of Jamestown, while Somers was the commander in charge until they reached Virginia. Eventually, some ten months later, Somers guided the two small ships, named *Deliverance* and *Patience*, to Jamestown, only to find that three-quarters of the colonists had starved to death. The survivors voted to abandon the settlement and return to England but as they sailed down the James river, they met the supply mission headed by Thomas Gates, who ordered the remaining settlers to return. Despite the stresses and difficulties that had gone before, the adept Gates managed to establish a lasting colony. Somers returned to Bermuda but fell ill on the voyage and died on Bermuda on 9 November 1610.

On 12 May 1611 Newport arrived back at Jamestown for the last time. On his return to England, he accepted a commission and joined the Royal Navy. He also joined a mission for the East India Company and sailed on the *Expedition* on 24 April 1609. The ship was captained by David Middleton, a man who knew the East Indies very well. Reaching the Cape of Good Hope, they stayed for eight days before sailing on to Bantam, arriving on 7 December. A month later Newport entertained the King of Button, one of the Andaman Islands, on his ship. Sadly no trade was accomplished, owing to the storehouses having been destroyed by fire.

The *Expedition* sailed on to Bangay, only to be confronted by a drunk and dissolute Dutchman who dominated the natives and swindled the King of Ternate. It was apparent that the Dutch were now in charge of the spice trade, having taken control of what is now Indonesia. Captain Middleton threatened to fight unless his ship was permitted to depart with her holds full of nutmeg and mace. A compromise was reached, but even so the Dutch navy threatened to intercept the *Expedition*. Middleton was no privateer, but he managed to avoid any maritime clash. In May 1614 Middleton and the *Samaritan* returned to the East Indies to collect spices from Bantam. Sadly, on the return trip the ship was dashed against the rocks of Madagascar and all the crew were lost.

In 1615 Christopher Newport sailed to India, and in November 1616, perhaps prophetically, wrote his will. Accompanied by his son, also named Christopher, he set out for Ternate in the Spice Islands. This was the island that Drake had visited thirty years before. But when Newport reached Java, he was struck down with an unknown illness and died. There can be no doubt that he was one of the great maritime seamen of the age.

Martin Frobisher

Born in either 1535 or 1539 at Altofts near Wakefield in Yorkshire, Martin is believed to have been the son of merchant Bernard Frobisher. Following the death of his mother Margaret (née York) in 1549, he went to live with his uncle, Sir John York, who was Master of the Mint in London. Martin had a good education, and took a great interest in exploration and navigation. In 1543 he was sent by his uncle to Guinea as a cabin boy with Thomas Wyndham's expedition, made up of three ships and 140 men. (Guinea was the name used for the western part of Africa which now includes Nigeria.) Wyndham traded with King Oroghbua of Benin and extended credit for 80 tons of pepper. Although three-quarters of the expedition's crew would perish of heat and disease, Frobisher survived. Wyndham himself died at sea in the Bight of Benin, probably from fever or drowning.

Despite this experience, in 1554 Frobisher took part in another trading expedition to Guinea, this time as an apprentice merchant. Accompanying the landing party, he went ashore at the town of Samma to trade with the Africans. During the negotiations, the Africans abruptly ceased talking and took Frobisher prisoner. The expedition was unable to secure the young man's release and abandoned him. His captors handed him over to the Portuguese at the Mina trading post, where he was imprisoned for nine months in the castle of Sao Jorge da Mina. In 1556–57 he was released and spent some time in Morocco as a merchant before arriving back in Portugal. From there he found a ship that took him back to England.

On 30 September 1559 Frobisher married a widow named Isobel Richard, who had two young children and a substantial settlement from her previous marriage. By the mid-1570s Frobisher had spent her inheritance on his ventures and abandoned the family, leaving them destitute.

Frobisher had set his heart on finding a shortcut to China (Cathay) and India via the North West Passage at the top of North America. Funded by his uncle and other backers, he applied for a Letter of Marque from the English Crown and, together with John Hawkins, preyed on French ships trading off the Channel coast. In May 1563 he seized five French ships, and spent time in a French prison for capturing the *Catherine* and despoiling tapestries intended for King Philip.

Frobisher purchased the *Mary Flower* in 1565 and in 1566 was interrogated 'on suspicion of his having fitted out a vessel as a pirate'. In 1571 and 1572 he was employed in the Irish Sea, supporting the stamping out of the rebellion. In 1574 he at last managed to obtain the privy council's approval to mount an expedition to find the North West Passage to the Southern Sea. The Council referred him to the Muscovy Company, which licensed his search for the fabled shortcut. With the help of Michael Lok (aka Lock), he was able to raise enough capital to fund two ships, *Gabriel* and *Michael*, each of about 20–25 tons, and an unnamed vessel of 10 tons. On 7 June 1576 the three vessels left Blackwall on the Thames, being waved off by Queen Elizabeth from a window in Greenwich Palace. Sailing north, they reached the Shetland Islands before heading west by north for three days. Within a few days the ships were engulfed in a severe storm that pounded them continuously until 8 July. Three days later they spotted the mountains of southern Greenland before crossing the Davis Straight. Encountering another violent storm, they lost the pinnace, presumably sunk, and the *Michael* was forced to turn back to England.

The *Gabriel* sailed on for four days and found the southernmost tip of Baffin Island before reaching the mouth of a bay, which Frobisher named after himself. Prevented from travelling north by a contrary wind and ice floes, the *Gabriel* sailed westward, still hoping to find the entrance to the North West Passage. On 18 August the ship reached Burche's Island, named after the ship's carpenter who first spotted it. Here they met the local Inuit, and persuaded one of them to guide them through the region. Five men who disobeyed Frobisher's orders and went ashore were captured by the Inuit. After days of searching for them, Frobisher gave up. (On a later expedition Frobisher learned that the five crew members had stayed with the Inuit for five years; finally they attempted to leave by boat, but it capsized and all were drowned.)

With winter approaching, Frobisher turned for home, bringing with him a black stone which he believed contained gold. On arrival, Frobisher gave the black stone to Michael Lok. It was examined by an Italian alchemist, who declared it to be gold-bearing, and on the strength of this declaration Lok was able to persuade investors to fund a second expedition. The fleet that sailed from Plymouth in 1577 was considerably larger, with a maximum complement of 120 men, including thirty Cornish miners. The queen's ship, the 200-ton *Ayde*, with the *Gabriel* and *Michael*, was used to collect the supposedly gold-rich ore; their holds full, on 23 August the expedition returned to England.

Frobisher's third and largest expedition was made up fourteen vessels: the flagship *Ayde*, *Michael*, *Gabriel*, *Judith*, *Dionyse*, *Anne Francis*, *Francis of Foy*, *Bear of Leicester*, *Thomas of Ipswich*, *Thomas Allen*, *Armenail*, *Soloman of Weymouth*, *Hopewell* and *Emanuel of Bridgewater*. There were 400 men aboard the ships, including 147 miners, four blacksmiths and five assayers. The fleet reached the south of Greenland on 20 June. After going in the wrong direction, Frobisher turned about and anchored in Frobisher Bay. The freezing cold and ice led to arguments and discontent among the men and any thoughts of establishing a colony in this frozen waste were dismissed. Once again, considerable amounts of ore were collected before the fleet returned to England, losing *Emanuel of Bridgewater* off the west coast of Ireland. The ore was taken to a specially constructed smelting plant at Dartford, where it was found to be valueless iron pyrite. In the end the rocks and ore were used to surface the road near Dartford. Michael Lok and his Cathay Company went bankrupt and he was sent to the debtor's prison.

Having blundered around Baffin Island without making any notable discoveries, Frobisher gave up on ever discovering the North West Passage. With his reputation in decline, he applied to Sir William Winter for a captaincy on one of the heavily armed ships bound for Ireland and the putting down of the Desmond rebellion. He was given command of *Foresight* and took part in the siege of Smerwick at Dingle, coincidentally near the spot where *Emanuel of Bridgewater* was wrecked. Although Frobisher disliked Francis Drake, mostly because of the latter's success, he joined him on the 1585 raids in the West Indies. As captain of the *Primrose*, he joined a select group of Drake's advisers, including Christopher Carleill, Nichols and Fenner.

After the defeat of the Spanish Armada, Frobisher visited his native Altofts in Yorkshire. Here he met and later married Dorothy Wentworth, the widowed daughter of the 1st Baron Wentworth. With another impressive marriage settlement, Frobisher and his new bride purchased the manor of Whitwood in Yorkshire and Finningley Grange in Nottinghamshire. Despite the country life, Frobisher still hankered after a life at sea. In 1592 he joined the fleet being sent to blockade the Spanish coast under the command of Sir Walter Raleigh, who was no great lover of the sea. Despite Raleigh being in command, the queen refused to allow him to join the fleet in person, and instead she recommended that Frobisher take his place. The fleet was divided in two, with Sir John Burgh and John Norton patrolling the Azores and Frobisher sailing off the Portuguese coast. Much to Frobisher's disgust, he learned that the Azores squadrons had captured the treasure ship *Madre de Deus*.

The siege of Morlaix took place from 6 to 17 September 1594. It was part of the French Wars of Religion, fought between the combined forces of the Catholic League of France and the Spanish against the Protestants. Part of the Catholic force was defending Morlaix when they spotted Martin Frobisher's fleet approaching with a siege train of heavy guns for Sir John Norreys. With no hope of being relieved, the Morlaix garrison surrendered.

The following month Frobisher's squadron was involved in the siege and relief of Brest. During the fighting at Fort Crozon Frobisher was shot in the thigh. The surgeon who extracted the ball left the wadding in his leg, and the resulting infection led to Frobisher's death on 22 November 1594. His heart and organs were buried at St Andrew's Church, Plymouth, and his body was taken to London to be buried at St Giles-without-Cripplegate.

George Clifford

George Clifford, born in Brougham Castle, Westmoreland, on 8 August 1558, was the son of Henry, 2nd Earl of Cumberland, and his second wife, Anne Dacre. The earl died in 1570, when George was just 12 years old. His wardship was acquired by Francis Russell, 2nd Earl of Bedford, who duly arranged a marriage between George and his daughter, Lady Margaret Russell. The marriage had been mooted in their infancy by their respective fathers but it was not a happy one. In his youth Clifford was sent to some notable academic schools, including Battle Abbey, as well as Cambridge and Oxford Universities. He showed a great aptitude for mathematics, which would serve him well in later years. As a peer of the realm, George spent most of his time in London or at court. He was tall, strong and active, although one courtier described him as 'the rudest Earl by reason of his northerly bringing up'. He was also a gambler, a spend-thrift and a faithless husband, who later separated from his wife. He took a great interest in jousting and became the queen's second champion after the retirement of Sir Henry Lee. A miniature painting by Nicholas Hilliard around 1590 shows Clifford in tilting attire, with the queen's diamond-encrusted glove pinned as a plume to his hat as a sign of her favour. He was made a Knight of the Garter and sat as a peer at the trial of Mary Queen of Scots. He was also involved in the formation of the East India Company.

The diaries of Anne Clifford, his only daughter, describe how much money he spent on gambling, and give details about his mistress and the hostility between himself and his wife. He may have made money from his voyages but he frittered it away in betting on horses, dice and the outcome of jousts. Already spending more than his estate could sustain, he attempted to re-establish himself on the outbreak of the war with Spain. In 1586 he sailed to Brazil with an expedition sponsored by Sir Walter Raleigh. Here he took part in capturing a Portuguese slaver and took a share in the profits. In 1588, during the pursuit of the Armada, he commanded the 600-ton *Elizabeth Bonaventure*, which gave him the impetus to take part in, and fund, further voyages of exploration.

In 1589 Clifford was put in command of an expedition to the Azores, also known as Cumberland's Third Voyage. This would involve a series of battles and skirmishes in the islands between August and September either to collect provisions or to steal prizes from the Spanish. Authorised by Elizabeth, Clifford was given command of the largest fleet he had ever fitted out. Leaving Plymouth on 6 March 1589, they made for the Spanish coast, where they learned that five carracks were leaving for the East Indies. The Spanish were warned that Clifford's ships were heading their way and instructed all shipping to remain in port.

Clifford then led his ships to the Canaries and the island of Lanzarote, where they bombarded a fortress and burned a nearby town. The fleet then sailed on to the Azores, where they waited for the expected *flota* from the Spanish Main. After several days Clifford decided to attack an island and selected San Miguel as the closest. Entering the capital's harbour, Ponta Delgada, flying the Spanish flag to fool the citizens, his ships captured four Portuguese carracks that were carrying olive oil, Madeira wine, cloth, silk and taffeta.

After stopping at the island of Flores for water and food, they learned that a number of Spanish and Portuguese ships were at anchor at Terceira Island. Entering the bay, Clifford trapped and bombarded the enemy's vessels, assisted by a merchantman, the Raleigh-owned *Barke of Lyme*. By misfortune, Clifford's cannon-fire was so accurate that it sank the largest galleon, which was carrying pearls, silver and 200,000 gold coins. A Portuguese carrack was boarded and found to contain silk, gold, silver and porcelain. Two other vessels were taken, carrying elephant tusks, grain, hides and coconuts bound for Brazil. While the fighting was going on, the English captives on the island managed to escape in a boat and were rescued by the *Margaret*.

After the capture and destruction of the enemy's ships, Clifford made for the island of Faial. On 6 September the English fleet approached Fort Santa Cruz and demanded its surrender. When the garrison refused, 300 troops were landed and attacked the fort and town. With the Spanish soldiers retreating, the fortress was easily overwhelmed. For four days the men plundered the town, demanding a ransom of 2,000 ducats from the governor, who duly paid.

The fleet next sailed to Graciosa Island, where the villagers produced a flag of truce, followed by gifts of wine and food. Unbeknown to Clifford, a Spanish treasure fleet had meanwhile stopped at Terceira for provisions. Clifford's fleet sailed on to Santa Maria Island and captured a small Portuguese carrack laden with sugar, but her crew put up stern resistance in which the English lost two men killed and sixteen wounded. The *Margaret* was left unfit to take part in any further action, and was sent back to England carrying the wounded and sick. Clifford decided to attack the island by climbing the cliffs, but as they ascended, his men were hit by rocks thrown down by the Spanish which forced them to retreat. During the encounter Clifford himself was struck in the side, arm and head before being taken back onboard his ship.

A few days later his men boarded another small ship and seized more than 400 chests of sugar and a large quantity of Brazil wood. Two days later they chased and caught the treasure ship *Nuestra Senora de Guia*, while rest of the *flota* managed to get away. They seized her cargo of silver, hides, plate and sugar; added to the rest of the expedition's plunder, it would produce a healthy profit. Satisfied with their destruction and their treasure, the fleet returned to England.

The 1590s proved a good decade for Clifford. Lacking a vessel able to support his hired fleet, he built himself a 600-ton galleon which he named the *Scourge of Malice*; it was the finest warship built at that time. Clifford went on several more voyages, and took part in both the abortive 1591 Battle of Berlengas Islands off Portugal and the more successful 1592 Battle of Flores in the Canaries.

In 1598 Clifford set off again with the largest expedition so far, consisting of twenty-one ships, including the *Scourge of Malice*. Heading west, they arrived at the island of Dominica, where they careened their ships. Clifford had instructed the soldiers that their main objective was San Juan on the island of Puerto Rico. On 6 June Clifford landed about 12 miles from San Juan with about 1,000 soldiers. They negotiated steep cliffs and rough terrain before they reached the city, spread out before them on a slope. The last obstacle for the attackers was the San Antonio channel, with a causeway and a drawbridge at one end. Instead of making the crossing under fire from the defenders, the English chose to wade through the water at the foot of the causeway. Clad in his armour, Clifford stumbled and fell. The weight of the armour dragged him down but he was rescued from drowning by the many hands that grabbed him and brought him to the surface.

The English laid siege to Fort San Felipe del Morro for two weeks, after which the governor surrendered. During the next two months a dysentery epidemic killed more than 400 men. After sixty-five days Clifford decided that the castle should be abandoned and the city sacked before being razed to the ground. Among the objects brought away were hides, ginger, sugar, eighty cannon, cathedral bells and 2,000 slaves. Once again, he arrived too late to intercept the treasure fleet. Unlike Francis Drake, who almost always captured Spanish treasure, Clifford mostly took sugar, hides and grain. A fellow courtier spoke of him as

> a man of admirable qualities, both in civil and military affairs. He knew as well how to fight as to govern, and had virtues capable of rendering him equally illustrious both in war and peace. He was so excellent a person that it can hardly be said what was lacking in him, and yet he had one considerable want: a steady gale of good fortune. Considering the vast expenses he was at in building, hiring and furnishing ships, it is a question whether his expeditions increased his estate.

Following the death of Queen Elizabeth, which Clifford's daughter described in her diaries (as well as her father's philandering with his mistress, 'a lady of high quality', and his addiction to gambling), Clifford went north to greet James VI of Scotland, soon to be England's new king, whose mother he had helped to condemn. Countess Margaret was not amused when their daughter was bypassed as Clifford's heir when he made his will. He bequeathed her £15,000, making her a wealthy heiress, but he ignored what should have been hers by right of birth. He may have done this because of the burden of debt that lay on the estate. On 30 October 1605, aged 46, George Clifford died at the Savoy Hospital overlooking the Thames. His embalmed body was taken to the family vault at Skipton Castle in Yorkshire and entombed in a highly decorated chest tomb monument in the Church of the Holy Trinity.

Interestingly, two of Shakespeare's plays were staged aboard Clifford's favorite ship, the *Scourge of Malice*: *Hamlet* on 5 September 1607 and *Richard II* on 30 September 1608. He was the first person outside England to put on such performances to entertain his crew. Eventually he sold the ship to the East India Company; renamed *Red Dragon*, she was on her way to the Spice Islands when she stopped on the Guinea coast due to an outbreak of scurvy. Captain William Keeling dosed his men with citrus fruits in the hope of stemming this awful shipboard malady.

William Monson

William Monson was born in South Carlton, Lincolnshire, in 1569, the third son of Sir John Monson and his wife Jane (née Dighton). Little is known of his early life but on 2 May 1581 he attended Balliol College, Oxford, at the young age of 14. After he matriculated aged 16, he ran away to sea. In his *Tracts*, which he compiled in the 1620s, he wrote on how officers and sailors should behave and was scathing about the Spanish and Portuguese mariners. Unlike the writings of the previous century, he wrote in a straightforward style, unlike the poetic prose of the Elizabethans.

He managed to get a captaincy on a merchant ship which went to the Canary Islands and then to Cezimba on Portugal's mainland. Disguised as a Portuguese man, he went into nearby Setubal to get supplies but unfortunately on the return journey they were almost shipwrecked and came close to starvation. He saw his first action in the Bay of Biscay when he and his fellow crew members boarded a Spanish ship. He wrote briefly about capturing the vessel:

> ... the Biscainer, I have formally spoken of in my First Book, in the voyage I first went to sea and the first fight I did ever see, in 1585. This ship had a flush deck fore and aft, which in boarding we won upon her, and her men being beaten into her other deck spent most part of their powder in making trains to blow us up; which, by fortune, we prevented, and with our fire pikes fired them before they could be brought to perfection. And thus after twelve hours fight in the night, we being upon the flush deck, and commanding their scuttles aloft that they could not come up to us, and they commanding the scuttles below that we could not go to them, what with wearisomeness, want of powder, and the death of their people they yielded as I have before described.

In 1588, at the age of 19, he took part in the pursuit of the Armada in the 70-ton vessel *Charles*, part of the queen's own fleet. As there was no regular naval service until 1590, the queen granted £8,970 per year to repair her ships. Monson then applied to join George Clifford's ship in the Azores expedition in 1589. Known as Cumberland's Third Voyage, it was a success and seven ships were captured from the Caribbean, netting gold, silver, silks and porcelain. Although the investors realised a healthy profit, many lives were lost to disease and storms.

Monson also went on Cumberland's other ventures to the Azores in 1591 and 1594. During the 1591 expedition Sir Richard Grenville sacrificed the *Revenge* to the Spanish fleet, as the rest of the English ships managed to escape. Monson was later captured by a Spanish galley during an engagement at the Berlengas Islands off the coast of Portugal. Taken to Lisbon, he was incarcerated in the castle until 1592, when he was ransomed. He again joined George Clifford at the end of his 1593 expedition to the Azores. In the Battle of Faial Island on 22–23 June 1594 the English attacked a 2,000-ton Portuguese carrack named *Cinco Chagas*. After a long and bitter fight, the carrack was eventually sunk in an explosion and the riches she held were lost.

Monson's father died in 1593 and he inherited property in Lincolnshire but ill-health laid him up for a year or so, although he did receive a Master of Arts degree from Oxford and entered Grays Inn as a would-be lawyer. In 1594, after a bitter argument with George Clifford, who considered Monson incompetent, he left his employ. Monson had hoped to succeed Sir John Hawkins as Treasurer of the Navy but it did not materialise. In 1595 he married a widow, Dorothy Wallop, who brought with her a stepson and some property.

Monson was appointed to command the 500-ton *Rainbow* in the spring of 1596, which marked twenty years of continuous service in the Royal Navy. It also marked the beginning of Monson's attachment to Robert Devereux, in the occupation of Cadiz. He received a knighthood from the earl just after the English had taken Cadiz and sailed with him to the Azores in 1597. The bad blood between Monson and Clifford spilled over after the latter made some disparaging remarks. Monson was incensed and challenged Clifford to a duel, but it came to nothing.

Although Monson was not implicated in Devereux's machinations regarding a Popish plot, there was a lull in his career. This came to an end when he returned to Parliament in 1601 and sought a new patron in Charles Howard, Earl of Nottingham, and his son-in-law Sir Richard Leveson, who had served with Monson at Cadiz. In 1603 Monson was elevated to the rank of vice-admiral by Leveson and took part in the capture of the carrack *St Valentine* of Lisbon. The treasure found on board settled Leveson's debts, but he still had to struggle not to fall into debt again.

Monson left the sea and returned to Parliament with a seat at Malmesbury. With the accession of James I, Monson's prospects seemed bright. Through his connections, he was made commander of the Channel Squadron, a post he retained for eleven years. But just as he seemed on the way up, Sir John Digby, the ambassador in Spain, revealed that Monson had been receiving bribes from Spain. With his benefactors already either dead or in disgrace over the murder of Sir Thomas Overbury, and Monson's own brother Thomas implicated in the killing and imprisoned, Monson himself was sent to the Tower. It is not clear whether or not he was implicated in Overbury's murder, but he remained in the Tower from January to July 1616. His own explanation was that he had incurred enmity through his writing about naval reforms and his hostility to the Dutch. He had also questioned Arabella Stuart's potential role as second in line to succeed Elizabeth. Some Englishmen felt she was more suitable than James to rule the country. Her fate was sealed when she secretly married William Seymour, 2nd Duke of Somerset; it was an unsuitable marriage in James's eyes, and the pair were placed under house arrest. When they attempted to flee to the Netherlands, Monson arrested them and Arabella Stuart was brought back and imprisoned in the Tower. Refusing to eat anything, she died of malnutrition.

Questioned about the matter of the Spanish bribes, Monson wriggled out of the charge and was pardoned by the king. Because of widespread political unrest, the king did not want such bribery to become public knowledge and Monson was released from the Tower. His only punishment was the loss of his command. In 1624 he began writing his *Naval Tracts*, an explanation of policy, strategy and administration, for which he is best remembered. In 1635, appointed vice-admiral by Charles I, he returned to sea, and spent his final years writing his lengthy *Tracts*. He died in February 1643 at Kinnersley and was buried at St Martin-in-the Fields.

Chapter Eleven

The Execution of Mary Queen of Scots

One of the most shocking incidents that precipitated the intended Spanish invasion was the trial and execution of Mary Stuart, Queen of Scotland and Dowager Queen of France. She had been implicated in the murders of two former husbands and had married a third, James Hepburn, Earl of Bothwell. This union was unpopular with the Scottish nobles and Mary was forced to abdicate in favour of her young son James. She had little choice but to cross the Solway Firth and enter England. Mary arrived in Cumberland in a humble fishing boat but, instead of being embraced by her cousin Queen Elizabeth, she was moved from castle to manor-house for eighteen years. As a figurehead for the Catholic cause, Mary became involved in some of the plots to assassinate the Protestant queen. Alarmed at the prospect of a Catholic uprising, Elizabeth imprisoned her cousin in a variety of locations. She was right to be alert, as Pope Sixtus V excommunicated her and urged Catholics to replace her with the Scottish queen. Philip II also encouraged Mary to claim the throne for her own and even proposed marriage with a view to including England in the Catholic cause. A description of Mary Stuart at the age of 45 was written by a contemporary: 'Tall, big made and somewhat round-shouldered, her face broad and fat, double-chinned and hazel eyed. She carried an Agnus Dei about her neck.'

The best description of Mary Stuart's last days was written by her doctor, Dominique Bourgoing, who was with her during her reign in Scotland and stayed with her until her death at Fotheringay Castle. He wrote of her conversations, reactions and travels during the last five months of her life. One of the last places in which Mary was imprisoned was Chartley Manor in Staffordshire. Her host and jailor, Sir Amyas Paulet, came to Chartley to see if it was big enough to accommodate both Mary's household and his own. It was noted that the manor had a deep moat, which helped security, and Mary spent almost a year there.

In August 1586 Francis Walsingham broke the code used in the letters sent by the participants in the Babington Plot, which implicated Mary Stuart. On the way to a hunt, Sir Amyas Paulet's party was intercepted on the road by a royal messenger, who delivered the news that the Babington Plot had been exposed and evidence found that incriminated Mary in the conspiracy. This gave Walsingham enough proof to accuse Mary of high treason. The leading members of her household were detained and their papers seized. Mary was arrested by armed soldiers who took her first to Paulet's house at Tixall and then back to Chartley. On 21 September Mary was taken from Chartley and travelled for three days to the castle at Fotheringay in Northamptonshire. This was a secure location, with the castle surrounded by marshland and a river. Although Mary did not yet know it, it was to be her final resting place. There are no surviving images of Fotheringay Castle but it was built in the Norman motte and bailey-style, and the village of the same name stood on the banks of the river Nene. It had long been an important site: on 2 October 1452 the Duke of York's youngest son Richard was born in the castle; he would grow up to become King Richard III.

Elizabeth was wary of Mary's devotion to the Catholic religion and alert to the danger that it could spill over into a religious war, as had happened in France. It was thought that the castle at Fotheringay was remote enough to hold Mary and oversee her trial. As Mary's carriage lumbered through the gloomy gateway, she must have thought that she would never again be released. Decades earlier, Catherine of Aragon had flatly refused to be imprisoned within its dank walls, declaring that 'To Fotheringay she would not go, unless bound with cart ropes and dragged hither.'

On 11 October the Commissioners arrived at the castle; the most prominent figures included Lord Burghley, Sir Francis Walsingham, Sir Christopher Hatton, the Earls of Leicester and Warwick, Robert Beale, the Clerk of the privy council, and William Davidson, the queen's secretary, plus about thirty others. They had come as an enlarged jury to question Mary about the Babington Plot and other intrigues against Elizabeth. On the first day of her trial, held in the large room in the keep, Mary responded very little, and as she retired Lord Burghley, the main spokesperson, made a final remark:

> The Queen, my Mistress, has punished those who contested your pretensions to the English crown. In her goodness she saved you from being judged guilty of high treason at the time of projected marriage with the Duke of Norfolk and she protected you from the fury of your own subjects.

On the second day Mary was again questioned by the lawyers over her relations with the King of Spain. She haughtily responded, 'It is not your affair to speak of matters concerning princes, and to enquire whether they have secret intelligences with each other.'

Burghley intervened and said, 'I do not blame you for this but if the Spanish army had entered the country, could you have answered for the life of the queen? Would not the country have been in danger of falling into the hands of strangers?'

Mary replied,

> I do not know of their intentions nor am I bound to answer them; but I am very sure that they would have done something for me, and if you wished to employ my services I should have been able to bring about a good understanding between you and them, as I have always offered to do. You should not have refused my offers.
>
> If you destroy me, you will place yourselves in danger, and will receive more harm than good. Of all that has been done by strangers I know nothing and am not responsible. I desire nothing save my deliverance.

While the trial was proceeding, the two Houses in Parliament were praying for Mary's execution: 'We cannot find that there is any possible means of providing for your Majesty's safety but the just and speedy execution of said Queen ...'

During the trial Mary Stuart gave a good account of herself, despite lacking any legal backing from lawyers, but she could not extricate herself from the various plots in which she was involved. As she left the room, she passed the table where the lawyers sat and spoke to them: 'Gentlemen, you have shown little mercy in the exercise of your charge and have treated me somewhat rudely ... but may God pardon you for it and keep from having to do with you all again.'

The Commissioners were now ready to delivery their verdict but Burghley had received a message from Elizabeth stating that she would suspend the sentence until she could hear and consider the report. The Commissioners were told to gather at the Star Chamber in Westminster in ten days' time to confirm the verdict. There followed a period of suspense for Mary Stuart, who showed little sign of sadness or depression. Paulet, although her jailer, allowed Mary and her retinue to use the large hall where the trial had taken place. Mary declared to Paulet,

> I have no occasion to feel troubled or disturbed. My conscience is at rest and I have answered my accusers. God and I know that I have never attempted nor connived at the death or murder of anyone. My

conscience is free and clear on this point, and being innocent, I have rather occasion to rejoice than be sad, having my confidence in God, the protector of the innocent.

Elizabeth, although she disliked Mary, was in a quandary about signing the death warrant. She harboured some hope that an official execution could be avoided by employing a hired assassin such as Robert Wingfield, who might sidestep the legal issues and simply smother the Scottish queen. She wanted to escape the responsibility for such an act. Mary rather reinforced this sentiment when she wrote to the Duke of Guise: 'I expect poison or some other secret death.'

Although she could not know it then, Mary would have to wait for three months before her execution. The dais in the large chamber where she sat during the trial had been dismantled. This upset her and she mentioned it in her letters sent on 24 November to Pope Sixtus V, Don Bernard de Mendonca and the Duke of Guise. Paulet was becoming increasingly anxious as the weeks went by and feared Mary's followers would attack the castle. He wrote to Burghley asking for additional soldiers, and 120 were provided. The death warrant remained unsigned as Elizabeth wrestled with the idea of executing one of her relatives. Rumours abounded up and down the country: Philip was preparing for an invasion of England and Palma was expected to rescue Mary; the Duke of Guise had actually landed in Sussex and the Scots had marched over the Border; Paulet had already put Mary to death. Of the latter, one of Walsingham's agents said, 'God grant that this is true for she has lived too long; good Protestants blame the queen for waiting so long, for God commanded rulers should govern with great severity.'

Elizabeth still hesitated, torn between a desire for her cousin's death, which would remove the plots against her, and the fear that the execution would trigger a determined invasion of her country by Catholic Spain. Her ministers understood that the queen wanted Mary put to death in a secret manner in a way that did not implicate her. It was very evident that she did not want the responsibility of signing the death warrant, and she hoped that her ministers alone would be held accountable for Mary's execution. Finally, on 1 February 1587 Secretary Davidson placed in front of Elizabeth a few letters that required her signature, among which was the death warrant. Pretending not to notice it, the queen swiftly signed it. Somewhat emboldened, she then instructed Davidson that the execution should take place in the great hall on the ground floor of Fotheringay Castle and not in the courtyard. The last thing she wanted was a public execution. Even at this late stage, Robert Beale noted that a secret way of killing Mary was still being considered:

> One Wingfield should have been appointed for the deed, and it seemed that Her Majesty would have done so rather than otherwise, pretending that Archibald Douglas, the Scottish Ambassador had advised her . . . by the example of Edward II and Richard II, it was not thought convenient or safe to proceed covertly but openly according to the statute.

On Monday, 7 February Mary received the dreaded news that her execution would take place the next day. That evening she wrote a letter to King Henry III of France, in which she stated, 'Today after dinner it was announced to me that tomorrow, without fail, I must die like a criminal. At seven o'clock of the morning.' She turned to her ladies-in-waiting and remarked, 'Did I not know that they desired to do as they had done? I knew they would never allow me to live. I was too great an obstacle to their religion.'

The hangman, Bull, and his assistant, George Digby, were housed at the local inn, while the witnesses were accommodated in the castle or in local manor houses. The night was filled with the sounds of hammering as a raised dais was constructed and the tramp of soldiers as they were posted around the castle. So the dreary night dragged by.

After a night of prayer, Mary rose early and reminded her ladies that she had only hours to live. She dressed carefully, as if to make a grand entrance, in a skirt and bodice of black satin worn over a petticoat of russet-brown velvet. Her headdress was white crape with a long veil and around her neck she wore a chain of scented beads with a cross and at her waist a golden rosary. The walls of the great hall were bedecked in black serge. Near the large fireplace stood the scaffold, raised off the ground and measuring 12ft sq. with a low balustrade. This too was covered in black serge, as was the oak execution block standing a few inches above the dais, and the stool and cushions. Bull and Digby, wearing black masks, were clothed in long black garments with white aprons. The headsman held a two-bladed axe with a short handle. Around the dais was stationed a guard of halberdiers brought from Huntingdon. To complete the scene, some 300 spectators were crammed into the great hall, while a large crowd gathered in the courtyard and outside the castle.

Supported by two guards, Mary descended the staircase to the first floor, accompanied by Melville, Dominique Bourgoing, Pierre Gorian, Jaques Gervais, Didier, Elizabeth Curle and Jane Kennedy. At the bottom, she was met by the Earls of Kent and Shrewsbury, who escorted her into the great hall. As she ascended the two steps onto the dais, she was met by Dr Fletcher, the Dean of Peterborough Cathedral, who had twice attempted to prepare her for death, but both times she had turned her back on him declaring that he was wasting his time trying to change her belief. Mary sat on the stool with Kent and Shrewsbury beside her and the sheriff in front. She asked for her chaplain but this was refused. Robert Beale climbed onto the dais and read aloud the royal commission for the execution. Turning to her two ladies, Mary said, 'I am happy to go from this world; you should rejoice to see me die for such a good quarrel; are you ashamed to cry?'

After more prayers, Mary began to disrobe. She removed the black silk outer-garments to reveal the bright russet-brown petticoat; the assembly was amazed by this splash of colour against the backdrop of black. She took the gold cross from her neck to give to Jane Kennedy, but Bull roughly grabbed at it, saying that it was his right; he put it in his shoe. Jane Kennedy produced a handkerchief and put it over Mary's face, pinning it securely at the back of her head. The executioners knelt before her and asked her forgiveness. Mary had thought she was to be executed by the sword, a privilege granted to French royal personages such as Anne Boleyn. Instead, she was led to the block.

Spread-eagled, she laid her head upon the block. As the executioner raised his axe, his assistant indicated that Mary's hands were under her chin. Digby gently moved her hands to the side so the axe-man could have a clear swing. Her last words were: 'In manus tuas Domine commendo.' The executioner then struck an ill-aimed blow which cut into her skull. His next blow severed her head and the third blow cut the sinew that still held it to her body. After her death her pet dog, a Skye terrier, crept out from beneath her dress. The poor animal was covered in blood and was rushed away to be washed as nothing was to be allowed to remain of Mary Stuart that could be venerated by the Catholics.

The executioner bent to pick up the head. Mary's auburn wig had fallen off and it was noted that the hair on her head was short and streaked with grey. One of the witnesses, Robert Wingfield, recalled: 'Her head fell from the wig and it appeared as one of threescore years and ten years old. Her lips stirred up and down for almost fifteen minutes after her head was cut off.' Then the Dean of Peterborough exclaimed in a loud voice, 'So perish all the queen's enemies.' In similar vein the Earl of Kent cried out, 'Such end of all the queen's and the Gospel's enemies.' Bull placed the head on a dish and showed it through the window to the crowd in the courtyard to prove that the Scottish queen was truly dead. In the afternoon her body was stripped, embalmed, wrapped in a waxed winding sheet and placed in a coffin. The assembled crowd began to disperse and the great drama that had been played out in the castle to its climax on 8 February 1587 was over.

For six months Mary's body remained in the coffin within the walls of Fotheringay Castle, neglected and apparently forgotten. But her execution gave the Catholics a huge propaganda boost. Cardinal William Allen fashioned for Philip a claim to the English throne through the Lancastrian line. He set up colleges to train English missionary priests to return to England to keep Roman Catholicism alive. He also assisted in the planning of the Spanish Armada, which ended so badly.

On Sunday evening, 30 July 1587, Mary's body was placed in a royal coach covered in black velvet and drawn by four horses. During the night it travelled 12 miles from Fotheringay to Peterborough Cathedral, where it was received by the Bishop of Peterborough. A vault had been prepared on the south side near the choir and opposite the tomb of Catherine of Aragon. The next day a ceremony was held in the cathedral, its walls draped in black cloth to a height of 6 yards. Every second pillar was covered in black baize, as were the walls of the choir.

It had always been Queen Elizabeth's intention to give her cousin a royal funeral, despite the passage of time. She herself did not attend the service, although many of the nobility did, along with thousands of mourners. When James I was crowned in 1603, he removed his mother's body from Peterborough and had her reburied in Westminster Abbey. By 1635 Fotheringay Castle was deserted and falling into ruins. Much of the stonework was used to rebuild the village, and all that now remains is the conical mound or motte.

Chapter Twelve

Cadiz

During the summer of 1586 Sir Francis Drake had been encouraged to form a fleet to go and 'singe the King's beard'. As was her custom, Queen Elizabeth avoided making the decision to send the ships, despite Burghley and Walsingham's advice that striking the first blow would destroy the Spanish ships and delay any invasion. Much troubled by the recent execution of her cousin, the queen brooded over Mary's death. It was now the spring of 1587, and the queen was still undecided. Barely on speaking terms with her leading councillors, she readily accepted the misadvised information sent by her ambassador in Paris, Sir Edward Stafford.

Nowhere during the Elizabethan years was one able to keep a secret. The Spanish Ambassador in Paris was Don Bernardino de Mendoza, a key figure in King Philip's plans. Like Francis Walsingham, he had informants to bring him intelligence, which he passed to his king. One of his most valued informants was Sir Edward Stafford, the English Ambassador, who was much burdened by gambling debts. Handsomely rewarded for passing on information, he had no compunction about sharing intelligence about England's intentions to Mendoza. Conversely, despite having full knowledge of the Armada's intentions, he did not pass on this information to Walsingham or Burghley. Walsingham was deeply suspicious of Stafford but found he was protected by Lord Burghley. Stafford was related to Elizabeth, and his sister-in-law, Katherine Sheffield, was a close female companion to the queen, as well being her second cousin. Despite his treasonous acts, the queen paid off his gambling debts. Stafford passed secret plans to Mendoza that Francis Drake's attack on the Spanish fleet at Cadiz would delay the Armada by a year. Despite this intelligence, Cadiz was not made aware and was taken by surprise.

It took a week to travel from London to Plymouth, 215 miles distant. A royal messenger changing horses every 10 miles could cover the same distance in thirty-six hours. Francis Drake left the Thames with 5,000 men and the rumour spread that they were heading for the West Indies. His fleet put into Plymouth to collect more ships and provisions, and his flag-captain, Thomas Fenner in *Dreadnought*, told Walsingham that Drake 'does all he can to hasten the service and sticks at no charge to further the same and lays out a great store of money to soldiers and mariners to stir their minds'. Drake was most anxious to leave Plymouth and there was a flurry of last-minute activity as the fleet made haste to sail and so avoid another postponement. The lengthy delays caused desertions to such an extent that Drake was forced to replace the missing crew members with soldiers from the local garrison. This gave him little time to get his fleet out into the Channel. He wrote a last letter to Walsingham before leaving:

> Let me beseech your honour to hold a good opinion not only of myself but of all these servitors in this action ... The Wind commands me away. Our ships are under sail. God grant we may so live in His fear as the enemy may have cause to say that God fights for Her Majesty as well abroad as at home. Haste!

A preliminary strike by Drake's fleet would destroy a large portion of the Armada fleet and delay any sailing that year. Drake's flag-ship was the 600-ton *Elizabeth Bonaventure*. His second-in-command was Sir William Borough, appointed as the queen's representative to prevent Drake from exceeding his mandate. A cautious and plodding but gifted navigator, he commanded the *Golden Lion*. The other ships were the *Dreadnought*, the *Rainbow*, the *Merchant Royal*, the *Susan and Edward Bonaventure* and the *White Lion*, as well as the smaller vessels *Spy*, *Makeshift* and *Cygnet*. Francis Drake supplied three ships commemorating his family: the *Drake*, the *Thomas Drake* and the *Elizabeth Drake*. In all, the fleet numbered more than eighteen ships, plus seven pinnaces, and it was the largest Drake had commanded. Leaving Plymouth, they encountered two vessels from Lyme Regis in the English Channel, which readily agreed to join the expedition, thus increasing the fleet to twenty-seven.

Every effort was also made to see that Spain's vast enemy fleet did not join up together in one body. As usual, this involved a combination of private enterprise and defensive aggression against the expected armada, and it was hoped that the amalgamation of Protestantism and patriotism would effectively blunt the axis of Catholicism. On 5 April a storm hit Drake's fleet off Cape Finisterre, but abated after forty-eight hours. Off the Iberian coast two Dutch merchantmen were intercepted and reported a large concentration of provision ships in Cadiz. This confirmed Drake's choice of attack. By 16 April the fleet was off Lisbon, the principal assembly port for the Armada. Lisbon was heavily defended, and could only be approached along the well protected river Tagus, with cannon on both banks. Drake refrained from launching an attack on the town as it would be costly, and instead turned his attention towards the Armada. In command of the Spanish vessels was the ageing Santa Cruz, the most experienced of the Spanish mariners, who had overseen the armament of the assembled warships and was ready for the all-important supply vessels from Cadiz.

The port of Cadiz stands within a narrow peninsula at the mouth of the Guadalquivir river and provides a safe shelter from Atlantic gales and tides. The city was built at the tip of the isthmus overlooking the sea and the harbour. Responding to the Dutch ship's report, the English fleet reached Cadiz on 19 April. The conventional Borough was shocked by the way Drake called a council to let his captains know his intention. Borough argued against an immediate attack but Drake would have none of it: 'Action this day. That is my opinion, though there are some would have us stay until morning.'

Drake's fleet arrived about an hour before sunset. The ships were instructed to fly no flags until the last moment to confuse any guards or lookouts on the ships. With his twenty years of experience, Drake knew the city was not aware of his presence and was confident of entering the port without being attacked. He confidently led the way into the harbour knowing that it was filled with supply ships, and told his followers to destroy what shipping they found there.

Drake's fleet sailed past the long spit of land screening the harbour, where some fifty to sixty ships lay at anchor. As they turned into the harbour, they were confronted by the galleys acting as a guards. Taken unaware by the powerful English fleet, they put up only a token resistance, losing two badly damaged vessels before retreating across the shallows where Drake's ships could not reach them. Once the English ships entered the 4-mile wide harbour, the unarmed supply ships were at their mercy. Some made a run for the upper harbour but the rest were trapped and helpless.

Only one vessel attempted resistance: a 700-ton Genoese transport laden with wood, hides, wool and cochineal (red die made from insects). But it was an unequal contest and she was quickly sunk, with her crew tumbling into the water, drowning or clinging to debris. There was little opposition after the sinking, and the crewmen began to board the vessels, transferring anything of value to their own ships. As dusk approached, the remaining transports were set on fire, the flames lighting up the white walls of the town. The cannon in the old fort and the various batteries continued to fire but they were inaccurate and at extreme range. The only Spanish success came when a galley crept out and captured a Portuguese caravel at the rear of the English squadron, but found just five wounded men on board.

The following morning, 30 April, Drake led his squadron to anchor, guarding the upper bay. Here they found Santa Cruz's own 1,500-ton flagship taking on board ordnance and soldiers. Moving from the *Elizabeth Bonaventure* to the *Merchant Royal*, which had a shallower draught, Drake closed on the galleon and opened fire. Before long the Spanish ship was surrounded by small ships and overrun by boarders. The looters grabbed what they could and then set fire to the ship as they departed. The smoke and flames were so intense it seemed like a volcano to the people onshore.

By this time the Duke of Medina-Sidonia had arrived with 3,000 soldiers and 300 cavalry. The city's citizens moved two huge bronze culverines to fire on the English ships. The *Golden Lion* was hit and the master gunner's leg was severed. The galleys attempted another attack, but to counter them Drake sent the *Rainbow* with six armed merchant ships and his own pinnace. Soon the advantage was with the English ships, with Drake and Borough forcing the galleys to shelter in the outer channel. It was now time for Drake and his fleet to put to sea but they were undone by a lack of wind. The Spaniards then launched fire-ships, which were easily intercepted and towed to the shore, where they burned harmlessly on the beach. The English ships remained becalmed for twelve hours until the wind finally got up and they made their way out to sea.

The galleys followed but Drake cut his sails and dropped anchor, which had the effect of stopping the galleys from attacking. When the wind freshened, Drake weighed his anchor and led his fleet towards Cape St Vincent. He knew that the Biscayan squadron of Juan Martinez de Recalde was at sea and expected to arrive in Cadiz. He was unable to intercept the squadron but did capture a small boat carrying orders for de Recalde's squadron to make for Lisbon. Giving up the chase, Drake returned to Cape St Vincent to capture the castle of Sagres. This was a prominent landmark, which all returning ships from the New World and the East Indies recognised as they reached their destination.

Once again Borough disagreed with Drake over the attack on Sagres, but this time he found himself the subject of a trial. Drake had grown weary of Borough's objections and had him placed under arrest in his cabin. His replacement was Captain Marchant of the military, who took command of the *Golden Lion*. Drake then landed more than 1,000 men some 15 miles along the coast with orders to march on Sagres. This was a diversion, and they made no attempt to scale the castle walls. However, as the defenders were busy firing at the English soldiers, Drake led his fleet to the attack. He offered the Spanish commander a chance to surrender, but when he declined, the soldiers opened fire with their arquebuses and muskets. Under cover of the firing, the crews made a great pile of pitch-soaked logs and bundles of sticks against the wooden gate and set it alight. When the gate was reduced to ash, the English entered the castle and set about destroying it. Most of the Spanish retreated and the crews dismantled the castle's cannon, which was lowered to the beach and loaded onboard the fleet. The next five days were spent repairing, provisioning and careening the ships and resting the crews.

In the meantime Drake sent out his pinnaces to patrol the coast. They attacked mainly fishing boats, burning or wrecking them and destroying their nets. Other targets included forty-seven barques and caravels transporting provisions for the Armada. One of the cargoes comprised barrel staves and hoops, which were necessary for transporting water and wine. It was estimated that Drake's men destroyed 100 vessels, greatly adding to the woes of the Armada, which relied on fish and water supplies to sustain their crews. Captain Fenner remarked: 'We hold the Cape so greatly to our benefit and so much to their disadvantage, as a great blessing was the attaining thereof, for the rendezvous is at Lisbon, where we understand of some twenty-five ships and seven galleys.'

Although Drake had been successful in preventing the Armada from sailing for another year, the officers and crews were becoming restless at the lack of treasure seized for their backers. Returning to anchor near Lisbon, which alarmed the Spanish, causing them to send men and cannon to defend one of the city's approaches, Drake went back to Sagres after a few days, stocking up with provisions and making repairs to his ships. Aware that the crews were growing weary of damaging Spanish shipping for little profit, he decided to sail for the Azores, where he hoped to find a treasure ship.

His fleet headed north and then due west. Some of the ships returned to England with what plunder they had managed to seize and many sick crews. On 3 June they ran into a severe storm that raged for two days and split the fleet. When the storm cleared, just seven galleons and some pinnaces remained. The crew of the *Golden Lion* had mutinied, reinstated Sir William Borough as captain and sailed for home. Drake was furious and held a court-martial in which he passed a sentence of death on Borough. Back in England, a Court of Enquiry subsequently exonerated the pedantic Borough and even promoted him.

Reaching the Azores, the new ships overseen by John Hawkins went on the attack. They were easily manoeuvrable and could deliver broadsides while the large Spanish galleons took twice as long to deliver their fire-power. This made it easy for Drake's remaining ships to intercept the *San Felipe* on 18 June near Sao Miguel. The huge transport ship from the East Indies had jettisoned its ordnance to make way for the mixed treasure it carried, including precious metals, jewels, ebony, silks and spices. After a brief fight, in which six Spaniards were killed, the *San Felipe*'s captain surrendered. The vessel was not plundered, but instead was accompanied back to England by Drake's remaining fleet. Her Spanish crew were given a small boat to reach the safety of one of the islands. Learning of the attack in the Azores, Santa Cruz gathered his Lisbon fleet and set out to confront Drake, but he was too late. Drake's fleet had left with the treasure ship and headed for England.

Elizabeth and Burghley went to great pains to say that they knew nothing of Drake's depredations on the Spanish coast. The Spaniards, naturally, did not believe them. Despite Elizabeth's feigned disparage-ment of Drake, she must have been delighted with the cargo of the *San Felipe*; it was worth £40,000, well over half an annual parliamentary subsidy. Meanwhile, Philip had to postpone the Armada for another year, during which time he strengthened the forts along the Spanish and Caribbean coasts.

The queen's disapproval contrasted with the public's celebration of Drake, although not everyone viewed him as a hero. Sir William Borough was accused of cowardice and desertion but he countered with reports of Drake's execution of Thomas Doughty and his desertion of John Hawkins at St Juan de Ulua. The court cleared Borough of all charges and he was even able to accept part of the *San Felipe* treasure, even though he had not taken any part in the attack.

Chapter Thirteen

The Spanish Armada

The Spanish Perspective

On 26 July 1582 Alvaro de Bezan, Marquis of Santa Cruz, won a victory over Filippo di Piero Strozzi's mercenary fleet at the Battle of Ponte Delgada in the Azores and so set the seal on the invasion of England. On 9 August 1583 he wrote to Philip with the first suggestion that an Armada should be sent to invade England. The only problem was the damage sustained by his ships in the battle; it would take more than a year to repair and refit them. On 29 December 1585 Philip authorised Santa Cruz to assemble a fleet of armed ships in Lisbon but it was still below the required strength. To increase the number of warships and vessels available to carry provisions and munitions, he began impounding all merchant ships found in Spanish ports. Dozens of vessels – English, Dutch, German, French, Genoese, Neapolitan, Venetian and Danish – were conscripted to serve in the Armada. No fewer than twenty-three ships from Ragusan (Croatia) alone were seized and either armed with cannon or prepared to carry supplies. For decades Spain and England had been involved in a state of hostility but by July 1586 both Spain and England had declared war.

News of the execution of Mary Queen of Scots did not reach Philip until March 1587, but when it did, it acted as a catalyst for the invasion of England. He did not conceal his claims to the double inheritance of the crowns of England and Scotland. His ambassador, Don Bernadino de Mendoza, wrote to him,

> God having been pleased to suffer this accursed nation to fall under His displeasure, not only in regard to spiritual affairs by heresy, but also in what relates to worldly affairs, by this terrible event, it is plain that the Almighty has wished to give your Majesty these two crowns [England and Scotland] as your entire possession.

Under Francis Walsingham, the English were well aware of Spain's preparations for a sea invasion from the nearby Spanish Netherlands. The numbers of troops were insufficient to invade England but the build-up of the Armada, with its large numbers of soldiers and ordnance, was to be one of the most pivotal naval encounters in the early days of naval combat. The 'vast good-fortuned fleet' ('Grande y Felicisima Armada') comprised 130 ships carrying over 30,000 men, including 19,295 soldiers, 8,450 mariners and 2,088 galley slaves, plus 3,000 noblemen, priests, physicians, pay-masters and officials. The 10,000 seasoned soldiers were bolstered by the reluctant indented peasants, shepherds and unemployed who made up the rest. They were to be joined by some 16,000 battle-hardened soldiers from the Spanish Netherlands, making a total of 35,000.

The ordnance included 2,830 cannon, 123,790 cannon balls and some 2,000 tons of gunpowder. The provisions carried by the lumbering, slow-moving merchant ships were barrels of salt-fish, salt-meat, biscuit, rice, beans, wine, vinegar and, most importantly, water. All this was to sustain the invasion from the Spanish Netherlands onto English soil. King Philip, the Duke of Parma and Santa Cruz produced a feasible plan to march on London, capture Queen Elizabeth and reconvert England to Catholicism. However, the plan was deeply flawed thanks to Philip's insistence that the much-diminished Armada should be sent in mid-winter to invade England. A large diversionary armada would also sail to Ireland, engage the English ships and then enter the Channel. This force would meet up with Parma's men and take London. It did not occur to the king that Parma had no navy to protect his soldiers.

Harried by Philip, Santa Cruz was unable to raise sufficient warships to undertake such a voyage. He was in Lisbon without the means of increasing his fleet when Francis Drake attacked Cadiz and destroyed many of the support ships. Ill and depressed by Philip's insistence on an 'instant' fleet, Santa Cruz died on 9 February 1587 at the age of 62. Spain's exceptional maritime commander was not a well-liked figure and at his funeral only four pall-bearers bore his body to the grave.

Philip had only a tenuous connection with the world outside the Escorial and rarely set foot outside the palace. In Santa Cruz's place he ordered his cousin, Don Alonzo Perez de Guzman, 7th Duke of Medina-Sidonia, to command the Armada. Of all the people he could have appointed, Medina-Sidonia was the last person he should have chosen. He could have chosen experienced seamen like Juan Martinez de Recalde, Don Martin de Padilla or Miguel de Oquendo. Instead, he appointed the wealthy 37-year-old Andalusian land-owner, who was a quiet, dutiful, decent man without a trace of aggression, charisma or leadership in him; he was content to enjoy his peaceful life amongst his grapevines and oranges. Nevertheless, he was an able administrator who oversaw the provisions and ordnance loaded aboard the merchant ships that had been confiscated at the Spanish ports. Medina-Sidonia himself reacted to Philip's appointment with reasons why he was unworthy of the command:

> I have not the health for the sea, for I know by the small experience that I have had afloat that I soon become seasick ... My family owes 900,000 ducats, and I am therefore quite unable to accept command. I have not a single *real* to spend in the King's service ... the undertaking is so important that it would not be right for a person like myself, possessing no experience of seafaring or of war to take charge of it. I cannot attempt a task of which I have no doubt I should give a bad account ... and should have to be guided by others, of whose good or bad qualities I know nothing.

Philip considered only Medina-Sidonia's high social rank, his administrative expertise, his modesty and, most of all, his reputation as a good Roman Catholic Christian. He also wanted a commander who would obey instructions, unlike the previous incumbent who was too temperamental a military commander. In the end Philip got his way and rejected his cousin's plea as 'an excess of modesty'. Medina-Sidonia had later written a letter to the king in which he pointed out that the 'Enterprise of England' was fatally flawed and that the English ships were superior. The letter never reached Philip; it was intercepted by his advisers, Juan de Idiaquez and Cristobal de Moura, who rebuked Medina-Sidonia for writing in such negative terms when the matter had been blessed by God. The two councillors effectively blackmailed him, writing: 'Your reputation and opinion which today the world has of your valour and prudence, which all be hazarded if it were known what you wrote.'

Medina-Sidonia was not alone in fearing a poor outcome. There was scepticism among senior Spanish officers and foreign observers, but still the preparations for the Armada went ahead. Although Spain had the largest and most numerous ocean-going ships in the world, she fell a long way behind in arming them. Hastily manufactured cannon often had flaws in the metal and the bore cast off-centre, which caused more danger to the crews than to their enemies. The writer I.A.A. Thompson commented:

> Some of their pieces are bored awry ... some are crooked ... others of unequal bores ... full of honeycombs and flaws ... they will either break, split, or blowingly spring their metals and will be unserviceable ever after.

The author Neil Hanson wrote that Spanish iron was often of poor quality and riddled with impurities. In most cases the impurities rendered their cannon weak. Even the flukes or teeth of anchors often sheared off under the stress of currents or the weather. To compensate for this, Spain used her wealth from the New World to purchase ordnance from other European nations, including England, the Netherlands and Venice. Although trade with Spain was prohibited in England, smugglers and privateers ignored the nation's interest and supplied their bitterest enemy with superior guns at a handsome profit. One Sussex iron founder even supplied a hundred cannon, while Bristol businessmen shipped nine vessels filled with muskets and shot to Spain.

Medina-Sidonia's attention to detail had melded together 134 ships into a formidable-looking fleet. The front-line ships were eight galleons which normally accompanied the treasure ships from the Spanish Main. They were joined by Portuguese and Castilian galleons, and the most formidable ship in the fleet was the *San Francisco*, taken from the Duke of Tuscany. The front line was divided up into three squadrons of ten ships each, plus four Neapolitan galleasses. The second line was made up of four squadrons of ten ships each from Biscay, Andalucía, Guipuzcoa and the Levant. Many of the second-line ships were large merchantmen that had been converted into warships by the addition of gun-platforms. The four galleasses were effective in the Mediterranean Sea, but were prone to swamping in the rough seas of the Atlantic and the Bay of Biscay.

The third line consisted of thirty-four pinnaces used for carrying dispatches and scouting. At the rear came the freight vessels carrying provisions, munitions and horses. The larger freighters transported the siege cannon with timbers to construct gun platforms and palisades, as well as all manner of weapons and tools and even a crude form of barbed-wire (pine trees with sharpened branches). The merchantmen were the slowest squadron, so the faster ships had to adjust their speed to their pace.

The Armada was not wholly Spanish-manned but drew its crewmen and soldiers from all over Europe, including Castilians, Basques, Sicilians, Italians, Portuguese, Dutchmen and Germans. The civil servant in Medina-Sidonia listed each ship, noting its tonnage, guns and personnel, right down to the number of bullets. The personnel included noblemen, gentlemen adventurers, their servants, priests and friars. Medina-Sidonia even included the strengths of the officers, their fighting men and all the great ordnance. The noblemen, gentlemen adventurers and a few English exiles expected a swift victory and were prepared to take possession of English properties with the return of Catholicism. So confident were the Spanish that they produced victory medals even before the Armada sailed.

When the Armada was nearly ready to depart Lisbon, a service of con-secration was held at the Dominican Convent, led by the King's viceroy, the Cardinal Archduke, accompanied by the Duke of Medina-Sidonia. Behind them stretched a long line of nobles, riding three or four abreast and representing all the grand houses of Spain. It was apparent that no Portuguese nobles had been invited, an insult that rankled with the spectators, who were few in number and resentful of the takeover of their country by their neighbours. As Medina-Sidonia emerged from the service, the fleets' guns fired a salute, the echoes rumbling around the sur-rounding hills. The consecration took place a fortnight before the Armada was ready to sail, and in between the river Tagus was alive with boats delivering provisions, munitions and soldiers to their allocated ships. The priests offered up prayers for the reversal of religion in England, mentioning not only the 'mortal sins' of Queen Elizabeth but also 'the blessed and innocent Mary Queen of Scotland who, still fresh from her sacrifice, bears copious and abounding witness to the cruelty and impiety of this Elizabeth'.

The Pope's special envoy consulted one of the highest officers in the fleet to ask who would win the battle:

It is very simple. It is well known that we fight in God's cause, so when we meet the English, God will surely arrange matters so that we can grapple and board them, either by sending some freak weather or, more likely, just by depriving the English of their wits. If we can come to close quarters, Spanish valour and Spanish steel and the great masses of soldiers we shall have on board will make our victory certain ... So we are sailing against England in the confident hope of a miracle.

Setting out on 11 May, Miguel de Oquendo's squadron reached the mouth of the Tagus and dropped anchor but the rest of the fleet faced a strengthening westerly wind which delayed their passage for another three weeks. In fact, the whole of western Europe was battered by storms which delayed most shipping in the Atlantic and the English Channel. Philip sent a letter to Medina-Sidonia, which almost every commander onboard the Armada repeated:

There is little to say with regard to the mode of fighting and the handling of the Armada on the day of battle ... it must be borne in mind that the enemy's object will be to fight at long distance, in consequence of his advantage in artillery and the large number of artificial fires with which he will be furnished. The aim of our men, on the contrary, must be to bring him to close quarters and grapple with him ... The enemy employs his artillery to deliver fire low and sink his opponent's ships. And you will have to take precautions as you consider necessary.

The king was quite adamant that the greatest threat was Francis Drake and that steps should be taken to avoid a fight with him:

Even if Drake should have sailed for these waters ... you should not turn back but continue on your course, not seeking out the enemy even if he should remain here. If, however, he should pursue and overtake you, you may attack him, as you should also do if you meet Drake with his fleet at the entrance to the Channel ... It is understood that you will fight only if you cannot otherwise make secure the passage across to England of the Duke of Parma.

When Portugal came under the rule of Spain in 1580, the Portuguese had just finished building the 1,000-ton *Sao Martinez*. When the Armada was being assembled, it was found she was the finest warship in the fleet; renamed *San Martin* by the Castilians, which offended the Portuguese, she was duly chosen as the flagship for the Duke of Medina-Sidonia.

With the weather improving, the 'Enterprise of England' finally got under way, albeit slowly. After thirteen days the Armada had reached Finisterre on the north-west coast of Spain. The snail's pace had affected the provisions, which had already become contaminated. The barrels that had been destroyed by Drake's raid were replaced with casks that were neither watertight nor airtight, and consequently the contents were mouldy and rotten. Water was a particular problem, being foul and undrinkable. Medina-Sidonia appealed to Philip for fresh supplies but to little avail. They had not even left Spanish waters and already they were lacking in provisions. Medina-Sidonia called a council of war and the various commanders came aboard the *San Martin*. Food and water were the main problems. It was agreed that all the ships would put into Corunna to take on what provisions were available.

On 19 June about half the ships managed to enter the port before it darkness fell. About midnight a south-westerly gale struck the rest of the ships out in the open sea, which had little alternative but to run before the storm. By the afternoon of 21 June the storm had passed and Medina-Sidonia sent out pinnaces to find the scattered fleet. Some had reached the port of Vivero and two had made it to Gijon, halfway along the northern coast. Juan Martinez de Recalde gathered another ten ships, which he led into Corunna. By 24 June they were still missing twenty-eight ships. Even the vessels in the harbour had suffered damage, including broken spars and masts, and many were leaking. The soldiers and crew were falling ill with scurvy and dysentery, and Medina-Sidonia wrote to Philip that the Armada was now in such poor condition that it should be postponed until the following year. On 5 July Philip replied in uncompromising terms:

> From what I know of you, I believe that your bringing all these matters to my attention arises solely from your zeal to serve me and a desire to succeed in your command. The certainty that this is so prompts me to be franker with you than I should be with another.
>
> I see plainly the truth of what you say, that the Levant ships are less free and staunch in heavy seas than the vessels built here, and that the hulks cannot sail to windward; but it is still the case that Levant ships sail constantly to England, and the hulks hardly go anywhere else but up the Channel. Indeed it is quite an exception for them to leave it to go to other seas. It is true that, if we could have things exactly as we wished, we would rather have other vessels, but under the present circumstances, the expedition must not be abandoned on account of this difficulty.

Philip also appointed Diego Flores de Valdes as 'naval adviser', stirring up jealousy and rancour among the rest of the commanders. De Valdes was an irascible man who treated Medina-Sidonia with such disdain that he barely consulted him. During the end of June and the first three weeks of July the missing ships showed up. The 600-ton *La Trinidad de Scala*, one of the Levant ships, limped back into Corunna after being battered by the storm, with her planks gaping and shipping water. Two of the group had been driven by the gale into the English Channel, before turning back to Corunna. The rest of the group had sailed between the Scilly Isles and the Lizard, waiting for the rest of the Armada to show up. They even boarded a couple of small ships and discovered that the English fleet was dispersed along the southern coast between Plymouth and the Narrow Seas. Rather than linger close to England, the group decided to return to Corunna.

The interval had lifted the spirits of the crews. They had fresh provisions, and the damaged ships had been caulked, some broken masts replaced and sick crewmen substituted. A few of the gentleman adventurers felt that they had seen enough of the sea and departed. On 19 July Medina-Sidonia called his commanders together and, with the weather looking fair, gave the order to sail for England the next day.

The English Perspective

England knew that Spain was amassing a huge fleet in Lisbon and most European observers expected the Spanish force to overwhelm the English and swiftly reinstate Catholicism in the country. With English merchants and businessmen in Spain, France and other Catholic countries reporting to Francis Walsingham about the state of Spain's shipping, the Sea Dogs had a shrewd idea when the invasion would come. Francis Drake's 1587 raid on Cadiz had delayed the 'Enterprise of England' for a year, which gave the English time to organise enough ships to counteract the Spanish fleet. The English had no standing army, and the ships were manned by seamen who used the cannon rather than boarding the enemy. Spain, on the other hand, sought to grapple with the smaller English ships, in order to board and capture them.

One of the revolutionary designs which brought the English victory was produced by the experienced John Hawkins, now Treasurer and Comptroller of the Navy. Assisted by his ship designer Matthew Baker, they introduced twenty-five 'race-built' vessels. These revolutionary new ships were longer in the keel, narrower in the beam and sat lower in the water than traditional warships, with a mast situated forward with a new style of rigging, and without the towering fore and after decks of the Spanish ships. The term 'race-built' derives from the word 'raze', meaning lowering the fore and aft decks so they were more streamlined than their Spanish counterparts. They were much faster and were easily able to avoid being boarded. These new ships harried the Armada vessels, pouring shots at them from their longer-range artillery but not sinking them. Being lower than the Spanish ships, they caused damage, particularly leaks below the waterline. Matthew Baker was the son of a ship builder and the first man to use blue prints, which enabled him to replicate the successful designs. Instead of having 'fighting castles', on race-built ships the fore-castle was reduced to a single deck and the sterncastle rose to a poop deck, accommodating the officers and helmsman. When the hull was under construction, the oak ribs were clad in a double layer of oak planks, the gap between being filled with a mixture of tar and horsehair to help preserve the hull from rotting. Only seasoned timber was used instead of used timber and green wood, which were prone to rotting and warping.

After the lengthy delay in leaving the Spanish coast, the Armada set sail for the tip of Cornwall, avoiding the shifting sandbanks on the French side of the Channel. Out of England's 226 vessels, only thirty-four were the queen's ships, or what was soon to be called the Royal Navy. The rest were merchant ships fitted with cannon. Written by an Englishman, the following report illustrates the state of England before the Armada was sighted:

> People here do not fear the Spaniard any more, as they are convinced that he had returned to Spain. The rumour was current that the Spaniards were at the Scilly Isles, and the Admiral [Howard] set sail to meet them, but, as he could get no news of them, he returned. All the principal Catholics have been sent to the Isle of Ely in the custody of Lord North. The Queen has caused the proclamation to be published against those who receive bulls from the Pope respecting the excommunication of the queen, or similar subjects. Offenders are to be hanged, and half their goods confiscated to the informer.

The command of the English fleet was given to Lord Charles Howard of Effingham as High Admiral. He may have been an inexperienced sailor but his vice-admirals were Sir Francis Drake (*Revenge*), Sir John Hawkins (*Victory*) and Sir Martin Frobisher (*Triumph*), all expert mariners. On 29 July Captain Thomas Fleming in the 50-ton *Golden Hinde* glimpsed the Armada through the swirling morning mist off the Lizard and raced to Plymouth to warn Lord Howard.

The *Revenge* was a good example of the new design. Despite her slender construction, she had an additional row of lighter cannon. Altogether, she carried forty-three guns, twenty on the lower deck and twenty-three on the upper deck. The guns were manned by specialist crews who could fire accurately three or four times faster than their European counterparts. It took some effort to get fifty-four ships out of Plymouth Sound as the south-west wind and the tide were against them, but they warped until they left the harbour. ('Warping' entailed sending one of the boats to drop the main anchor as far forward as possible, then the crew would pull the cable in, drawing the ship forward with sheer muscle power; then the whole process was repeated. By this laborious means they brought their ships out of the harbour.)

Once the 'Floating Forest' of masts was spotted off the Lizard, the chain of beacons from Penzance in Cornwall to Berwick in Northumberland were lit to give warning of the Armada's approach as mainland England prepared for the invasion. There were beacons inland as well, to alert major towns, and it took twelve hours to alert York from the south coast. As a sea-going nation, England relied on her sailors to keep the Spaniards at bay. Militias had been recruited throughout the land as a back-up but they were, at best, untrained and under-armed, although willing to fight. England's regular soldiers numbered far fewer than those of Spain and the Spanish Netherlands, and it was fortunate for England that they were not called upon to fight. The Armada had a relatively smooth crossing across the Bay of Biscay but on 27 July a storm separated a number of ships, including three galleys. The *Santa Ana* was blown almost to Le Havre, where she stayed for the remainder of the campaign. Three galleys had to seek shelter in the ports in the Bay of Biscay before rejoining the Armada. At about 4pm on 29 July, as the storm was blowing itself out, the coast of England was spotted. Medina-Sidonia ordered his fleet to form into a crescent formation some 7 miles in length. Warships were stationed on the wings and in the rear of the formation to prevent attack and those vessels carrying soldiers and supplies were kept safely in the centre. This defensive deployment was difficult to attack. The Tudor writer William Camden described the Armada as being 'built high like towers and castles, rallied into the form of a crescent whose horns were at least seven miles distant'.

The Armada spotted English ships to windward and another dozen or so to leeward. The contrast between the two fleets was striking. The Armada was very colourful, the ships' upper-works richly decorated and gilded. The sails were gaily painted with the Burgundian saw-toothed cross (which was mistaken for the Cross of St George), and the royal Spanish emblem. The galleasses were resplendent with shields, red oars and sails that depicted bloody swords. The officers and nobles wore silks and velvet, with jewellery around their necks. The commanders wore violet clothing, with crosses sewn on their sleeves, to show the crusade on which they had embarked.

The English fleet, although decked with pennants and flags, was much less colourful. The queen's ships were painted with geometric patterns in green and white, but the paint had begun to crack and fade. The hulls were tarred black from the deck to the waterline and the sails were painted with the Cross of St George. Although Lord Howard and other nobles wore their finery, men like Drake and Frobisher preferred plain utilitarian clothes. The crew wore what they always wore: loose clothing in brown and green. The most colourful men were the master gunners, who wore banded hats and clothes trimmed with gold embroidery.

The first to open fire was a pinnace, followed by a number of English cannon. These inflicted some cosmetic damage on the Spanish vessels but none was disabled. Unlike the English gunners, the Spaniards were unable to reload their cannon quickly and suffered three times the battering from the enemy guns. Drake wrote that the gunners were English, and not drawn from the various nations of the Habsburg Empire:

> They made good use of the most reliable quality of their most excellent and speedy ships, not crowded out with useless soldiers, but with decks clear for the use of artillery, so that they could safely play it any hour to harm the enemy, at any moment when it suited them best to do so.

By 30 July the English fleet was off Eddystone Rocks in poor weather conditions – foggy and rainy. To get into a position to attack, the English had to tack to gain the weather gauge (a position upwind of the enemy). Lord Howard wrote to Walsingham, putting the most favourable outlook on the day's events:

> At nine of the clock we gave them fight, which continued until one ... we made some of them to bear room to stop their leaks; notwith-standing, we durst not adventure to put in among them, their fleet being so strong. But there shall be nothing either neglected or unhazarded that may work their overthrow ... For the love of God and our country, let us have with some speed some great shot sent us of all bigness; for this service will continue long; and some powder with it.

At daybreak on 31 July Drake's *Revenge* with eleven ships attacked from the north, while Howard with the rest of the fleet harried from the south. They were at too great a distance to be effective but the Spanish did lose two ships to accidents. A spark from a gunner's smouldering match on the *San Salvador* caused an enormous explosion which blew out the poop deck and two decks in the stern castle and wrecked the steering-gear. The explosion killed about 200 men and wounded many more. The wounded were taken off the wrecked ship and she was abandoned. At one point Lord Howard and members of the *Ark Royal* boarded the *San Salvador* but it was a distressing sight, with torn bodies and limbs scattered about. The overpowering smell of brimstone hastened their departure. Eventually one of the ships towed the wreck into Weymouth, still filled with dead and dying crewmen.

The other accident involved the flagship of the Andalusia Squadron, the 1,150-ton *Nuestra Senora del Rosario*. Sailing in close formation, she collided with the *Santa Catalina* and broke her spritsail and cross-yard. Her steering was badly affected; barely under control, she collided with another ship which brought down much of her rigging. The unsecured foremast broke and fell against the mainmast, which immobilised the vessel. At that moment the explosion aboard the *San Salvador* diverted attention away from the *Rosario*. Although attempts were made to tow her, the proximity of the English fleet hastened her abandonment.

Howard called a council to discuss tactics and Drake was ordered to lead the pursuit in the dark by showing a lighted lantern on the stern of the *Revenge* so the rest of the ships could follow him. But privateering was too deeply engrained in Drake, causing him to extinguish the lantern while he went in search of the *Rosario*, perhaps expecting to net a handsome profit. Certainly, there was no one more adept at taking a Spanish ship than Drake. However, the *Margaret and John*, a 200-ton privateer captained by John Fisher, had already approached the *Rosario*, finding her escorted by four Spanish ships that were trying to fix a tow to bring her back into the Armada. Seeing the English ship, the Spanish concluded that the rest of the English must be following; abandoning their attempts to tow the stricken ship, they made haste to catch up with the Armada. Richard Tomson, an officer on the *Margaret and John*, looked at the seemingly deserted ship and later wrote that his ship kept to the windward,

> hard under sides of the ship ... which by reason of her greatness and the sea being very much grown, we could not lay aboard without spoiling our own ship. Seeing not one man show himself nor any light appearing in her ... we discharged 25 or 30 muskets into her cage-work, at one volley, with arrows and bullets ... They gave us two great shot, whereupon we let fly our broadside through her, doing some hurt.

The *Margaret and John* remained close to the crippled ship until midnight, before turning back to join the English fleet. Meanwhile, the *Revenge* appeared with the 300-ton *Roebuck*, captained by another West country-man, Jacob Whiddon. Pulling alongside the stricken ship, he persuaded Don Pedro de Valdes to surrender by identifying himself as the dreaded Drake. De Valdes felt he had little option but to surrender and Drake and his crew boarded the huge galleon. They found the deck was a tangled mess of rigging and spars, which was one of the reasons for her abandonment. Drake took possession of the precious powder and cannon balls, and also found some 25,000 gold ducats.

At daybreak, the rest of Drake's squadron found themselves too close to the Armada but with no sign of their commander. There was much rancour about Drake's actions that night, none more so than Martin Frobisher's comments, mostly about the allocation of spoils:

> He thinks to cozen us of our shares of 15,000 [*sic*] ducats, but we will have our shares ... He hath used certain speeches of me which I will make him eat again or I will make him spend the best blood in his belly.

Drake made his excuses to Lord Howard. He had observed the dim out-lines of the Armada and feared they were gaining the weather gauge. He had extinguished his lantern to avoid leading the fleet astray. He had also challenged a ship that turned out to be an innocent German cargo vessel. Then he had fallen in with the 300-ton *Roebuck* and together they had boarded and captured the *Rosario*, which was taken by the *Roebuck* into Tor Bay. Drake's explanation was partially believed but the fall-out from his privateering act during England's moment of jeopardy rumbled on for years. The abandonment of the Andalusian flagship was a further blow to the morale of the men in the Armada. In the space of twenty-four hours two major warships had been abandoned and allowed to fall into the hands of the enemy. Already any thought of invading England was fading fast, and the only hope was that Palma would appear with his soldiers and invasion barges. Incidentally, de Valdes himself spent some agreeable time as Drake's prisoner until £3,000 was paid for his ransom. He was given a sumptuous farewell banquet by the Lord Mayor of London before being exchanged for Edward Wynter, who had been captured by the Spaniards.

Meanwhile, the battle was moving up the Channel. Off Portland Bill, Martinez de Recalde commanding the *San Juan de Portugal* decided to provoke the English into coming close enough so he could grapple and board them. Not tempted, the *Revenge* and *Victory* concentrated on main-taining a withering fire which took down the *San Juan*'s rigging and damaged the masts. Other vessels of the Biscayan squadron, including the *El Gran Grifon*, turned to help, but the English ships moved away so as not become involved in fighting at close range.

In a separate skirmish Frobisher in the *Triumph*, accompanied by five other vessels, was attacked by a Spanish galleass squadron supported by some larger galleons. Only the combination of a tidal race and unfavour-able winds prevented the Spaniards from boarding Frobisher's ships. Despite a frenzy of close-range bombardment little damage was done and both sides withdrew.

On 3 August Diego Flores de Valdes wanted the Armada to take the Isle of Wight, which would give them a stepping stone onto mainland

England, but Medina-Sidonia vetoed this plan, as he had been instructed by the king himself to rendezvous with the Duke of Parma at the Narrows between Margate and Flushing. Once again Drake, ever to the forefront of the action, closed in on the *El Gran Grifon*, an 1,150-ton armed merchant ship. A prolonged exchange of fire ended with Drake's main mast being hit and he had to withdraw for repairs. Hawkins and Frobisher took up the brunt of the firing, which culminated in a galleon towing the *El Gran Grifon* back into the shelter of her companions.

By the end of 4 August both sides were badly short of ammunition and little in the way of fighting occurred. On 6 August Medina-Sidonia dropped anchor off Calais and sent an urgent plea to the Duke of Palma for more ammunition and flyboats. The duke was unable to leave Flushing harbour as he was bottled up by the flyboats of Justinus van Nassau, whose contribution to the defeat of the Armada was considerable. He not only prevented the Duke of Parma from combining with the Armada to invade England, but also captured the *San Mateo* and *San Felipe*, which had run aground on the sandbanks of Walcheren Island off the Dutch coast.

The English fleet was joined by Sir Henry Seymour's ships, which were tasked with maintaining a watch on the Flanders coast. Their number brought the English fleet up to the same number of ships as the Armada. Lord Howard ordered one of Seymour's captains to sail to Dover and collect brushwood, pitch and tar and other combustible materials. With the Armada at rest outside Calais, eight of the least useful ships were selected for use as fire-ships. With the English covering the north-west, west and south-west, Medina-Sidonia guessed that fire-ships would soon feature. He warned that no ships should move from their moorings, while small boats were to drag the fire-ships away from them. The fire-ships were coated in pitch and tar, filled with brushwood and combustible material, and sent on their way with all cannon fully loaded. Two captains, Prowse and Young, were put in charge of preparing the fire-ships. A dozen men on each boat started out before midnight and, carried by the following wind, approached the mass of Spanish ships at anchor off Calais. At a given signal the crews ignited the combustible material, lashed the helm and made their escape in the small boats towed behind the fire-ships.

Medina-Sidonia spotted the approach of the fire-ships and sent out pinnaces with grappling hooks to divert them. The Spaniards successfully pulled away the two ships on either wing and they were beached. The rest, driven by the wind, hurried towards the anchored ships; in panic, the crews cut their anchors and escaped to the north-east. Despite the explosions and debris, not one Spanish vessel was engulfed by the fire-ships, which sailed on until they burned themselves out on the beach. Even so, the close-knit formation of the Armada had been breached and the fleet scattered.

The galleass *San Lorenzo* had been struck by one of the merchantmen off the Lizard, which destroyed her rudder, and she spent days struggling to keep up. She managed to avoid the fire-ships but ran aground beneath the ramparts of Calais Castle. Howard sent his longboat, with privateer Amyas Preston in charge of about a hundred seamen. There was a short scuffle involving the Spanish crew, soldiers and galley slaves, during which the commander, Don Hugo de Moncada, was shot in the head. As the rest of the soldiers, crew and some galley slaves tried to escape they were either drowned or killed. The rest of the imprisoned galley slaves were released by the English and in the ensuing hunt for valuables they found a considerable quantity of gold ducats.

After the ordeal of the fire-ships, which caused little damage but created great terror, the Armada was scattered. Some headed into the North Sea, but most moved eastwards. Following the *San Martin*, the surviving ships sailed for another 7 miles until they were off Gravelines. Here, they had little option but to turn north to avoid running foul of the shoals and sand bars off Flushing. The Dutch added to the Spaniards' woes by removing buoys from the shallows, which caused more groundings and chaos. Despite the English ships' powder shortage, they poured rounds of shot at the enemy fleet 'and tore many of their ships so dreadfully that the water entered all sides; and some, flying for relief towards Ostend, were shot through and through again by the Zealanders'.

Medina-Sidonia may have been no seaman but he displayed great bravery, pushing his ships into some sort of formation and then confronting the English fleet. The English ships moved closer than they had during the pursuit through the Channel and fired round after round, riddling the Spanish ships. Medina-Sidonia's first adversary was Francis Drake's *Revenge*. The *San Martin* was reportedly hit with 200 cannon balls but was unable to reply, having very little powder and shot left. Instead, her soldiers peppered the *Revenge* with musket fire, but to little effect. Drake then ordered chain and bar shot to be fired, which shredded the rigging, sails and spars. The heavier cannon continued to pummel the sides of the *San Martin*, loosening the 4-inch planking. One cannon shot from the *San Martin* blasted through the wall of Drake's cabin, and in the impact one of the officer prisoners taken from the *Rosario* lost his toes.

Having sustained damage, Drake pulled away, leaving Frobisher to take up the challenge. Still smarting from the loss of so many ducats from the

Rosario, the latter declared that Drake was a coward and traitor, accusations later dismissed by the Board of Enquiry. As the *Revenge* withdrew, the *Nonpareil* and the *White Bear* continued the bombardment without success. The battle lasted for eight hours, until a brief squall enveloped the two sides. The rain became torrential and when it had passed, the Spanish ships had moved towards Dunkirk. Howard's fleet, unwilling to engage and already low on powder and shot, followed them. Another council of war was held among the Spanish commanders but opinions were split, with some wanting to sail for Norway or Denmark. However, Medina-Sidonia had made his choice: they would sail north, around Scotland and keep well clear of Ireland.

The Spanish lost more ships during the battle of Gravelines and the manoeuvring around the Netherlands sand-banks. A Biscayan carrack ran aground near Blankenberge, while *La Maria Juan* foundered and sank among the Zeeland shoals. Two major Spanish ships, the badly damaged *San Felipe* and *San Mateo*, were driven onto the sandbanks and captured by the Dutch. Around 300 men were taken from these ships and were subsequently murdered. Gleeful Zeelanders filled the streets of Flushing and celebrated a cheaply won victory, wearing the finery seized from the Spanish ships.

Moving away from Gravelines with the wind at their back, the Armada headed up the North Sea, with the English fleet keeping a watchful eye but unable to open fire through paucity of shot and powder. As they followed the Spanish, there was an outbreak of disease on the English ships, no doubt due to the cramped quarters that the seamen and soldiers had to endure. Something akin to the plague caused a devastating epidemic that resulted in some 6,000 dead. As a result, some ships put into ports along the east coast. After the fighting along the Channel, in which they lost about 100 men, the seamen were later denied their pay by the queen and Hawkins and Drake had to help out.

The English wanted to make sure the Armada did not return to the Thames or Kent coast, but the Spanish just wanted to sail around the British Isles and return home. John Hawkins led nine of the queen's ships into Harwich, while others put into Margate, and then Howard's ships trailed the remnants of the Armada as far as the Firth of Forth before turning back. As the Armada disappeared into Scottish waters, Francis Drake speculated that,

> The only thing that is to be looked for is that if they go to the King of Denmark, he is a prince of great shipping and can best supply their

wants which now the Duke of Medina-Sidonia standeth in need as great anchors, cables, masts, ropes, and victuals. What the King of Spain's hot crowns will do in cold countries for mariners and men you can best judge thereof.

The Spanish may have thought they had escaped the worst, but further horrors awaited them.

Chapter Fourteen

Ireland and Scotland

Medina-Sidonia desperately tried to maintain formation but bad weather, and the slowness of the merchant ships, split the fleet. Instead of heading to the north of the Orkney Islands and then west, as advised by Medina-Sidonia, most of the ships sailed between Fair Isle and the Shetlands. Medina-Sidonia held another meeting of the squadron commanders and issued fresh orders:

> The course that is first to be held is to the north/north-east until you have found under 61 degrees and a half; and then take great heed lest you fall upon the Island of Ireland for fear of the harm that may happen unto you upon that coast. Then, parting from those islands and doubling the Cape in 61 degrees and a half, you shall run west/south-west until you be found under 58 degrees: and thence to the south-west, making for the Cape Finisterre, and so to procure your entrance into The Groyne at Corunna or to Ferrol, or to any other port on the coast of Galicia.

Once out in the Atlantic, the ships were to steer to a point 400 miles beyond the Shannon estuary, giving them a clear run to northern Spain. The navigators had only latitude to plot their course and they were headed for 61½ degrees north, which should keep the fleet well to the west of Ireland. Navigation was very crude by today's standards, with few tools to help in plotting a course. Poor weather in the Atlantic Ocean continued to hamper the navigators, and by this point the Armada was in the hands of these ocean-going specialists. It was mid-summer, but there were an extraordinary number of storms, particularly around Scotland and Ireland. To lighten their loads and save on water, the ships jettisoned all the cavalry horses and mules by flinging them into the sea and leaving them either to drown or to swim for the nearest shore. A passing fishing boat reported that, although the Armada had disappeared, the sea was black with the desperately struggling horses and mules trying to keep afloat.

Several ships were lost along the stormy north coast of Scotland, the most prominent being *El Gran Grifon*. On 1 September she went to the assistance of the *Barca de Amburgo*, which sank during a storm south-west of Fair Isle. Alongside *La Trinidad Valencera*, she managed to rescue the *Barca's* crew and then continued towards Ireland. Off Galway Bay a strong gale from the southwest drove *El Gran Grifon* back up the west Irish coast and along the north coast of Scotland. By 28 September she had been blown back to Fair Isle and was in a deplorable condition. In making a desperate attempt to drop anchor, the *El Gran Grifon* was driven ashore and ended up smashed against the cliff at Stroms Hellier. Most of the crew managed to scramble ashore before their ship disappeared beneath the water. Fair Isle was the most southerly and remote part of the Shetland Isles and the native islanders were usually welcoming, but as winter approached food was beginning to run out. In order to cut down on the numbers of Spanish guests, some were condemned to die of starvation, some were murdered, and others were pushed over the cliffs.

Accompanying *El Gran Grifon* to the Irish coast was *La Trinidad Valencera*. Leaking, and with considerable damage to her upper works, *La Trinidad Valencera* headed for Kinnogoe Bay in County Donegal, where she grounded a short distance from the beach. The 260 sailors and soldiers on board managed to land safely but most were killed by the Anglo-Irish soldiers who found them. Only thirty-two managed to escape to Scotland, and from there they returned home to Spain. As the main bulk of the Armada made its way round Scotland's north coast, several vessels became separated during the bad weather. *Castillo Negro*, a Flemish merchant ship converted to a warship, had been with *El Gran Grifon*. She carried 239 soldiers, the second largest number in the squadron of hulks. On 4 September she foundered off the Donegal coast and sank.

One ship that turned south along the west coast of Scotland was the *San Juan de Sicillia*, an Adriatic merchant ship previously named *Brod Martolosi*. The largest of the Levant fleet, she was rumoured to be carrying a huge treasure of gold and silver plate and the paymaster's chest containing a hoard of 30 million ducats in gold coin. On 23 September the ship sought refuge in the Bay of Tobermory on the Isle of Mull. The senior officer was Diego Tellez Enriquez, commanding a crew of sixty-two, mainly Slavonic. The military contingent was made up of Flemings, Sicilians and Spaniards. Sir Lachlan MacLean of Duart, the Maclean leader on Mull, agreed to provide water and provisions to the Spaniards if they would help attack the Macleans' hated rivals, the MacDonalds. Enriquez agreed and received a surety of five hostages from Sir Lachlan. For more than a month the *San Juan de Sicillia* remained in Tobermory port. With Sir Lachlan's agreement, 100 soldiers set out to attack the islands of Eigg, Muck, Rhum and Canna, destroying crops and villages. The troops were later used to attack Mingary Castle on the mainland, and for three days they laid siege to the castle until forced to withdraw.

On 18 November there was an enormous explosion at Tobermory, which sank the Spanish ship. Although it was never explained, it seems likely that one of Walsingham's agents, a merchant named John Smollet, had infiltrated the provisioning of the ship prior to its departure and managed to lay a fuse to the powder store. The explosion killed most of the 300 men on board and sent the ship to the bottom of the bay. Of the survivors, Sir Lachlan kept fifty and used them in his feuding for another year before sending them back to Spain.

The Armada was fragmenting, but the bulk of the ships stayed together around Scotland and Ireland, despite storms and violent winds that caused twenty-four wrecks along the Irish coast. Many of the survivors of these wrecks were put to death by Anglo-Irish soldiers, while the remainder fled across the sea to Scotland. The English feared that if Spanish soldiers were to land in sufficient numbers on the west coast, they might raise a rebellion with the Irish. Although it was a wild and underpopulated coastline, reliable intelligence was received that the Spanish ships were running aground all along the 300-mile coastline from Ulster, through Clare to Kerry. The Lord Deputy, William Fitzwilliam, ordered that all Spaniards captured should be immediately hanged and anyone who aided them would be tortured and charged with treason.

On 15 September the *Santa Nicolas Prodaneli* was forced onto Erris Head (or Broad Haven), County Mayo, by a fierce storm. The wretched Spaniards came ashore only to be imprisoned and later slaughtered. Out of 355 crewmen and soldiers, only sixteen survived. Further south on 20 September three galleons were wrecked. One, *San Esteban*, was driven by the great storm into the estuary of the Doonbeg river, County Clare, where she sank. Many of the survivors were killed but most were hanged, according to tradition, on Gallows Hill by the High Sheriff of Clare, Boetius MacClancy.

Newly built in 1585, the *San Marcos* was also shipwrecked on 20 September at Lurga Point, County Clare. One of the escorts for the treasure ships which sailed twice a year from the Spanish Main, she was regarded as one of the most formidable ships in the Armada. She weighed 790 tons and carried sixty guns, with a complement of 490 men. King Philip saw her as the natural choice to provide heavy firepower and support for the Armada. The survivors were captured and executed.

The third ship to founder on the 20th was the *Annunciada*. Any attempt to land was repulsed, although some supplies were allowed. The ship was in a very poor state and there was little alternative but to set her on fire off Kilrush at the mouth of the Shannon. The crew were transferred to the *Barco de Danzig*, which managed to get back safely to Spain.

One of the oddities of the Armada was the 37-year-old supply ship *Santiago*. Instead of following the route laid down by Medina-Sidonia, she was forced by the North Sea weather to seek shelter elsewhere. Built in 1551, she was one of the oldest and slowest ships in the Armada. She carried a variety of supplies, including twenty-four artillery mules, gunpowder, horseshoes, nails and parts for wagons and artillery. She had also been armed with nineteen cannon. She carried thirty-three crew and thirty-two soldiers with their wives, whose presence earned the ship the sobriquet 'the ship of the women'. As they travelled north they were ordered by Medina-Sidonia to jettison the mules as they drank too much water and took up much space. They had planned to sail around the Orkneys but a strong storm, dwindling supplies and many leaks drove them towards Norway. They made landfall at Skudeneshavn, where they picked up a local man to guide them north to Bergen. As they limped up the coast, they encountered another storm which left the *Santiago* riding even lower in the water. She was barely afloat, but the crew turned her into Hardanger Fjord and beached her near Mosterhamn. All on board survived and spent several months in Bergen. A passing German ship collected most of the crew but ran into another storm and was wrecked at Halmsad in Sweden. The Swedes detained the survivors and sent them to Buxtehude near Hamburg, where they were finally released to find their own way home.

Unable to withstand the terrible storms, the battered and leaky ships were held together with ropes which passed under the hulls and were fastened to the masts. With water seeping in as fast as it was being bailed out, the crews had no idea that they were heading into one of the most ferocious storms ever to hit the west of Ireland. Having little knowledge of the Irish west coast, the navigators did not realise that the Gulf Stream and the westerly winds were drawing some of the ships towards this dangerous coast. The 'Great Gale' began on 21 September 1588. Sir Richard Bingham, the provincial governor of Connacht, observed 'a most extreme and cruel storm the like whereof hath not been heard a long time'. He was a veteran mercenary who had served with Don Juan of Austria at Cyprus and Lepanto, but also fought with the Dutch against Palma's Army of Flanders.

All the Armada ships had left their best anchors at Calais when the duke had ordered them to cut their cables to avoid the English fire-ships. Four ships, the *San Juan Bautista*, *San Juan de Ragusa*, the *Santa Maria de la Rosa* and the hospital ship *San Pedro el Mayor*, took cover in the lee of Great Blasket Island off the Dingle Peninsula. Captain Marcos de Arambaru of the *San Juan Bautista* recalled, '*San Juan de Ragusa* gave us two cables and an anchor, since we had only one cable which was in the sea, and I gave him [*San Juan de Ragusa*] an anchor of 30 quintals, which was useless to us, but of which he had the greatest need.'

At midday the *Santa Maria de la Rosa* came into the Sound,

> by way of another entrance somewhat nearer the mainland from the northwest. Coming in she fired a piece as if asking for help, and further on she fired another. All her sails hung in pieces except for the fore mainsail. She came to a stop with one anchor, which was all she had, and, with the tide coming in from the southwest, she held steady for a while. At 2 o'clock the tide turned, she began to swing on her anchor and then dragged to within two cable lengths from us, and we dragged with her.

The two ships were dragged three-quarters of a mile down the Sound. De Recalde managed to hold his position but the *Rosa* hit the rocks off Dunmore Head, ripping a hole in her hull. She filled with water and sank so quickly that the crew did not even have time to launch any boats. The watching crews were overcome with shock:

> She went down straight away with every man on board, not a soul was saved, a most extraordinary and frightening thing; we were dragged over on top of her in great danger to ourselves … At this moment the ship of Miguel de Aranivar arrived which was identified as the *San Juan de Fernando Horra*. Her mainmast had gone and as she came in, her fore mainsail ripped to pieces. She dropped anchor and stopped. With the fierce weather we were not able to hail her or give her any assistance. Without her mainmast she was in a hopeless position. She transferred her crew to Recalde's ship and the patache (a light, two-masted, shallow-draught boat used for delivering messages). The *San Juan* was scuttled and burned. Lost were *San Juan de Fernando Horra* and *Santa Maria de la Rosa*.

Out of 297 men on board the *Santa Maria*, there was only one survivor. He stated that one of the military captains called the pilot, Francisco de Manona, a traitor and ran him through with his sword just as *la Rosa* sank.

De Recalde, having made repairs, took the chance to head for the open sea and managed to reach Corunna on 7 October; he died a few days later of fever. De Arambaru managed to sail the *San Juan Bautista* to Santander a week later.

The captain of the hospital ship, the *San Pedro el Mayor*, a 213-ton hulk carrying 100 soldiers and twenty-eight crew, realised that she would never reach Spain in her leaking condition, so set a course for France instead. On 28 October, in a sinking condition, she was driven aground at Hope Cove, about 5 miles from Kingsbridge, at the southern tip of Devon. Hearing of the sinking, George Clifford, the Earl of Cumberland, hurried from Plymouth in the hope of finding treasure but he found only 140 survivors. They were initially sentenced to death but ransoms were paid and some later returned to Spain. The last prisoners of the *San Pedro el Mayor* were released but did not see Spain until 1597.

On 21 September the 900-ton *Duquesa Santa Ana*, battered by strong westerly winds, with its crew at starvation point and others badly injured, put into Blacksod Bay, County Mayo. She was under the command of Don Alonzo de Leyva, who had already lost the *Santa Maria Rata Encoronada*, whose surviving crew were crammed into the *Duquesa Santa Ana*. Leaving Blacksod Bay and setting a course for Scotland, they ran into another storm and were driven into Loughros Mor Bay, County Donegal, where the overcrowded ship was wrecked. Don Leyva himself was crippled by a flying capstan and was carried ashore. They found a deserted castle by Kiltoorish Lake and were fed by a friendly chieftain named MacSweeney Bannagh, who set them on their way.

The seven Armada vessels that either sought shelter or were unable to avoid destruction on the Irish coast were mostly from the Levant Squadron. They were mainly used in the calmer Mediterranean and Baltic Seas, and were not designed for the rougher waters of the Atlantic Ocean. On 22 September the carrack *Ciervo Volante* was wrecked on a sandbank off Streedagh Strand in County Sligo, and on the 25th the *Concepcion de Juanes del Cano* sank in the storm off Spanish Point, County Clare. *Falcon Blanco Menor* sank off Freaghillaun Island, County Galway, and the entire crew were killed by Anglo-Irish soldiers. *El Juliano* was torn apart between Spanish Point and Black Rock, while *La Lavia*, *San Juan de Ragusa* and *Santa Maria de Vision de Biscione* were driven ashore and wrecked at Streedagh Strand near Dingle, with the loss of 1,000 lives. Only one of the Levant Squadron survived to return to Spain.

On 26 October *La Girona*, one of the four galleasses from Naples, became the last ship to be wrecked on the Irish coast. She had 280 men on board, including the rowing slaves. Entirely unsuited for the Atlantic, she had been damaged during the storms off Corunna, and she played little part in the fighting in the Channel and off Gravelines. She managed to cross from Scotland to Ireland, where she picked up 800 men, including some from the *Duquesa Santa Ana* and the *Santa Maria Rata Encoronada*, who had taken refuge in an abandoned castle after their ship had run aground in Blacksod Bay, County Mayo. Continually battered by storms and struggling with a broken rudder, *La Girona* was forced to seek shelter at Killybegs. After some hasty repairs, she attempted to cross to Scotland but soon ran into yet another storm – they seemed to lash Ireland every few days. In the storm-lashed sea the repaired rudder broke and, despite frenzied rowing by the 200 galley slaves, the vessel was hurled against the reefs of Lacada Point by the Giant's Causeway. She was carrying more than a thousand men, but fewer than a dozen of them survived. One or two settled in Ulster and married local girls, while others escaped to Spain.

There are two accounts written by the survivors of the Spanish wrecks on the west coast. One, which details the adventures of the survivor, was written by Captain Francisco de Cuellar of the 530-ton galleon *San Pedro*, part of the Squadron of Galleons of Castile. When he broke the Armada formation in the North Sea, he was accused of disobedience and sentenced to death by hanging by the commander, Major General Francisco Arias de Bobadilla. Cuellar was entirely innocent, as he had been asleep when his pilot allowed the *San Pedro* to surge ahead of the leading vessel. Nevertheless, Cuellar was sent to the *San Juan de Sicilia* for execution, but the sentence was not carried out, thanks to the intervention of the Auditor-General, Martin de Aranda. Along with De Aranda, Cuellar was later put on board *La Lavia*, one of the Levant Squadron ships. She would be wrecked, along with *Santa Maria de Vision*, on Streedagh Strand between Sligo and Bundrowse. On 25 September Francisco de Cuellar was aboard *La Lavia*:

> In the morning it began to blow from the west with a most terrible fury ... such a great gale arose from our beam, with the sea running as high as heaven that the cables could not take the strain nor the sails serve us, and we were driven ashore with all three ships on a beach of fine sand with great rocks at each end. Such a thing was never seen for in the space of one hour all three ships were broken in pieces, less than three hundred escaped and more than one thousand were drowned. I placed myself on the top of the poop of my ship,

after having commended myself to God and Our Lady, and from thence I gazed at the terrible spectacle. Many were drowning in the ships, others, casting themselves into the water, sank to the bottom without returning to the surface; other on rafts and barrels, and gentlemen on pieces of timber; others cried out aloud in the ships calling to God; captains threw their jewelled chains and crown-pieces into the sea; waves swept others away, washing them out of the ships ... men trying to save their coins, gold chains and jewellery only to be weighed down and drowned by them. Seventy men found a boat with a covered deck; they jumped in and closed the hatch hoping to reach land safely. Even a boat this size was tumbled by the surf and eventually cast up on shore with its keel upwards so that the men could not get out. It was not righted until two days later; all were dead except one, but he died at that moment.

While I was watching this sorrowful scene, I did not know what to do, nor what means to adopt as I did not know how to swim and the waves and storm were very great; and, on the other hand, the land and shore were full of enemies, who went about jumping and dancing with delight at our misfortunes; and when one of our people reached the beach two hundred savages and other enemies fell upon him and stripped him of what he had on until he was left in his naked skin. Such they maltreated and wounded without pity, all of which was plainly visible from the battered ships.

The choice of drowning or confronting the waiting soldiers on the shore was not a cheerful prospect. Cuellar managed to cling on to a hatch cover and was washed ashore unobserved. He scrambled into some reeds and was joined by another survivor, traumatised and naked, who soon died of hypothermia. In his half-conscious state, Cuellar saw about 200 horsemen riding across the Strand. Hours later he saw the 800 corpses littering the sand being eaten by ravens and wild dogs.

Moving at night, he came to a small church, where he saw twelve of his countrymen hanging from nooses tied to the iron bars of the windows. He met a local woman driving cattle; she warned him to keep off the road as the Anglo-Irish soldiers were about and had already killed 100 captured survivors. He also encountered two naked Spaniards who had seen 400 corpses at another beach. Travelling through a wood, he was attacked by a man and stabbed in the leg. The robber took all his clothes, his gold chain and forty-five gold crowns. He was saved by a young village woman, who sent a young boy to treat his wound with a poultice and to give him some food.

When he could walk again, he made his way to a deserted settlement by a lake and was surprised to find there three of his fellow countrymen. He joined up with them, and soon they came to O'Rourke's territory where they found greater safety at 'a village belonging to better people. Christian and kindly.' Here they found a further seventy Spaniards seeking refuge. Cuellar was given a lice-infested cloak and trousers and set off northwards with a party of Spaniards. Without the hospitality of the local 'savages', he and his fellows would not have survived:

> As to ourselves, these savages liked us well because they know we came against the heretics, and were such great enemies of theirs; and if it had not been for those who guarded us as their own persons, not one of us would have been left alive. We had goodwill to them for this, although they were the first to rob us and strip to the skin those who came alive to land … In this country there is neither justice nor right, and everybody does what he likes.

By November Cuellar had moved into MacClancy territory and stayed at Rosclogher Castle. Eight Spaniards had resolved to defend the castle against the Anglo-Irish soldiers while MacClancy departed for the mountains. The castle was difficult to besiege as it was surrounded by bogs, and after a week the Anglo-Irish troops gave up and departed. When MacClancy returned, he offered his sister in marriage to Cuellar, but he declined. After months of travelling across Ireland, Cuellar arrived in Derry and, with seventeen others, sailed for the Hebrides. After six months he was given passage to Flanders and in August 1589 he arrived off the Flanders coast. Unfortunately the Dutch were waiting to attack any returning Spanish ships. In the ensuing firefight, Cuellar's ship was wrecked on the sands and once again he had to cling to some flotsam, this time floating into the safety of Dunkirk. When he finally returned to Spain, he wrote down his experiences and his account was later published.

The Armada had set off proudly with some 130 ships; despite the disastrous start from Lisbon, the commanders were confident of overwhelming the English, replacing Queen Elizabeth on the throne and reinstating Catholicism in the country. Instead the atrocious autumn weather had exacted a heavy toll, destroying many ships, and leaving the battered survivors to limp home. Of the 30,000 sailors and soldiers carried by the Armada ships, 20,000 never made it back to Spain. According to Garret Mattingly's *The Defeat of the Spanish Armada*, Spain lost forty-four ships, mostly on the Irish coast, but those that did make it back had suffered so badly from the English gunfire and the storms that they were unfit for future service. One ship that almost made it back to Spain was the *Doncella*, part of the Squadron of Guipuzcoa commanded by Miguel de Oquendo. Battered and damaged, she had managed to sail around the British Isles, somehow weathering all the storms, but on reaching Santander she was wrecked on the rocks at the entrance to the port.

On 21 September the pride of the Spanish fleet, the *San Martin*, bedraggled and splintered by English cannon fire, limped into Santander. Medina-Sidonia, commander of the Armada, was suffering from fever and dysentery, and was weighed down with depression. His crew were so afflicted by starvation and fever that they were barely able to perform their duties, and were unable to heave overboard the bodies of the 180 seamen who had died. With a heavy heart, Medina-Sidonia was rowed ashore with never a glance back at the ship that had once been the pride of the Spanish navy.

Chapter Fifteen

The Deaths of the Sea Dogs

After the Armada scare of 1588 Queen Elizabeth felt her country to be in danger. The years 1594 to 1595 were anxious times as Spain regained her superiority and threatened England once again. The queen gave orders for a fleet to sail to the Spanish coast and destroy enemy shipping while keeping a lookout for the incoming *flota*. This did not sit well with Hawkins and Drake, and after much discussion, the queen gave her permission for the two Sea Dogs to attack Spain's possessions in the Caribbean. By Elizabethan standards they were old men – Hawkins was 63 and Drake 56 – and they perhaps lacked the adventurous drive they had once had. Thomas Maynarde, who knew both men well, wrote about their last voyage together:

> Sir Francis Drake, a man of great spirit and fit to undertake the matter . . . But assuredly his very name was a great terror to the enemy in all those parts, having heretofore done many things to his honorable fame and profit. But entering into them as the child of fortune, it may be his self-willed and peremptory command was doubted, and that caused Her Majesty to join Sir John Hawkins in equal commission, a man old and wary, entering into matters with so leaden a foot that the other's meat would be eaten before his spit could come to the fire, men of so different natures and dispositions that what one desireth the other would commonly oppose against the other would commonly oppose against whom the one loved the other smally esteemed.

As Naval Treasurer, Hawkins was left with the task of paying off his sailors and was rewarded with a firm rebuke from Lord Burghley, who was very careful with the queen's money and thought Hawkins over-generous. Hawkins was given a year's leave in order to sort out the muddled accounts arising from the English fleet's hounding of the Armada. As well as Treasurer of the Navy, he was also Comptroller of the Navy and Port Admiral of Plymouth, both posts that had been awarded to him by Burghley. It was a way of demonstrating Lord Burghley's esteem, and it helped to deflect the sniping Hawkins had to endure over his part in the Armada. Feeling his age, he tried several times to be relieved of his naval duties but Elizabeth always refused. In 1591 Hawkins' wife died after thirty-two years of marriage. Unable to live alone, he married Margaret Vaughan, a bedchamber lady to the queen, but it was a short-lived relationship.

On 9 June 1595 Hawkins received news that his son Richard had been captured by the Spanish after seizing a large amount of treasure. His ship, the *Dainty*, was forced to surrender and he was imprisoned in Seville and Madrid until 1602, when he was released. As Hawkins and Drake were planning their expedition to capture ports and treasure in the Caribbean, he saw a way of securing his son's release. Evidence had come into their possession that a disabled galleon containing 2 million ducats had been forced into San Juan by bad weather. When the queen learned of this, she could not resist the temptation and gave the two men permission to mount a raid on the disabled treasure ship. The fleet consisted of twenty-six ships led by Sir Francis Drake's *Defiance* and Sir John Hawkins' *Garland*, with the land forces commanded by Sir Thomas Baskerville, a greedy, self-centred man. Both seamen promised 'to engage very deeply in the adventure, both with their substance and persons; and such was the opinion everyone had conceived of these two valiant commanders, that great were the expectations of the success of this voyage.'

The fleet left Plymouth on 28 August 1595, with instructions to take 2 million ducats from San Juan. The commanders sailed on different ships; their personalities and ideas were dissimilar, and when they did meet, there were misunderstandings and arguments. The first disagreement occurred at Canaria Grande in the Canary Islands. Instead of heading for the West Indies as agreed, Drake and Baskerville decided to land and plunder the island, much to Hawkins' disgust.

Now short of provisions, they finally set sail for the island of Dominica. Arriving on 29 October, they spent too long building pinnaces and trading with the natives. Five Spanish ships that were on their way to collect the silver from the disabled galleon came upon the small barque *Francis* and soon discovered that the English fleet was going to attack Puerto Rico and take the treasure. A fast caravel was sent to warn San Juan that the English fleet was after the riches from the damaged treasure ship. Sensibly, the treasure was removed and stored in 'La Fortaleza' (the island's fortress). The town also prepared for its defence by sinking a large ship at the entrance to the port and constructing a boom to impede the English fleet's progress.

On 31 October the already infirm Hawkins fell ill with fever onboard the *Garland*. His condition deteriorated and two days later he was unable to leave his bed. On the afternoon of 12 November John Hawkins died and his body was commended to the deep off Puerto Rico. The fleet became a funeral procession and Hawkins, who had despaired of any enthusiasm for the raid, was laid to rest in the waters that he had once dominated.

On the day that John Hawkins died, Drake took over command of the fleet and sailed to Puerto Rico, where the ships anchored before the harbour entrance. As they approached, they were met with a cannonade from the Moro Castle and the obstacles which prevented them from making their way into the harbour. On the same evening, as some of the officers were enjoying beer with Drake, a lucky shot landed in his cabin. Sir Nicholas Clifford and Captain Brutus Browne were mortally wounded but by great good fortune Drake escaped without injury, although his stool was smashed. On the 13th Sir Thomas Baskerville, with twenty-five pinnaces full of pikemen and musketeers, pulled into the harbour to attack with cannon and small arms the five Spanish ships anchored broadside-on. The Spaniards fired numerous shots at them but their aim was wayward and Baskerville's men managed to board the ships – only to find empty holds, as any treasure had been off-loaded. There was much close-fighting and many men died by drowning and burning. There was little to gain, so the English withdrew.

Giving up on investing San Juan, Drake withdrew his fleet to La Hacha in New Granada (Nicaragua), where they burned and destroyed the small port. They repeated their depredations at La Rancheria, where Drake seized many slaves and some pearls. Sailing on to Nombre de Dios, a town familiar to Drake, he searched for plunder but found none. Once again, he set fire to the town and sank all shipping. In a watch-tower outside the town he found twenty bars of silver, two bars of gold, some plate and money – not a great haul but better than had been gained in the other raids.

Drake landed Sir Thomas Baskerville's troops and watched as they disappeared into the jungle, heading towards Panama on the other side of the isthmus. Four days later the half-starved survivors returned, beaten off by a Spanish force in a small fort that had blocked their progress. Disappointed with the lack of treasure, Drake decided to sail to Escudo de Veraguas, a small island off the coast of New Grenada, where he planned another raid. By this time Drake himself was suffering from the 'bloody flux' (dysentery) and he died on 27 January 1596 in Portobello Harbour,

Panama. When he realised he was not going to survive, he asked to be dressed in his armour. He also asked to be buried on land, but in the event he was buried at sea in a lead coffin. Towards the end he dictated his last will and testament:

> In the Name of God, Amen. The seven and twentieth day of January the eighth and thirtieth year of the Reign of Our Sovereign Lady Elizabeth by the Grace of God of England, France and Ireland, Queen, Defender of the Faith, etc.
>
> I Francis Drake of Buckland and Monathorn, in the County of Devon, General of Her Majesty's Fleet, now in service for the West Indies, being of sound mind and memory (Thanks be therefore unto God), although sick in body, do make and ordain my last Will and Testament in manner and form following, viz.: First. I commend my soul to Jesus Christ my Saviour and Redeemer, in whose right-eousness I am made assured of everlasting felicity, and my body to the earth to be entombed at the discretion of my executor. Item 1, I give, devise and bequeath unto my well-beloved Cousin, Francis Drake, the son of Richard Drake of Eshire [Esher], in the County of Surrey, Esquire, one of the Esquires of Her Majesty's Stable, all that my Manor of Yarcombe, scituate [situated] lying and being within the County of Devon, with all the rights, members and appurtenances to the same, belonging, or in anywise appertaining. To have and to hold all and singular the said Manor of Yarcombe, with all the rights, members and appurtenances unto the same belonging, unto the said Francis Drake, Son of Richard Drake, his heirs and assignees forever.

Appropriately, both these great sea commanders died and were interred close to the Spanish Main. Sir William Monson wrote of Francis Drake's funeral that,

> He had no other funeral, than that which falls to the lot of those who die at sea, save his remains were cased in a heavy coffin of lead, and then cast overboard with volley of shot and firing of cannon in all the ships of the fleet; so he happened to find his grave near the place whence he had borrowed so large a reputation by his fortunate successes.

With both admirals dead, the command of the fleet devolved upon Sir Thomas Baskerville. After a meeting with his council, he decided to return to England. They sailed through the Caribbean until they passed the Isle of Pines off the southern coast of Cuba. Here they were confronted by twenty Spanish ships from Cartagena which had been sent to intercept them. In an engagement that lasted just two hours, Thomas Baskerville in *Defiance* and Captain Troughton in *Garland* led the English fleet in a fierce attack. One of the Spanish ships was set on fire and burned down to the waterline, while others had their sails and rigging reduced to tatters. The Spanish fleet had little alternative but to withdraw. In May 1596 Baskerville brought the failed expedition home. It was a sad conclusion for Elizabeth's veteran Sea Dogs. The following year Baskerville commanded the English army in Picardy, during the siege of Amiens, but he died of fever on 4 June.

Chapter Sixteen

The Capture of Cadiz

The argument between the queen and the two veteran Sea Dogs over whether the treasure ship in San Juan harbour was more important than blockading the Spanish ports had eventually been resolved, but in the end there was no treasure. After the deaths of Hawkins and Drake in the Caribbean, Queen Elizabeth ordered another attack against Spain in order to prevent another Armada, which just might succeed in overrunning England and deposing the queen.

On 13 June 1596 some 150 ships, one of the largest fleets ever to sail from England, set out for Spain, led by Elizabeth's favourite courtier Robert Devereux, 2nd Earl of Essex, a rash and daring young man. The fleet was divided up into four squadrons, led by Lord Charles Howard, High Admiral of England, in the *Arc Royal*, Devereux in the *Repulse*, Lord Thomas Howard in the *Mary Honora* and Sir Walter Raleigh in the *Warspite*. The squadrons carried 6,360 soldiers, with another 1,000 volunteers and 6,772 sailors. These forces were augmented by twenty ships from the Dutch United Provinces, with 2,000 men on board under the command of Admiral John de Duyvenvoorde. For the first time in recorded history the captains of the ships had sealed orders, which were not to be opened until they had reached Cape Finisterre.

Three of the swiftest ships, the *Litness*, the *Truelove* and the *Lion's Whelp*, were sent ahead as scouts. Keeping away from the coast, they captured three Hamburg fly-boats, which reported that the harbour at Cadiz was quiet and no attack was expected. They also intercepted an Irish ship, which yielded the information that the port held some fifty-six galleons, galleys and merchant ships. There were no soldiers in the town except the garrison.

By 30 June the fleet arrived off Cadiz in the teeth of a gale. It was decided to first attack the shipping and then land the soldiers. The gunners in the Moorish castle began firing at the ships but to little effect and after two hours the Spanish fleet retreated into the interior of the port. During the fighting the galleons *San Felip* and *Santo Tomas* were set on fire to prevent the English capturing them. At about eight in the morning the

English managed to enter the bay and attacked the moored vessels. At midday the Duke of Medina-Sidonia sent raw troops, poorly armed, as reinforcements. A while later another 5,000 men were deployed from the garrison.

Sir Walter Raleigh recalled,

> Here did every ship strive to be headmost, but such was the narrowness of the channel that neither the admiral's nor any other ship could pass one another. There was a command given that no ship should shoot but the queen's, making account that the honour would be the greater that was obtained by so few.

Steering his ship in mid-channel, Raleigh ran the bows of the *Warspite* with a terrible crash into one of the Spanish galleons, pouring fire into her from his forecastle guns and driving her from her anchorage. Sir Francis Vere attempted to engage the galleys, but they had taken shelter beneath the castle and the cannonade made it too hot to approach. Some of the Spanish ships escaped by entering the 200-yard wide channel, sailing under the bridge spanning the San Pedro Channel and, with the help of the raised drawbridge, managing to exit the port. This escape route was then blocked by Sir John Wingfield's *Vanguard*. Medina-Sidonia ordered the trapped ships to be burned to prevent them being captured by the English. The bombardment between the ships ended with the Spanish vessels so badly mauled that their captains set them on fire or scuttled them. Often they did so without warning their crew and soldiers, and many of the latter, weighed down with armour, were drowned when their ships went down. While the bombardment was in progress, the *San Philipo*, 1,500-ton galleon, was blown up and the debris from the blast sank three nearby ships. During the bombardment, one English ship was burned and a Dutch ship was accidentally blown up by her own powder. The Dutch commander, de Duyvenvoorde, bravely attacked the anchorage at El Puntals, while the English ships were battering the nucleus of the new Armada.

The English troops, their colours flying, were landed unopposed on the narrow neck of land that led to Cadiz town. The strongly fortified walls extended across the isthmus from sea to harbour, and great crowds of citizens were hurrying to enter the town. On Vere's advice, the regiments went to the bridge and drawbridge and destroyed them, leaving the ships within the port at the mercy of the English. As the soldiers advanced on the town they could see that the Spaniards were drawn up along the dry ditch in front of the walls. Once again Francis Vere came up with a solution. He ordered 200 men to advance and skirmish with the Spanish troops, while another 300 soldiers hid behind the series of sand dunes along the isthmus. The third 500 men were held in reserve.

Led by Sir John Wingfield, the first wave engaged the Spaniards but then deliberately fell back. The Spaniards gave chase but as they reached the sand dunes, the second squadron suddenly appeared, forcing the Spaniards to flee back to the ditch. At the same time the reinforcements appeared and the retreat became a rout. The officers vainly tried to persuade their men to turn and fight, but the troops tumbled into the ditch and tried to scramble up the other side. All the English soldiers followed, pursuing the remaining Spaniards through a gate and into the town. Soon hand-to-hand fighting raged in all the streets and alleys, before the Spanish were overwhelmed. The Spanish troops did put up a fight, firing from the windows and rooftops, and one of the casualties was Sir John Wingfield, who was fatally shot in the head.

Soon Cadiz was in the hands of the English, with the soldiers joined by the seamen to eject the Spanish troops from the city. Instead of the usual bloodletting, the troops and seamen were ordered to treat the unarmed citizens with respect. The capture of Cadiz was a great blow to Philip's plans to launch another invasion of England. The English fleet had threatened to return to England with the captured Spanish ships; to prevent this, Medina-Sidonia ordered the destruction of thirty-two ships, including the galleys and the vessels of the treasure fleet.

Some 1,200 pieces of ordnance were taken and either carried away or sunk. The plunder taken by the English fleet was substantial and would doubtless have satisfied the queen. Finally the fleet left Cadiz on 14 July with artillery, stores and treasure loaded onto the victorious ships. Cadiz offered a mournful scene as the city was put to the torch, made even bleaker by the wrecks of Spanish ships littering the shore. The main English warships remained, and next day the town's officials agreed to allow the citizens to leave unmolested in exchange for 120,000 ducats and the freedom of fifty-one English prisoners, probably oarsmen from the galleys. The poor organisation by the authorities had made the English victory inevitable and Medina-Sidonia stated later,

> The disorder had been, after the will of the Lord, the cause of the loss of this city, because all were heads of command and none were feet that would follow, and that is how they lost, for not having either feet or head.

Robert Devereux, Sir Francis Vere and the Dutch commanders were in favour of keeping Cadiz as an Anglo-Dutch port, but Lord Howard and the rest of the commanders thought it was too dangerous and vulnerable to a Spanish counter-attack. Together with the attack on Cadiz in 1587 and the destruction of the Armada, the sacking of Cadiz was one of the worst defeats inflicted on Spain during the Anglo-Spanish War. It was estimated that the economic loss was some 5 million ducats, which contributed to the bankruptcy of the Spanish Treasury.

On the return journey the fleet called at Faro in Portugal and burned the town. King Philip, determined to send an invasion force from Ferrol, managed to assemble what was left of his navy and various foreign ships trapped in Spanish ports. Under the command of Martin de Padilla, this Armada encountered hurricane force winds and seas in the Bay of Biscay that destroyed half the fleet and rendered the rest of the ships unserviceable. Even this set-back did not deter Philip, who rushed to assemble a third Armada; this was dispersed by storms off the Irish coast. It took the signing of the Treaty of London in 1604 to bring the Anglo-Spanish War to a conclusion.

Chapter Seventeen

The End of an Era

The dispersal of the Armada in 1588 was a reason for great celebration among the populace, with many watching from the south coast as the Armada made its slow passage up the Channel. The English had harried the Spanish without inflicting much damage, and just two ships were captured, the *San Salvador* and *Nuestra Senora del Rosario*. One person who quibbled over the victory against Spain was Queen Elizabeth. Already she was thinking about sending ships to intercept the treasure fleet from the New World but, with all her vessels in need of careening and repairs, it was a poor suggestion. There would be a lull anyway as the treasure ships from the Caribbean had all but stopped, their warship escorts crippled by the Sea Dogs and severely damaged by the Great Gale. Elizabeth was also far from satisfied by the performance of the Plymouth fleet and she asked a lengthy list of questions, including:

> What losses of men and ships have been made on the Spanish side ... and what powder, munitions and treasure have been taken from them? And though some of the ships of Spain may be thought too large to be boarded by the English, yet some of the queen's ships are thought very able to have boarded several of the meaner ships of the Spanish navy.

Remote from the action, the queen was entirely ignorant of the Sea Dogs' strategy, as were the non-sailing sycophants at her court. One tactic was to keep the Armada away from the Isle of Wight, which would have given the Spanish a foothold to invade England. Both Drake and Frobisher managed to position themselves to prevent any landing and push the Armada towards Calais. England gave thanks that Medina-Sidonia vetoed any thought of a landing and followed his cousin Philip's order to link up with Parma's army in the Spanish Netherlands.

In 1614, eleven years after the death of Elizabeth, Sir Walter Raleigh wrote a criticism and apology for the way English seamen had behaved:

> In like sort had the Lord Charles Howard, Admiral of England, been lost in the year 1588, if he had not been better advised than a great

many malignant fools were, that found fault with his demeanour. The Spaniards had an army aboard them and he had none, they had more ships than he had and of higher building and charging; so that, had he entangled himself with those great and powerful vessels, he had greatly endangered this kingdom of England ... But our admiral knew his advantage and held it, which had he not done, he (symbolising the Armada invasion), had not been worthy to have held his head. Here to speak in general of sea-fights ... I say that a fleet of twenty ships, all good sailors and good ships, have the advantage on the open sea, of an hundred as good ships and of slower sailing.

Smarting from the failure of his invasion of England, Philip raised taxes to pay for a new ship-building project that would give Spain an even larger fleet than the Armada. Taking note of the performance of the English ships, Philip vowed to improve his navy. An inspired ship constructor named Pedro Menendez Marques designed a new kind of ship which he called a *gallizabra*, which was long in the keel, sat low in the water and could use oars. It was smaller than the lumbering treasure ships, could out-run the Sea Dogs and, armed with twenty cannon, it could take on any privateer.

Meanwhile, Elizabeth was advised by Francis Drake to attack and destroy the ships that had made it back to the northern ports of Spain. She was told that most of the Armada ships had arrived in the ports of Santander and San Sebastian. Drake, ever keen to capture treasure ships in the Azores, decided first to enter Corunna, the westernmost port on Spain's north coast. Here he found only one survivor of the Armada, the *San Juan*, which was destroyed by her own crew to prevent her falling into English hands. He and John Norreys burned most of Corunna but came away with very little. They then sailed to Lisbon and, after a lengthy delay, failed to take the city. Drake's attempt to reinstate Don Antonio, the pretender to the Portuguese throne, failed to inspire the Portuguese population, who declined to rally to their new ruler and the enterprise ended in a whimper.

Having attempted to fulfil his monarch's wishes, Drake took this as an excuse to go and look for a treasure ship. However, after setting sail for the Azores, Drake's ships ran into a severe storm and were forced back. From the start the voyage was plagued by sub-standard supplies, high winds, poor planning and disease. With his crews starving or dying of fever, the expedition was a costly failure; the loss of lives totalled some 6,000 men, and many Dutch ships were sunk. Drake returned to Plymouth to face the queen's disapproval. At a meeting of the privy council they demanded to know why he had focused on land attacks rather than destroying the survivors of the Armada as instructed. Also, why had Lisbon not fallen? The answer seemed to lie in the lack of communication between the soldiers under John Norreys and the fleet. By his neatly fudged answers, which seemed to be accepted by the Council, Drake escaped punishment.

In 1590 Drake retreated to Buckland Abbey to complete the construction of the 27-mile freshwater leat, or channel, from the river Meavy. In fact Plymouth had plenty of fresh water from wells and springs, but the leat was an excuse for constructing six new mills along its banks. The Water Bill consisted of four items: to provide a supply of water for naval and merchant shipping; to provide water for fire-fighting; to scour Sutten Harbour of silt; and to improve the poor quality of land on Dartmoor. Drake had already leased a mill in the Millbay area of Plymouth and needed the leat to drive it. Millbay was tidal, and it was under increasing threat as the sea levels dropped throughout the second part of the century. Drake explained to Parliament the need for fresh water but discreetly played down the problem with his Millbay mill. For years afterwards the last day in April was celebrated in Plymouth as the Leat Feast.

Just as important was the defence of the port and Drake contributed £100 to this end from his own pocket. As a gesture, he even took the first spell of sentry duty when a fort was built on St Nicholas Island – now Drake Island – in the Sound. There was a scare when the Spanish threatened an invasion, but Drake and his wife left Buckland Abbey and moved into their town house to allay the fears of the citizens of Plymouth.

The Armada defeat did not harm Philip's control over his empire. It may have been temporarily inconvenienced but Spain was to remain the dominant, if declining, power for a further century. Although Philip rebuilt his fleet, the Armadas of 1596 and 1597 were both destroyed by dreadful storms. Thanks to the hurricanes that hit the Armada off Ireland, the English could not defeat Spain in the English Channel and the war dragged on. In 1595 a small Spanish force attempted to invade England from Cornwall. In a letter written to King Philip, Tristram Winslade, the grandson of John Winslade who had led the Cornish army during the Prayer Book Conflict, stated that there were people in Cornwall who would support a Spanish invasion. A small force of 400 soldiers sacked and burned Newlyn, Paul, Mousehole and Penzance. At Penzance the local militia attacked the Spaniards on the beach but were soon routed. The Deputy Lord Lieutenant, Sir Francis Godolphin, made a stand with twelve men but was forced to withdraw. One of the reasons for the

Spanish invasion was to recapture the cargo ships that had been seized by the English privateers at Pernambuco in northern Brazil four months earlier, and retrieve the treasure they had carried. The Cornish raid greatly concerned the queen and Lord Burghley, who immediately improved the defences in the West Country. There was no let-up, however, in the privateering attacks against the treasure ships. The defeat of the Armada was not the beginning of an English empire, as it was in no position to fund such adventures. Instead the Sea Dogs blockaded the Spanish coast and raided ships crossing the Atlantic. Although the privateers benefited from their attacks, a proportion of the captured treasure went to the queen and was used to fund the exchequer.

One important reason why the English were able to defeat the Armada was that the wind blew the Spanish ships northwards. To many English people this proved that God wanted them to win and pictures and medals were made to celebrate this fact. The investment of the British naval medal began with the defeat of the Spanish Armada. Although the Sea Dogs had harried the Armada down the Channel and seriously weakened Spain's intention of invading England, it was the hurricane storms that caused the wrecking and damage to the enemy fleet.

The 'Dangers Averted' medal minted in 1589 by the miniaturist artist Nicholas Hilliard, was made in gold, silver and copper. Gold medals were probably given to the senior officers who faced the Armada, while copper medals were probably given to petty officers and seaman. This was probably the first naval award medal, although the distribution was not exclusive to men of the sea. On the obverse is depicted the queen in her ruff with all her titles, while the reverse shows an island with a bay tree (which was supposed to ward off lightning and disease). It bears the Latin inscription '*Non Ipsa Pericula Tangunt*' ('Not even dangers affect it'). There were several other medals struck that showed English ships fighting against the Armada or the enemy's vessels being dashed against the rocks of Ireland. The Dutch produced their own medal. The obverse showed a scattered fleet on a stormy sea, bearing the inscription 'Jehovah blew with His wind and they were scattered'. On the reverse was a Protestant Church, unmoved in a storm (symbolising the Armada invasion). The inscription reads *Allidor non laedor* ('I am assailed but not injured').

After her initial burst of bad temper about the failure to destroy the Armada, Queen Elizabeth relished the adulation the population felt towards her and England's role in the world. She would not involve herself in continental affairs, although she did send John Norreys to the Low Countries as Ambassador to the States-General to thank them for their efforts in thwarting the Armada. For the next fifteen years she allowed her Sea Dogs to continue their trading and privateering, and the wealth generated would elevate the Elizabethan Age into one of the most out-standing periods in English history.

During the autumn of 1588 a series of thanksgiving services were held in cathedrals and churches throughout England. In London the final triumphal service was held on 4 December in St Paul's Cathedral. It was a double celebration, commemorating Elizabeth's accession to the throne on 27 November 1558 and the victory over the Spanish. Known for her desire to dress spectacularly, the queen wore silks and velvets bejewelled with gold, silver and pearls, no doubt part of her treasure captured by her Sea Dogs. She rode through the city in a mock-chariot drawn by four white horses, and in her wake followed Robert Devereux, Earl of Essex, the Lord Mayor, the privy councillors, officers of the livery companies, nobles, ladies-in-waiting and all the officers of the English fleet. Although she frequently stopped to hear verses praising her wisdom and courage, there was also a fear that she would be assassinated.

The hundreds of troops who were demobilised were dismissed without pay, leading them to sell their arms. On 9 August 1588, when Elizabeth addressed her troops at Tilbury, her address included the promise of reward: 'I know that already for your forwardness you have deserved rewards and crowns, and I assure you in the word of a prince you shall not fail of them.' But she either forgot her speech or was cynical enough to deny her military men and seamen any recompense. By this time the Armada was already approaching Scotland and the danger had passed. The same parsimony applied to the seaman who were dismissed in Kent and London but had no way of returning to the West Country. Starving, unpaid and diseased, the men who had signed on to keep the Armada at bay were dying on the streets of the ports along the east coast. Such were the false economies of the queen and her privy council. The treasury was almost bare but the queen spent a great deal of money on herself, with a wardrobe that contained 3,000 dresses and 628 items of jewellery. She remained indifferent to the plight of the men who had saved her country from invasion. Not for another five years would the survivors receive any recompense, and that was through gritted teeth. Lord Howard – as mer-cenary as any courtier – paid the officers from his own purse, but not the seamen. After a meeting with his commanders, he wrote to the queen:

> My most gracious Lady, with what grief I must write unto you in what state I find your fleet here. The infection had grown very great

and in many ships it requires speed and resolution of Your Majesty. The most art of the fleet is grievously infected and men die daily, falling sick in the ships by numbers; and the ships of themselves be so infected and so corrupted as is thought to be the very plague; and we find that the fresh men that we draw into our ships are infected one day and die the next, so as many of the ships have hardly men enough to weigh the anchors ...

In 1590, as a result of the government's parsimony, Hawkins and Drake founded a charity for the relief of sick and elderly mariners. The two Sea Dogs, who relied on their seamen to do their duty, were shocked at the way the sailors were released without pay, particularly as nearly half were sick with typhus or dysentery. Two years later they opened a hospital in Plymouth and another in Chatham. The charity still continues today, although the terms of the charter have been expanded.

During the 1590s seven of Elizabeth's Sea Dogs, mariners and soldiers died: Francis Drake (1596), John Hawkins (1595), Thomas Cavendish (1592), Martin Frobisher (1594), Richard Grenville (1591), Christopher Carleill (1593) and John Norreys (1597). Her close advisers Francis Walsingham and William Cecil passed away in 1590 and 1598 respectively. Robert Cecil inherited his father's political acumen and served the last days of the queen's reign and nine years under James I. He was ridiculed because he suffered from scoliosis, and his hunchbacked meant he stood just 5ft 4in tall. Elizabeth called him 'my pygmy', while James referred to him as 'my little beagle'. When Elizabeth was in decline, Robert told her she must go to bed, to which she replied, 'Little man, little man, 'must' is not a word to use to princes.' Despite his infirmities, he was exceptionally astute and, with the queen's support, he prepared the way for a smooth succession for the Scottish king, James VI. Unfortunately the new king had little interest in maritime matters and the Elizabethan navy went into a decline.

On 30 November 1601 Elizabeth delivered her last speech to Parliament, making what became known as the 'Golden Speech' in the palace council chamber to 141 members of the Commons. A highly accomplished speaker, she chose to talk not about the poor state of the economy, but rather to mark the symbolic end of the Elizabethan era:

> I know the title of king is a glorious title, but assure yourself that the shining glory of princely authority had not so dazzled the eyes of our understanding but that we well know and remember that we are also to yield an account of our actions before the Great Judge. To be a

king and wear a crown is more glorious to them that see it than it is a pleasure to them that bear it. For myself, I was never so much enticed with the glorious name of a king or royal authority of a queen as delighted that God has made me this instrument to maintain His truth and glory, and to defend this kingdom, as I said, from peril, dishonour, tyranny, and oppression. There will never queen sit in my seat with more zeal to my country or care to my subjects, and sooner with willingness yield and venture her life for your good and safety than myself. And though you have had and may have many princes more mighty and wise sitting in this seat, yet you never had or shall have any that will be more careful and loving.

At the age of 59, Queen Elizabeth died in the early hours of 24 March 1603 at Richmond Palace, drawing to a close the last of the Tudors and the era of her Sea Dogs.

Bibliography

Bawlf, Samuel, *The Secret Voyage of Sir Francis Drake 1577–1580* (2003).

Cooper, John, *The Queen's Agent – Francis Walsingham at the Court of Elizabeth I* (2011).

Coote, Stephan, *Drake* (2003).

Cordingly, David, *Life Among the Pirates* (1995).

Cumming, Alex, *Sir Francis Drake and the Golden Hinde* (1987).

Dean, James S., *Tropics Bound – Elizabeth's Sea Dogs on the Spanish Main* (2010).

The Diary of the Lady Anne Clifford, ed. V. Sackville West (2011).

Fletcher, Francis, *The World Encompassed by Sir Francis Drake* (1652).

Gosse, Philip, *Sir John Hawkins* (1930).

Grant, James, *British Battles on Land and Sea* (1894).

Hanson, Neil, *The Confident Hope of a Miracle – The True Story of the Spanish Armada* (2003).

Kelsey, Harry, *Sir Francis Drake – The Queen's Pirate* (2000).

Konstam, Angus, *Elizabethan Sea Dogs 1560–1605* (2000).

Mattingly, Garrett, *The Defeat of the Spanish Armada* (1959).

Maxwell Scott, Mary, *The Tragedy of Fotheringay* (1895).

Nuttall, Zelia, *New Light on Drake* (1914).

Sugden, Dr John, *Sir Francis Drake* (2006).

Tazon, Juan, *Life and Times of Thomas Stukely 1528–1578* (2003).

Thompson, I.A.A., 'The Spanish Armada Guns', *The Mariner's Mirror*, vol. 61 (1975).

Thomson, George M., *Sir Francis Drake* (1973).

Turner, Michael, *In Drake's Wake – the Early Voyages* (2005).

Wagner, Henry R., *Sir Francis Drake's Voyage Around the World – Its Aims and Objectives* (1926).

White, Alex, *Sir Francis Drake – Devon's Flawed Hero* (2003).

Williams, Patrick, *Armada* (2000).

Index

Allen, Thomas, 85
Almansa, Don Martin Enriquez de, 26
Anton, Juan, 66–7
Aragon, Catherine of, 1, 2, 128, 133
Arambaru, Marcos, 163, 164
Aranda, Martin, 165

Babu, Sultan, 71
Baker, Matthew, 148
Bannister, Robert, 85
Barret, Robert, 27
Baskerville, Thomas, 170–3
Bingham, Richard, 100, 162
Blondel, Robert, 25, 27, 28
Boleyn, Anne, 1, 94, 132
Borough, William, 136–7, 138, 139–40
Bourgoing, Dominique, 127, 131
Brewer, Thomas, 65
Burchett, Peter, 32
Butler, John, 84

Carder, Peter, 40–1
Carew, George, 13, 105, 111
Carleill, Christopher, 8, 100–4, 118, 184
Cavendish, Thomas, 12, 77–81, 184
Cecil, Richard, 100
Cecil, William, Lord Burghley, 2, 13–4,
    18–19, 22, 29, 30–1, 32, 33, 55–6,
    58, 60, 75, 91, 101, 128–9, 130, 135,
    140, 169, 182, 184
Champernowne, Arthur, 31–2, 104
Clerc, Francois de, 6
Clifford, Anne, 120
Clifford, George, 77, 88, 119–23, 124,
    164
Clifford, Nicholas, 171
Cockeram, Martin, 15
Coligny, Gaspard, 6, 104

Cuellar, Francisco, 165–7
Curtis, Anne, 90

Davis, John, 80–1
Dee, John, 36, 55
Devereux, Robert, 107, 124, 175, 177, 183
Devereux, Walter, 95
Doughty, Thomas, 55–61, 64, 140
Drake, Edmund, 43–4
Drake, Francis, 2, 10–13, 18, 22, 27–9,
    33, 39–40, 42, 49, 55–64, 66–7,
    70–2, 74–5, 78, 82, 86–7, 101–3,
    113, 116, 122, 135–41, 146, 149–53,
    155–6, 169, 171–2, 175, 179–81
Drake, John, 50, 73
Drake, Richard, 172
Drake, Thomas, 57
Dudley, Guildford, 2
Dudley, John, 90
Dudley, Robert, 18, 19, 30, 90, 96

Edward VI, 1, 89, 90
Elizabeth I, 1–4, 9, 11, 13–14, 18–19, 31,
    45, 55, 73–5, 77, 85–6, 89, 91, 93–4,
    98–9, 105, 110, 117, 120, 122,
    127–8, 130, 133, 135, 140–1, 145,
    167, 169–70, 173, 175, 179, 182–4
Enriquez, Diego Tellez, 160

Farnese, Alexander, 7–8, 96, 98, 142, 146,
    154
Fenner, Thomas, 118, 135, 139
Fisher, John, 152
Fitzgibbon, Maurice, 92
Fitzmaurice, James, 85, 92, 109
Fitzwilliam, George, 22, 30
Fitzwilliam, William, 161
Fletcher, Dr, 132

Fletcher, Francis, 64, 65, 71, 72
Fleury, Jean, 5, 9
Flood, Thomas, 65
Frobisher, Martin, 75, 110, 116–19, 149,
    150, 153, 154, 155–6, 179

Garret, John, 48
Gates, Thomas, 115
Geare, Michael, 111–13, 114
Gilbert, Humphrey, 84, 104, 108–11
Gilbert, John, 106
Godolphin, Francis, 181
Gonson, Benjamin, 17, 19, 32
Gonson, Katherine, 17
Goodall, Thomas, 39
Grenville, Fulke, 85
Grenville, Richard, 74–5, 77–8, 84–9,
    104, 108, 124, 184
Grey, Lady Jane, 2, 90

Hakluyt, Richard, 35–6, 77
Hartrop, Job, 37, 39
Hatton, Christopher, 32, 56, 61, 128
Hawkins, John, 10, 12, 15–16, 18–26, 29,
    34–5, 43–4, 47–8, 67, 91, 101, 124,
    140, 148–9, 156, 169–71, 175, 184
Hawkins, William, 15–16
Henry VIII, 1, 9, 15, 89
Hepburn, James, 127
Howard, Charles, 41, 124, 149, 150, 151,
    152, 153, 154, 155, 175, 177, 179–80,
    183
Howard, Thomas, 31, 87–8, 92, 105, 175

Ingram, Davy, 35–6

James I, 106, 125, 133, 184

Keeling, William, 123
Kemys, Lawrence, 106, 107
Kennedy, Jane, 131, 132

Laudonnière, Réné, 21
Le Testu, Guillaume, 52
Lee, Henry, 119
Lok, Michael, 117–18
Lovell, John, 46

MacClancy, Boetius, 161, 167
MacDonnell, Sorley Boy, 95
MacLean, Lachlan, 160–1
Mainwaring, Henry, 11
Mandingo, Pedro, 51
Mary Tudor, 1–2, 5, 10, 16, 44, 90, 104
Mary, Queen of Scots, 2, 14, 30, 55, 86,
    120, 127–8, 130, 133, 135, 141, 145,
    150
Mayne, Cuthbert, 85
Medina-Sidonia, Duke of, 138, 142, 143,
    144, 145–6, 147, 150, 154–5, 156–7,
    159, 162, 168, 176, 177, 179
Mendoza, Don Bernardino, 135, 141
Middleton, David, 88, 115–16
Monson, William, 88, 123–5, 172

Newman, Mary, 48
Newman, Mary, 48, 75
Newport, Christopher, 112–16
Norfolk, Duke of, 30, 31, 92, 128
Norreys, John, 8, 94–100, 101, 119, 180,
    181, 182, 184
Northumberland, Duke of, 1–2, 89–90

O'Neill, Shane, 90, 91
Oquendo, Miguel, 142, 168
Overbury, Thomas, 125
Oxenham, John, 51, 83–4, 86

Parma, Duke of, *see* Farnese, Alexander
Paulet, Amyas, 127, 128, 129–30
Perrot, John, 97, 101
Philibert, Emmanuel, 90
Philip II, 2–3, 7, 9, 16, 22, 30–1, 46, 53,
    91–2, 95, 117, 127, 133, 141, 143,
    145, 147, 181, 179–81

Raleigh, Walter, 20, 48, 84, 104, 108,
    110, 113, 119–20, 175–6, 179
Ranse, James, 48–9
Recalde, Juan Martinez, 138, 142, 147,
    153, 163–4
Ridolfi, Roberto, 30, 31, 91
Rilesden, John, 112
Roberval, Jean-Francois, 5
Russell, Francis, 43, 44, 74–5, 119

Saracold, John, 58
Seymour, Edward, 89
Seymour, Henry, 154
Seymour, William, 125
Shakespeare, William, 85, 104, 115, 123
Sherwell, Thomas, 84
Sidney, Henry, 91, 95, 108, 109
Sidney, Philip, 97
Silva, Nuno da, 57, 63, 67, 69
Smith, John, 114–15
Somers, George, 115
Sores, Jaques, 6
Sparke, John, 19–20
Specott, Nicholas, 84–5
St Leger, Mary, 85
Stafford, Edward, 135
Sydenham, Elizabeth, 75

Tomson, Richard, 152

Unton, Edmound, 85

Valdes, Diego Flores, 147, 153
Vere, Francis, 8, 105, 176, 177
Vicary, Leonard, 60

Walsingham, Francis, 2, 33, 35–6, 73, 86,
      95, 100–1, 127–8, 130, 135, 141,
      148, 184
Watts, John, 111–12
Willem van Oranje, 6, 7, 8, 101
Wingfield, John, 177
Wingfield, Robert, 130, 131, 132
Winter, John, 60
Winter, William, 19, 64, 118
Winterhay, Richard, 59, 61